Education Law

EDUCATION LAW

GEORGE M. JOHNSON

EAST LANSING

Michigan State University Press

1969

Acknowledgements

I first became interested in writing this book during my efforts to gather material for a graduate seminar dealing with the legal aspects of education. It was suggested that the seminar should include a discussion of some of the legal problems encountered by educational administrators at all levels in both public and non-public education. The legal problems in such important areas as educational finance have not been discussed primarily because of the desire to keep the book to a moderate size.

I am indebted to Dr. John E. Ivey, Jr., Dean of the College of Education of Michigan State University, for his encouragement and support, and to my colleagues in the Department of Administration and Higher Education for their criticisms and suggestions. I am especially grateful to Professor Robert O'Neil for his willingness to read and criticize drafts and redrafts of material for this book. His interest in the fields of law discussed here remained unabated as he moved from Professor of Law at the University of California at Berkeley to Assistant to the President of the State University of New York at Buffalo.

Needless to say, I am solely responsible for any deficiencies the book may have. The book profited greatly, however, from the capable research and editorial assistance of Kathleen Dunlop, and the secretarial assistance of Faith (Kathi) Ensworth and Mildred Peterson.

Finally, I am grateful to my wife, Evelyn, for her patience and understanding during the many months of this book's incubation.

GEORGE M. JOHNSON

Contents

Foreword

TRENDS of two distinct types have profoundly altered the character and content of education law within the past decade. There has, on the one hand, been a remarkable change in the relationship between the educational system and legislative bodies, both federal and state. This change is partially reflected—but only partially—in the growth of direct state support for public higher education, from 1.4 billion dollars in 1959–60 to 4.4 billion in 1967–68. Federal spending for support of all levels of education has accelerated at a corresponding rate. Predictably, however, the legislative beneficence which has produced this increased financial support has also brought an expansion of legislative and administrative surveillance of the educational process. The enactment of new laws and issuance of new regulations affecting higher education alone now justify, for example, the weekly publication of a loose-leaf *College and University Reporter*. The appearance of this comprehensive service reflects both a corpus of materials and a rate of change in the law of education comparable to the extent and growth of income tax or labor law. Consequently, it is no longer possible for the busy educational administrator to keep up to date on the law which governs his activities by reading an annual magazine summary or attending a panel at an annual professional convention.

The scope and character of education law have been reshaped at least as much by actions in the courts as those in legislative halls. To an unprecedented degree, courts have been called upon, within the past few years, to review legal disputes between students and educational officials. College and university disciplinary cases have understandably provided the bulk of this developing case law, but a surprising share of the cases have come from the secondary school level. The recent and vigorously contested case about a pupil's right to bring an attorney with him to a suspension hearing in a New York City public school is illustrative. It is also indicative of the increasing willingness of the courts to re-examine, and subject to constitutional scrutiny, internal admini-strative decisions once thought sacrosanct. Today, in fact, college and university officials—at least in publicly supported institutions —must simply assume that any student who is expelled or sus-pended for a substantial period may seek and obtain judicial re-view of the charges against him and of the disciplinary proceeding.

The concern of the courts has not by any means been confined to the claims of students. Faculty members, too, have increasingly sought judicial redress of their grievances against arbitrary or insensitive administrators. The contours of academic freedom have been greatly enlarged, for example, through the wave of cases challenging the constitutionality of state loyalty oaths and other political tests for public office. Elementary and secondary school teachers have raised in court a comparable set of issues with far greater frequency and ease than ever before. In the spring of 1968, for example, the United States Supreme Court was called upon for the first time to define the constitutional limits to a teacher's right to criticize publicly the policies of the school board or superin-tendent without jeopardizing his teaching position. Lower courts were struggling, meanwhile, with the resolution of a whole range of legal controversies involving the liberties and privileges of aca-demic personnel at all levels.

Many observers view these rapid and fundamental changes in the law of education with a keen sense of satisfaction. Others view these developments with a mixture of concern and foreboding. President James A. Perkins of Cornell University recently com-mented: "None of us, least of all the faculty and administration, much mourns the demise of the tradition of *in loco parentis*. But we do view with some alarm the spectre that seems to be rising out of its ashes and taking the form of a rash of court cases challenging decisions in areas that were once considered the educational world's peculiar province. The filing of these cases seems to suggest that judicial processes can be substituted for academic processes."

In any event, whether an educational administrator lauds or fears these profound changes, he can hardly overlook their impact upon the educational system. The law of education was once a rather simple and neatly defined collection of tort and contract problems—focusing upon such mundane questions as acquiring adequate insurance for the school bus and consummating contract negotiations with prospective employees. But now all that has changed. The principal must still worry about insuring the school bus, of course; and the dean must know something about signing contracts with incoming faculty members. But these rather simple, stable questions have been dwarfed by the welter of public law issues that now dominate the corpus of education law. The legal problems of the school and college have really come to mirror those of the society in which they function and educate. No longer can one readily isolate a distinct and insular body of "school law." Nor can he intelligently approach most legal problems that arise in the school or college setting without reference to a wide variety of legal disciplines once thought remote and irrelevant to the educator.

The central achievement of Professor Johnson's book is to serve as a bridge from the old concept of education law to the new. While the school bus and the teacher contract have not been omitted—for they are still part of the total legal context—they have been for the first time placed in appropriate perspective. The subjects of constitutional law, administrative law, and analysis of statutes have received the emphasis in this volume that they have recently achieved in the reported (and unreported) cases.

Lawyers have too often and too long kept this kind of information to themselves. There is a deep-seated fear that the role of the professional will be diluted if the tools of his trade are exposed to the layman's view. This prospect might be a cause of legitimate concern were this book designed to serve as a "do-it-yourself kit." But nothing could be further from the author's aim. The object of this study is clearly to make the lay reader more sensitive to situations in which the advice of a professional counselor is needed —rather than to supply the tools with which the nonlegally trained administrator can solve his own legal problems without an attorney's aid. The fact is that lawyers who practice education law will be helped rather than hurt by an increasing sensitivity and sophistication on the part of administrators and others who daily encounter increasingly complex legal problems in their school and college work. Yet only a book which is up-to-date and which comprehensively covers the current range of education law problems could adequately serve this purpose. Narrower coverage would most likely leave the layman with a false and dangerous sense of security in a half-knowledge about the simpler and more traditional legal issues.

Professor Johnson's book makes a very substantial contribution as a survey of the current state of the law. But its value does not stop there. It is certain to be extraordinarily useful to teachers and students of higher education in several respects. First, it will provide them a ready collection of case and statutory references. Second, it contains a catalog of stimulating and exciting research possibilities for those who seek to probe the frontiers of education law. And third, it suggests the many ways in which the preparation of professional educational administrators—guidance counselors, student personnel administrators and many others—must, in turn, be prepared to recognize and respond to administrative problems fraught with legal implications. To the extent this volume serves these three vital functions, it will, of course, transcend its immediate contribution as a text for the study of the new law of education.

Finally, the book imparts a sense of excitement about the interaction and interdependence of educational and legal institutions. Their growing proximity and cooperation are only partially reflected by the sharp increase in statutes and court decisions. The expanding and changing character of education law may well be the best index of what is happening, albeit an imperfect one. The decade ahead will undoubtedly bring commensurate changes, perhaps at an even faster rate. Other books must be written to keep pace with this process of evolution, but future authors will owe a substantial debt of gratitude to Professor Johnson for first recognizing and codifying the legal trends that are so central to the development of American education.

ROBERT M. O'NEIL

Professor of Law
Assistant to the President
State University of New York
at Buffalo

Introduction

THE PURPOSE of this book is to examine the laws—federal, state, and local—that regulate some of the important relationships in elementary, secondary, and higher education in the United States today. While the emphasis is on public education as it has been developed in the several states, it has seemed appropriate to include some of the laws relating to private, nonprofit education, which on occasion is closely related to public education. No attempt is made to examine the laws relating to profit-making education institutions, many of which are industrially or professionally sponsored. Although not insignificant, these proprietary enterprises are not yet relied upon by the national or state governments to supply the educational needs of our democratic society.

In early societies, education was not as important as it is today. The process of instruction, training, and learning has developed through time in response to the needs of different societies. The differences in educational practices and customs of particular societies reflect the differing ways in which civilizations have developed. As education has expanded in response to society's needs, so also has law—an independent instrument of social control—developed in response to the needs of civilizations.

The need for interaction between group members has been at the foundation of all societies. At first, this need was satisfied by familial relations, which proved the dominant bond of social cohesion. In early kinship societies, the function of education was essentially the transmission of culture, a task for which the family unit was adequate. Education, at this point in history, was not a matter of social concern. When the transmission of the culture and religious secrets of the tribal group grew beyond the competence of the family unit, members of the elite in the tribal hierarchy became "teachers," and priests took on the task of "educating" select students; learning was in large part accomplished through imitation. This type of education was regulated by the norms of custom and religion.

As civilizations developed and societies became more complex, the social importance of education increased and its regulation by custom and religion became inadequate to meet society's needs. Law emerged as a separate and distinct instrument of social control, principally because it possessed certain capabilities not associated with custom or religion. Unlike the injunctions of religion and the social sanctions of custom, the rules of positive law are applicable throughout the society which adopts them. The sanctions of law are confirmed by the right and the ability of a society to use its maximum power, if and when necessary, to compel obedience to the laws. Law thus became supreme in the hierarchy of social controls. In general, the application of law to particular relationships in education reflects society's conclusion that the legal regulation of those relationships is of primary social importance. A survey of the evolution of the American democratic society will reveal the concurrent and inter-related development of education and education law.

The early colonial societies in America were theocratic and class-constructed. Education was primarily a family responsibility, but where families were, for some reason, unable to educate their children, education became a matter of social concern, for the theocracies were predicated upon the Christian belief of each of their members. The dominant belief was that every child should receive enough education to enable him to read the Bible and be guided thereby to Christian faith and belief. In response to the needs of children whose parents were unable to educate them in this manner or who were unable to send them to private tuition schools, the colonies enacted apprenticeship laws in the late seventeenth century; they also enacted laws requiring townships of more than fifty householders to underwrite the wages of a teacher for the children of the poor. As different religious sects struggled for control of government and sought to make their religion the predominant one, local communities established separate religious schools, each dominated by a different sect. Because religion, government, and education were so closely inter-related during the colonial period, it is not unreasonable to assume that the "education laws" enacted during this time had religious bases.

During the latter part of the eighteenth century, however, the interest in religious freedom increased, and there were many efforts toward ending the conflict between religious sects. As the interest in religious freedom continued to grow, religion's place as the primary influence in all areas of early American society began to diminish. The period during and immediately following the American Revolution witnessed the development of a non-religious base for education, as many national leaders propounded the theory of natural right and respect for truth and reason. It was argued, with evident success, that for truth to prevail, whatever the sphere of life, man had to be educated so that he could debate and argue intelligently with information and insight. Having established a foundation for education in "truth and reason" rather than religion, a major problem remained for the as-yet class-structured American society. The dispute centered over the classes of persons believed to be the rightful beneficiaries of public education. It was contended by some that education should be reserved for the intellectually elite, while others argued that public education of a practical nature should be made available to all, without any stigma of charity. There was, at this time, controversy over state legislation for public-supported elementary and secondary education and over compulsory attendance laws; controversy over the same issues still exists.

Today, education has a high priority among the social needs of our democratic society. The education process includes governing bodies, professional academic and administrative personnel, non-professional personnel, students, buildings, laboratories, and other equipment. Law, as an independent instrument of social control, regulates a wide range of educational activities and relationships. However, the nonlegal norms of professional ethics and academic policies and practices regulate many of the activities and relationships involved in the education process. Much of what is currently referred to as "creeping legalism in education" is the result of the inadequacies of nonlegal educational norms.

Laws, including education laws, are both prescriptive and proscriptive. Education law constitutes the legal structure within which teachers, administrators, and other education personnel discharge their responsibilities. Members of the legal profession, trained to advise on legal matters and to represent persons in litigation, are available to educators when their professional services are required. However, the education laws are important guides to educators in carrying out their day-to-day responsibilities. Educators should have a sufficient understanding of the legal

principles underlying education law to appreciate the consequences of educational decisions and to know when a lawyer's
services are required. Educators should know enough about education laws to determine whether such laws promote or retard the
development of sound educational policies and practices.

The prevailing view among those who write about education is
that the power to determine the basic purposes of education in the
United States is vested in "the people." Under this view, the
members of the education profession have the limited responsibility of determining how these purposes are to be achieved. The
correctness of this view aside, there is some question as to whether
certain education laws are consistent with this allocation of educational responsibilities. There is evidence that the practical effect
of some education laws is to authorize nonprofessional agencies
such as governing bodies of systems and institutions of public
education to make professional decisions as to the methods for
achieving the basic purposes of education. Even if educators accept
the view that the broad purposes of education are for the public to
decide, there is merit in the contention that members of the education profession have a professional responsibility to examine education laws and, at the least, recommend changes in those laws
which vest in nonprofessional bodies the power to make admittedly professional decisions as to the means for accomplishing
publicly determined purposes.

The decision to limit this book to an examination of the education laws in the areas selected was made after conducting six
graduate seminars over a period of three years. A substantial
number of the students who were enrolled were employed in
administrative and supervisory positions in elementary and secondary public school systems. Others were qualifying for positions
in institutions of higher education. Their suggestions, often based
upon practical problems confronting them in their positions, were
of great value. Advice and suggestions were received from colleagues in the faculty of the College of Education of Michigan
State University and from fellow members of the National Organization on Legal Problems in Education. Criticisms and suggestions
were also solicited and received from members of law school
faculties.

The seven chapters include references to more than four
hundred and forty federal and state court decisions, forty-eight

percent of which have been decided within the past eight years. Briefly, the chapters deal with the following areas of education law:

Chapter I, American Educational and Judicial Systems, includes a brief analysis of the American educational system comprising elementary and secondary schools and institutions of higher education. The structure of American federal and state legal systems is summarized. The sources of education law as discussed include federal and state constitutional provisions, federal and state legislative enactments, federal and state court decisions, and federal and state administrative regulations and decisions.

Chapter II, The Organization and Administration of Educational Systems and Institutions, examines the laws relating to the structure and administration of these systems and institutions. It is observed here that, in public elementary and secondary education, state legislatures, with plenary power over education, provide for the delegation of decision-making power between state, intermediate, and local administrative agencies, i.e., boards of education. When such delegations of power have been properly challenged, it has been necessary for courts to determine their legality. Thus, in *Nord* v. *Guy*, discussed in Chapter II, the court was required to determine whether a state legislature could legally delegate to a constitutionally created state board of education the authority to determine what and where education facilities should be built and what they should cost.

Under the "separation of powers doctrine" which is recognized at both the federal and state levels, courts represent the judicial branch of government and are responsible for making final decisions in cases and controversies. Nevertheless, the laws of several states delegate to state education agencies or officials the power to make final decisions in certain types of cases and controversies. In construing these laws, courts frequently hold that the judicial review of such administrative decisions is limited to a determination as to whether the administrative decision was arbitrary or capricious. This was the court's holding in *Gable et al.* v. *Raftery et al.*, discussed in Chapter II.

Public institutions of higher education in several states are established under express provisions of state constitutions. The extent to which these "constitutionally autonomous" institutions are free from legislative supervision has been a much litigated question. In *Peters* v. *Michigan State College et al.,* discussed in Chapter II, it was held that a constitutionally autonomous university, despite its constitutional status, was nevertheless subject to a workmen's compensation law enacted by the legislature.

A supplement on *de jure* and *de facto* racial segregation in public educational systems and institutions appears as Appendix I. It is included here because the law that has developed and is still developing in this area involves organizational and administrative problems, as well as problems relating to teachers, which are considered in Chapter III, and problems relating to students, with which Chapter IV is concerned.

Chapter III, The Employment, and Rights and Responsibilities of Administrative and Teaching Personnel, deals with laws relating to the certification, employment, tenure, and dismissal of teachers in elementary, secondary, and higher education. At the elementary and secondary education level one of the most important legal developments has been the enactment of statutes in several states *requiring* school boards to negotiate or bargain collectively with representatives selected by teachers. A special supplement devoted to this development appears as Appendix II.

Another area in which there have been significant legal developments with respect to teachers at all levels of education embraces court decisions in which the rights of teachers that are protected by the Federal Constitution have been involved. Members of the U.S. Supreme Court have been sharply divided in many important decisions in this area. Thus, the Court stood five to four in *Keyishian et al.* v. *Board of Regents of the University of the State of New York et al.,* discussed in Chapter III, wherein the majority held unconstitutional a state law requiring the dismissal of teachers from employment in public education if such teachers are members of organizations known by them to have subversive purposes.

Chapter IV, The Admission, and Rights and Responsibilities of Students, examines the laws relating to attendance requirements and pupil discipline at the elementary and secondary levels, and the requirements of "due process" in actions against students in higher education. In *Dixon* v. *Alabama State Board of Education,* discussed in Chapter IV, the court held that "due process" requires that a student in a public institution of higher education must be given a timely notice and an opportunity to be heard before being dismissed for nonacademic causes. Several commentators on the legal aspects of education have been critical of the prevailing judicial position that the rights of students in non-public educational institutions are governed by principles of the law of contracts. However, there is little evidence in the decided cases that the courts have been moved by such criticism.

Chapter V, Tort Liability of Education Agencies and Personnel, summarizes those principles of the law of torts that are most frequently applied in education cases. The doctrines of governmental immunity and of charitable immunity, as they are applied in public and non-public education respectively, are analyzed. Reference is made to the "save harmless" statutes enacted by the legislatures of some states.

Chapter VI, Relations Between Church and Government in Education, examines the limitations imposed by the religious freedom provisions of the First Amendment of the Federal Constitution on cooperation between governments and church-related educational institutions. Examined also are the limitations imposed on such cooperation by state constitutional and statutory provisions. It has not been easy for state courts to apply the tests laid down by the U.S. Supreme Court in this controversial area. In 1966 the highest court of the State of Maryland applied the tests in a somewhat novel fashion in *Horace Mann League* v. *Board of Public Works of Maryland,* discussed in Chapter VI. Whether the U. S. Supreme Court approves this novel application of its tests is not known, because it subsequently denied a petition for certiorari when asked to review the Maryland decision.

Chapter VII, Federal Education Legislation, summarizes the constitutional bases for federal action relating to education. There is little doubt today that Congress has the power, under the Federal Constitution, to appropriate federal funds in aid of state and local education. However, a question has been raised as to the constitutionality of some conditional appropriations made by Congress in recent years. Some of the provisions in recent federal education legislation are examined in relation to the question of conditional appropriations. The special problems involved in getting this question before the U.S. Supreme Court for a definitive answer are also examined.

Appendix III contains a note on locating education law, and Appendix IV is a glossary of legal terms.

CHAPTER I

American Educational and Judicial Systems

I N the United States formal education is offered, in general, at three levels—elementary, secondary, and post-secondary; at each of these levels, it is offered under both public and non-public auspices. Many laws, both federal and state, constitute the legal framework within which this formal education is offered through educational systems and institutions.

American Educational Systems and Institutions

Most formal education in the United States, both public and non-public, is regulated by state laws. However, a few educational systems and institutions have been established and are regulated by the Federal Government.[1] In the exercise of the powers reserved to them by the Tenth Amendment of the U.S. Constitution, each of the fifty states, by constitution and/or by statute, has developed its own legal framework for education. The general pattern in all fifty states is essentially the same. State constitutions, in varying degrees of specificity, recognize the importance of education and provide for the financing of public education. Typically, the actual development of public education is left to state legislatures, subject only to limitations imposed by federal and state constitutions. The constitutions of a few states provide for constitutionally "independent" public institutions of higher education, but in most states public education at all levels is subject to regulation by the state legislature. In general, public elementary and secondary education is regulated by three levels of state education agencies: (1) a state or central agency, (2) an intermediate agency, and (3) a local agency. In some states, the state or central agency is established by the state constitution and is not subject, therefore, to state legislative regulation. The local agency is the local school district whose governing body is the local school board or school committee. In general, state legislatures delegate considerable responsibility to local school districts or boards, and they are responsible for the direct administration and operation of public education in their respective districts.

Non-public education preceded public education, and is now conducted at all levels. The right to engage in non-public educational activity is protected from arbitrary state interference by the "due process clause" of the Fourteenth Amendment of the Federal Constitution. Non-public education, however, is subject to reasonable state regulation, although it is not subject to the limitations of the Federal Constitution on state action.

American Federal and State Judicial Systems

An important characteristic of the governmental structure provided by the United States Constitution is the federal system under which there are two complete structures of government: one for the nation as a whole and another for each state. The national government is a government of enumerated powers delegated to it by the Federal Constitution. In contrast, the Constitution reserved to the states and to the people all powers "not delegated to the United States by the Constitution nor prohibited by it to the States."[2] As a general rule, federal and state governmental powers are allocated to the three traditional branches of government, pursuant to the separation of powers doctrine: executive powers are allocated to the executive branch, legislative powers to the legislative branch, and judicial powers to the judicial branch. The American judicial system, then, is made up of both federal and state courts. Under the widely accepted doctrine of judicial review, the United States Supreme Court is the final arbiter when federal or state action is challenged on the ground that such action violates some provision of the Federal Constitution.

THE FEDERAL JUDICIAL SYSTEM

Article III, Section 1 of the Federal Constitution provides, in part, that "The judicial power of the United States shall be vested in one supreme court, and in such inferior courts as the Congress may from time to time ordain and establish." The Supreme Court's original jurisdiction is fixed by Article III, Section 2, Clause 2 of the Federal Constitution, but its appellate jurisdiction, as well as the original and appellate jurisdiction of the inferior federal courts, is subject to control by Congress. The jurisdiction of the courts which make up the federal judicial system is a rather complex subject, and those with special interest in it are advised to consult a publication devoted to the subject. For the limited purposes of this book, it seems sufficient to observe that, in general, there are two levels of federal courts below the Supreme Court. As of January 1968, there were eighty-eight federal district courts which are essentially trial courts. In addition, eleven federal courts of appeals, one in each of the ten federal judicial circuits and an additional one in the District of Columbia, hear most of the appeals from the district courts. Congress has provided for a special three-judge court to hear and decide certain types of cases. Section 266 of the Federal Judicial Code prohibits a single judge from enjoining the enforcement of a state law alleged to violate some provision of the Federal Constitution, and requires the convening of a three-judge court to determine the question. The section also provides for a speedy review by the Supreme Court.

STATE JUDICIAL SYSTEM

Typically, the separation of powers is followed by state governments, and provision is made for a state judicial system. Most litigation is begun in state trial courts of general jurisdiction, but many large cities have established their own courts of limited jurisdiction. At the apex of the judicial system in each state is the state's highest court, which is called the state supreme court in most states, although in a few states it is called the court of appeals. Many states have established intermediate courts between their trial courts of general jurisdiction and their highest courts. These intermediate courts are called courts of appeals, except where that title is given to the state's highest court. Trial courts of general jurisdiction normally are presided over by a single judge who, with or without the assistance of a jury, must determine the facts, usually from conflicting evidence, apply the law to the facts, and render a decision. If a party to the litigation is dissatisfied with the decision of the trial judge, he may appeal the decision to a higher court. In general, the court to which an appeal is taken, whether it is the state's intermediate or its highest court, is bound by the facts as found by the trial court and is limited to a determination of the correctness of the trial court's application of the law.

It is also often the function of state appellate courts to review the decisions of administrative agencies to determine whether the agency has the authority to make the decision complained of and, if so, whether there has been an abuse of that authority. A decision by the highest court of a state is final unless it involves an issue over which the U.S. Supreme Court has jurisdiction. On appeal to the U.S. Supreme Court, that Court may decide the case on the merits, decline to hear the case because no *substantial federal question* is present, or certiorari may be denied without any stated reasons.

LEGAL METHOD

The American legal system embraces procedures for applying laws to the conflicts which arise in relationships between people and governments. Members of the legal profession are trained in these matters.

A lawyer, after consultation with a client, can determine whether a conflict should be presented to a court or other decision-making tribunal or official for decision. He may decide that the matter should be settled "out of court." If court action is indicated, it is the lawyer's responsibility to prepare the necessary papers for the proper court. In preparing for the possible trial or hearing, the lawyer must determine the witnesses to be called and the documentary evidence to be introduced. In the federal courts since 1938, and in some state courts, the courts may, at their discretion, direct the attorneys for the parties to appear before them for a "pre-trial conference" for the purpose of narrowing the issues and possibly settling the case without going to trial. If there is a commission, agency, or official involved, statutes frequently require that the matter be heard before such commission, agency, or official before it is brought to the courts.

The rules of evidence designed to confine court presentations to legally significant and material facts are familiar to lawyers, but sometimes appear overly technical to non-lawyers. Lawyers understand the distinction between jury trials and court trials and the legal principles that a jury is the trier of the facts, while a judge applies the law to the facts found. Where the application of the law results in a money judgment, there are procedures for seizing the judgment—debtor's property—and selling it; where it results in the issuance of an injunction, failure to obey may result in a fine and/or imprisonment. The procedures for appealing adverse decisions are also familiar to lawyers.

Lawyers often specialize in those fields where the legal issues have become complex or unique. Typically, however, all lawyers have received legal education in such substantive courses as contracts, torts, agency, corporation, and administrative and constitutional law. With such basic legal education, general practitioners are prepared to handle effectively most of the legal problems currently arising in the field of education. Proper handling of some of the legal issues relating to school bonds, however, requires the professional services of a school bond specialist.

The Sources of Education Law

The laws affecting education, either directly or indirectly, are the result of: (1) federal and state *constitutions* adopted by "the people," (2) federal and state *legislation* enacted by legislative bodies, (3) federal and state *court decisions* rendered by judicial bodies, (4) federal and state *rules, regulations, and decisions* promulgated or rendered by administrative bodies authorized to promulgate or render rules, regulations or decisions, and (5) federal and state attorneys' general *opinions* issued after proper request.

FEDERAL AND STATE CONSTITUTIONAL PROVISIONS

The Preamble to the Constitution of the United States proclaims, among other things, that "We the People of the United

States . . . do ordain and establish this Constitution for the United States of America." Article V provides for changes in the Federal Constitution: "The Congress, whenever two thirds of both houses shall deem it necessary, shall propose Amendments to this Constitution, or on the Application of the Legislatures of two thirds of the several States, shall call a Convention for proposing Amendments, which, in either Case, shall be valid to all Intents and Purposes, as Part of this Constitution, when ratified by the Legislatures of three-fourths of the several States, or by Conventions in three-fourths thereof, as the one or the other Mode of Ratification may be proposed by the Congress; . . . ." Provisions in the Federal Constitution and amendments thereto, as construed by the U.S. Supreme Court, have had a substantial effect on education. Moreover, provisions in the constitutions of all states and the amendments thereto may directly affect education in the states to which they apply.

FEDERAL AND STATE LEGISLATION—THE LEGISLATIVE PROCESS

Within constitutional limitations and consistent with the separation of powers doctrine, the U.S. Congress and the legislatures of the several states enact legislation on a variety of matters, including education. However, such legislation may actually result from recommendations by the executive departments of government. Also, in some states, it may result from the exercise of popular referendum. Legislatures are, of course, subject to pressures of special interest groups. The Federal Congress and the legislatures of the several states have committees responsible for handling specific types of legislative proposals. These committees may hold hearings on proposals before reporting actual bills to legislative bodies for final action. Therefore, groups with a special interest in proposed education legislation have several opportunities to participate in the development of such legislation.

FEDERAL AND STATE COURT DECISIONS—
THE JUDICIAL PROCESS

Generally speaking, courts, whether they are established by the constitution or by legislative action, declare the law and determine the rights of the parties to a controversy, but only when such controversy is properly before the court. Unless authorized by constitutional provision or statute, courts do not have the power to render advisory opinions.

Article III, Section 2 of the Federal Constitution limits the jurisdiction of federal courts to cases and controversies of specific types.[3] The jurisdiction of state courts is provided for in the various state constitutions and statutes. Where a case or controversy, properly before a state court, requires an interpretation of a state constitutional provision or state statute, the interpretation given by the state's highest court is final. However, the question whether the constitutional provision or statute, as interpreted, violates any provision of the Federal Constitution is, in the final analysis, for the U.S. Supreme Court to decide.

Subject to the rules of evidence and rules of the court, special interest groups may offer expert testimony to the trial court and may submit *amicus curiae* briefs to aid the court in reaching its decision. Here again is an opportunity for education organizations to participate in decision-making.[4]

ADMINISTRATIVE REGULATIONS AND DECISIONS—
THE ADMINISTRATIVE PROCESS

In the distribution of governmental powers at the federal and state levels, the separation of powers doctrine contemplates three branches of government: the executive, the legislative, and the judicial. However, for some time, legal recognition has been given at the federal and state levels to an administrative branch of government, consisting of a variety of administrative agencies established by the executive and legislative branches. A considerable body of law has been developed in relation to these agencies and is classified as "Administrative Law." It has been said that "The three large segments of administrative law relate to transfer of power from legislatures to agencies, exercise of power by the agencies, and review of administrative action by the courts."[5] Because relations in education are frequently regulated by administrative agencies and officials, it is important for persons with responsibilities in the field of education to have some familiarity with the general principles of administrative law.[6]

Notes

1. Congress has established five service academies: (1) the Military Academy at West Point in 1802, (2) the Naval Academy at Annapolis in 1845, (3) the Coast Guard Academy at New London, Connecticut in 1915, (4) the Merchant Marine Academy at Kings Point, N.Y. in 1942, and (5) the Air Force Academy at Colorado Springs in 1954.

   In 1857 Congress established what is now Gallaudet College, a special educational institution for the deaf in the District of Columbia.

   In legislating for the District of Columbia, Congress provides for the regular public school system of the District.

   Howard University in the District of Columbia was chartered by the Federal Government in 1867. It is supported in large part by federal appropriations but its governing body is a self-perpetuating board of trustees which is responsible for the institution's educational policies and practices.

2. See the Tenth Amendment of the U.S. Constitution.

3. See *The Constitution of the United States of America, Analysis and Interpretation*, 1964, pp. 599–620.

4. An analysis of court decisions in the field of education law reveals that, during the calendar year 1966, there were at least one hundred and sixty-six cases in which judicial decisions were handed down in matters involving education. Of these, one hundred and fourteen cases were decided by the state courts and fifty-two cases were decided by the federal courts, including one by the U.S. Supreme Court. Included in this analysis were eighty-three cases of direct concern to pupils in public schools and students in publicly financed institutions of higher education: forty-four were state court decisions and thirty-nine were from the federal judicial system. The other eighty-three cases, with rare exceptions, involved teachers or other professional school personnel in the public elementary and secondary schools and in publicly financed institutions of higher education; seventy of these cases were decided in state courts, and thirteen decisions came from federal courts, one of which was from the U.S. Supreme Court. Research Report 1967-R6, *The Teacher's Day in Court: Review of 1966* (Washington, D.C.: National Education Association, 1967). Research Report 1967-R7, *The Pupil's Day in Court: Review of 1966* (Washington, D.C.: National Education Association, 1967).

5. Kenneth Culp Davis, *Administrative Law Treatise*, I, Section 1.01, p. 1.

6. Persons interested in a detailed analysis of any specific problem or problems in administrative law should consult one or more of the many publications on the subject, for example, *Administrative Law Treatise, ibid.*

CHAPTER II

The Organization and Administration of Educational Systems and Institutions

I~N~ the United States the regulation of relationships involved in the education process is primarily the responsibility of the several states exercising the powers reserved to them under the Tenth Amendment of the Federal Constitution.[1] States, by constitutional, legislative, and administrative action, have provided the legal structure for the organization and administration of public educational systems and institutions and also have provided regulations relating to non-public education. Provisions of the Federal Constitution as interpreted by the U.S. Supreme Court impose limitations upon state regulations relating to education, but the limitations relating to public education are different from those relating to non-public education. As discussed in more detail in subsequent pages, the limitations imposed by the "equal protection clause" of the Fourteenth Amendment are applicable to public schools and institutions established by states because such schools and institutions are state agencies and their actions are "state actions." The actions of non-public schools and institutions, on the other hand, are not limited by the "equal protection clause." State regulations regarding non-public schools, however, are limited by the "due process clause" of the Fourteenth Amendment which protects private persons and organizations against unreasonable state regulations. The distinction between public and non-public education is important, although often difficult to determine.[2]

Public Education

Typically, state constitutional provisions commit the state to the support of education, set forth broad education policies, and direct the state legislatures to develop public school systems and institutions of education. The organizational and administrative patterns of public education that have developed in the several states are similar in many respects, with provision generally being made for three levels of education—elementary, secondary, and higher. Elementary and secondary education is generally free and compulsory. The constitutions of some states provide for public institutions of higher education under the supervision and control of their own governing bodies. Legislative efforts to regulate these "constitutionally autonomous" institutions are often challenged.

ELEMENTARY AND SECONDARY EDUCATIONAL SYSTEMS

In general, state legislation provides for the organization and administration of elementary and secondary educational systems by three levels of agencies and/or officials: the state or central agency, the intermediate agency, and the local agency.[3]

State or Central Agencies and Officials. The development of state agencies has been uneven but every state now has some form of state agency.[4] The chief state school officer has the title of either state superintendent of public instruction or state commissioner of education. The constitutions of some states provide for the state agency and chief state school official, while in other states such provisions are found in the acts of the legislatures. There is, thus, considerable variation from state to state in their responsibilities.[5]

A responsibility frequently vested in state agencies or officials is the distribution of state educational aid funds. The power of state agencies to withhold such funds as a means of enforcing legislative enactments and state agency regulations is frequently challenged on the ground that the exercise of this power is, properly speaking, the exercise of a legislative power which cannot be delegated to an administrative agency such as a state board of education. The legal basis for such challenges is the separation of powers doctrine adopted in most states. Under this doctrine, legislative powers must be exercised by the legislature and it is improper for a legislature to delegate legislative power to an administrative agency. In *Nord* v. *Guy*,[6] a state legislature empowered a constitutionally created state board of education to (a) request the sale of bonds and use the proceeds from the sale of such bonds to build educational facilities at state institutions of higher education and (b) provide for an annual facility fee to be paid by students for the use of such facilities. It was held that this legislation was an unconstitutional delegation of legislative power to an agency vested by the constitution with administrative powers only. The basis for this holding was that the legislation, without providing any guidelines, gave the state board of education the authority to determine what educational facilities should be built, where they should be located, and what they should cost. The same conclusion has been reached where state legislation authorizes the state superintendent of public instruction to formulate standards for approving schools for state aid.[7] The test in these cases is whether the legislature has established the policies and furnished the guidelines so that the administrative agency or official can fill in the details without exercising too much discretion. In *Wall* v. *County Board of Education of Johnson County*,[8] the legislature delegated authority to county boards and superintendents to fix boundaries of reorganized school districts *after study of educational conditions in the areas in question and hearings on whatever petitions had been filed*. The court held that the legislature "has adopted sufficient policies, prescribed necessary conditions as to administration, and supplied adequate requirements as to study, investigation and hearings before action." Under these circumstances the court held that the delegation of quasi-legislative authority was not only proper but necessary for the effective operation of the legislative policy.

As a general rule, the members of state boards of education are not required to have educational qualifications or to be members of the education profession. Typically, however, state boards are authorized to and do employ professional staff personnel. State superintendents of public instruction and state commissioners of education, as a general rule, are professionally trained. It is appropriate, therefore, for legislatures to delegate to administrative agencies with professional personnel and to professionally trained state officials, the responsibility for administrative actions that require professional judgment. The decisions referred to above in which courts have held that there was an unconstitutional delegation of legislative power are not necessarily in conflict with this view. Such decisions do emphasize the importance of drafting legislation so as to establish the policy and furnish the guidelines for professional implementation.

State agencies and officials are often empowered to make final decisions with respect to certain educational matters. Such delegations of power are sometimes challenged as unconstitutional delegations of judicial power to non-judicial agencies or officials in violation of the separation of powers doctrine. Administrative law principles support the view that it is appropriate for a state legislature to provide that certain controversies may or shall be heard and decided by an administrative agency or official, rather than by a court.[9] The attitude of the courts toward this type of statute depends to a large extent upon the language of the statute and the particular court involved. *Gable et al.* v. *Raftery et al.*[10] was concerned with the action of a district board of education in dismissing certain teachers for budgetary reasons. Some of the dismissed teachers challenged the method used in selecting those to be dismissed and appealed to the state commissioner of education. When the commissioner decided adversely to the interests of the teachers, action was brought to obtain a judicial review of his decision. The relevant statute stated that the decision of the commissioner "shall be final and conclusive and not subject to question or review in any place or court whatever." It was held that under this statute the commissioner "is made the practical administrative head of the educational system, and it is settled by the Court of Appeals (the state's highest court) that his determinations should not be interfered with unless shown to be purely arbitrary or capricious." Aside from the language of the statute involved, the reaction of the court may depend on the issues involved in a case brought before it. In *City of Dallas et al* v. *Moseley et al.*,[11] a taxpayer's suit was brought to enjoin a local school board from establishing a department of health as part of a high school's curriculum. One of the school board's contentions was that a statute provided that the state superintendent should hear and determine all appeals from decisions of school officers and that appeal from the superintendent's ruling should be to the state board of education. (This procedure had not been followed by the plaintiffs in this suit.) The court held that the statute referred to "purely administrative matters in the conduct of the schools" and that it was not the intention of the legislature "to close the door of the courts to taxpayers in cases of misappropriation of public school money by public officers." The court went on, however, to uphold the board in establishing the health department.

Intermediate Agencies and Officials. As indicated above, a majority of the states provide for three levels of agencies for the administration of public education. The intermediate school district is the middle agency in these states. In many states this middle agency corresponds to the county school district which is under the direction of the county superintendent of schools. The chief function of the intermediate agency has been to provide specialized services for the local school districts within its boundaries.[12] With the increase in the size of many local school districts as the result of school district reorganizations, there has been a reduction in the number of intermediate school districts in many states. On the other hand, there has been a trend toward new and expanded programs for intermediate districts in some states. This expansion has been reported in such fields as "data processing, instructional material centers, and special programs for physically and mentally handicapped children."[13]

In some states with three levels of agencies the county board of education and the county superintendent constitute the intermediate or middle agency and official, and their functions are different from those of the local board and the local superintendent. Thus, in *State ex rel. LeBuhn* v. *White*,[14] it was held that the duties and powers of a county board are so incompatible with those of the local school board that it is contrary to public policy for one person to hold membership on both boards. It was pointed out that in many important matters the local board is subordinate to the county board and subject to its revisory powers in some degree. It has been held, in another case, that a county school board may abolish a local school district under its jurisdiction in order to provide adequate educational facilities for pupils resident in the district.[15] Intermediate agencies and officials are frequently charged with specific responsibilities in relation to local school district reorganizations, and where such duties have been delegated to the intermediate agency or official, the general rule is that such authority must be strictly adhered to.[16]

Local School Districts. Education in the United States began as a local activity and, although today the state has the final responsibility for the development of education within its borders—and local school districts are agencies of the state and not of the local communities—the direct management of elementary and secondary public schools has to a large extent been made the responsibility of local school districts. In recognition of this responsibility the legislatures in most states provide for the participation of the residents of the district in school district matters. It has already been noted, however, that such participation does not give residents of the district any constitutional right to participate.[17] Normally a school district's educational facilities are available only to the children residing in the district, but in *Child Welfare Society of Flint* v. *Kennedy School District*,[18] the court upheld a statute requiring a local school district to accept for enrollment children not domiciled in the district but who resided in a children's home maintained in the district.

The Local School District's Relations With Other Governmental Units. Consistent with the rule that local school districts are state agencies, it is generally held that they are not subject to regulations promulgated by other governmental units within which they may be located in whole or in part. Thus, it has been held that a city zoning ordinance providing for a "restricted residence" area did not apply to property in such an area belonging to a school district upon which the school district sought to install a gasoline pump to service the district's school buses.[19] The court held that "A municipal zoning ordinance is not applicable to the state or any of its agencies in the use of its property for a governmental purpose unless the legislature has clearly manifested a contrary intent." Likewise, it has been held that a school district is not subject to a local amusement tax on all forms of entertainment for which an admission is charged.[20]

In contrast with the above cases are those in which it is held that local ordinances enacted to protect public safety, health and welfare are applicable to school districts. In *School District of Philadelphia* v. *Zoning Board of Adjustment, City of Philadelphia*,[21] the court, with one dissent, held that a school district was subject to that part of the building regulations requiring every building to have off-street parking space. The dissent expressed the view that the effect of the majority opinion would be to enable the city to prohibit the construction of public school buildings in certain areas, but the majority held that such a possibility was highly doubtful. It has been held in another case that a school district is subject to an assessment for the installation of a sewer system and for fees for connecting and using the sewer system because these are public health measures.[22] It has also been held that a school district is liable for inspection fees for the inspection of its fuel-burning facilities pursuant to a city ordinance.[23]

School District Reorganization. Population shifts, economic changes, improvements in transportation, the demands of citizens for more and better education for their children, and other related factors result in the periodic alteration and modification of the boundaries of local school districts. The trend has been toward larger and fewer school districts.[24] It is customary for state legislatures to provide for district reorganizations through the transfer of territory from one district to another, consolidation, merger, annexation, or dissolution. Reorganization statutes differ widely from state to state and the solution to a particular issue usually depends on the language of the statute involved. However, there are a few reorganization principles that have general application.

Frequently reorganization statutes set out broad policies and delegate to administrative agencies the responsibilities of implementation. Reference has already been made to the necessity for the legislature to establish policies and guidelines to avoid the successful challenge of delegation of legislative power.[25] Another principle of general application is that a reorganization must not impair the obligation of the holders of outstanding school district bonds. In *Canal National Bank et al. v. School Administrative District No. 3 et al.,*[26] the court, with two dissents, held a reorganization statute unconstitutional because it authorized the withdrawal of territory from a district that had an outstanding bonded indebtedness and made the withdrawn property only contingently liable for the bonded indebtedness. This arrangement was held to impair the bondholders' security in violation of Article 1, Section 10 of the Federal Constitution, even though the value of the remaining property was greatly in excess of the total amount remaining due on the bonds.[27] The principle as applied in the *Canal National Bank* case may seem overly cautious but any other rule would be difficult of general application and might deter prospective purchasers from buying school bonds.

Another legal principle of general application in reorganization cases relates to the requirement that reorganizations should result in districts that are made up of compact and contiguous territory. Because of this requirement, reorganizations have been challenged on the ground that the territories comprising a reorganized district are not contiguous or not adjoining. In disposing of such challenges, courts frequently give a liberal construction to the term "compact and contiguous." Thus, in *State ex rel. Badtke et al. v. School Board of Joint Common School District No. 1 City of Ripon et al.*,[28] it was held that territory which touches a school district only at its corner is adjoining territory and appropriately annexed. On the other hand, a reorganization has been invalidated where the annexation by one district of territory from another district leaves that other district in four unconnected "islands."[29] In the recent case of *Forest Oil Corporation v. District Boundary Board of Sweetwater County*,[30] the court refused to approve a reorganization plan that would annex non-contiguous territory forty-five miles away from the annexing district. The court concluded that such an annexation would be "a gross usurpation of powers" on the part of the annexing district even though there was no express requirement in the law requiring districts to consist of compact and contiguous territory.

Powers and Duties of Local School Districts. Local school districts, like state and intermediate education agencies, are state agencies and as such they are subject to the plenary power of state legislatures. The governing bodies of local school districts are generally referred to as local boards of education although they are sometimes given the title of local school committees. As subordinate state agencies, local school boards can exercise only those powers delegated to them by the legislature or such powers as can reasonably be implied from the powers expressly granted. Statutes provide for the manner in which local school boards are created and, as a general rule, school board members are elected by the voters residing in the school district. Statutes usually confer upon school boards the status of corporate entities. One result of this status is that school boards are required to act in a body, and actions approved by the majority are binding on the minority. However, in *Thomas v. Board of Education of Township of*

Morris,[31] it was held that a majority of the members of a local school board could not, against the wishes of a minority, rescind a superintendent's probationary contract. The decision of the court in *Funchess* v. *Lindsay*[32] conforms more to the recognized principles of the law of contracts and the law of corporations. There, a school board attempted to rescind a contract made by a predecessor board under which a superintendent was elected for a four-year term. In holding that the board could not rescind the contract, the court pointed out that the board of education is a corporate body which continues always the same regardless of the change in the individuals composing it, and the employment of the superintendent could not be rescinded without cause.

Where a statute prohibits any board member from having any pecuniary interest in a company making sales to the school board, it has been held that a board member may be removed from office for being a principal stockholder in a bottling company that sold soft drinks to the schools even though the profits from the sale of soft drinks were used for school improvements.[33] A contrary decision was reached in *Dials* v. *Blair*,[34] where a board member had a pecuniary interest in a public utility required by law to provide water to the schools under the board's control. It was held that it was not intended for such a case to come within the meaning of the statute in question. The conflict of interest rule is a sound one but, as the court observed in the *Dials* case, it was not intended to apply to situations similar to the one presented in that case.

Duties Imposed by Brown v. Board of Education of Topeka, Kansas.[35] The impact of these decisions on public education is discussed in detail in Appendix I, entitled "Before and After *Brown* v. *Board of Education of Topeka, Kansas*." It is sufficient here to point out that these decisions impose upon school boards the affirmative obligation to eliminate practices and policies that require or permit the segregation of students in public education on the basis of race. This duty has been interpreted to extend to the appointment and distribution of teaching personnel. The lower federal courts and state courts are divided on the question of whether or not school boards have a duty to eliminate *de facto* segregation or adventitious school segregation, but the majority view is that school boards have the power to relieve racial imbalance in the public schools should they decide to exercise such power. Illustrative decisions are referred to and discussed in the special note.

PUBLIC INSTITUTIONS OF HIGHER EDUCATION

Public institutions of higher education at the state and local level include state universities and colleges, normal schools, and municipal and junior colleges. However, the following discussion is limited to degree-granting institutions.

It has been estimated that there are more than three hundred and eighty degree-granting state universities and colleges in the United States today.[36] Some of these institutions were created by constitutional provisions, others by legislative action. In a few states institutions created by constitutional provision are referred to as "constitutionally autonomous" institutions because of their freedom from legislative supervision and control. The extent to which these institutions are in fact subject to state legislation depends on the language of the relevant constitutional provisions and on the particular state legislation in question as judicially construed.[37]

The Constitution of the State of Michigan, for example, provides for the establishment of certain universities to be governed by elected governing bodies which shall have the general supervision of the universities and the direction and control of all expenditures. The judicial construction of this constitutional language has been required in several situations. It has been held to prevent the legislature from conditioning appropriations so as to require a university to relocate certain operations.[38] In the early case of *Board of Regents of University of Michigan* v. *Auditor General*,[39] the court used the following sweeping language: "By the provisions of the Constitution . . . the board of regents is made the highest form of juristic person known to the law, a constitutional corporation of independent authority, which, within the scope of its functions, is coordinate with and equal to that of the legislature." However, in *Peters* v. *Michigan State College et al.*,[40] an evenly divided court upheld a lower court decision holding that the university was subject to a legislatively enacted workmen's compensation law. Moreover, in *Branum* v. *State*,[41] it was held that the state law making employers liable for torts of their employees in the operation of motor vehicles was applicable to constitutionally independent universities. The court observed that "(w)ithin the confines of the operation and the allocation of funds the University is supreme. Without these confines, however, there is no reason to allow the Regents to use their independence to thwart the clearly established public policy of the people of Michigan."

Non-Public Education

It is firmly established that private persons and organizations have the constitutional right to organize and operate non-public schools and institutions of higher education free from arbitrary or unreasonable governmental regulations. This right is protected by the "due process" clauses of the Fifth and Fourteenth Amendments.[42]

In the leading case of *Pierce* v. *Society of Sisters of the Holy Names of Jesus and Mary* and *Pierce* v. *Hill Academy*,[43] the U.S. Supreme Court held unconstitutional a state statute requiring all school-age children to attend public schools. It was held that the right to operate non-public schools was a property right and was not an inherently harmful undertaking which the state could prohibit. By way of dictum the Court stated that a state does have the power "reasonably to regulate all schools, to inspect, supervise and examine them, their teachers and pupils; to require that all children of proper age attend some school, that teachers shall be of good moral character and patriotic disposition, that certain studies plainly essential to good citizenship must be taught, and that nothing be taught which is manifestly inimical to the public welfare."

Municipal Zoning Ordinances and Non-Public Schools. On occasions local zoning ordinances and building codes have been challenged when applied to non-public schools. It has been held that a municipal building code and zoning ordinance when applied only against private non-sectarian schools is invalid.[44]

However, in *Tustin Heights Association* v. *Board of Supervisors of County of Orange et al.,*[45] it was held not unconstitutional to deny a permit to construct a non-public school in a residential area even though the city could not prohibit the construction of a public school in such area. The court observed that the construction of public schools is a sovereign state activity not subject to municipal control, and that "equal protection of the law does not require an equating of private rights with those of the sovereign." An ordinance excluding church-related schools might be challenged on the ground that it interferes with the First Amendment guarantee of freedom of religion but the decisions to date have not used this ground.[46]

State Regulation of Non-Public Education. It is customary for state legislatures to require private persons and organizations engaging in education to obtain a license or to incorporate and obtain a charter. Legislation may prescribe the conditions to be met before a license is issued or a charter granted. The conditions must be reasonable and whether they are reasonable is a legal question to be decided by the courts in cases properly presented to them for decision. State laws may reserve to the state the right of periodic inspection and the right to revoke the license or charter for cause.[47] Frequently, educational judgments must be made in connection with issuing or revoking licenses, granting or revoking charters, the formulation of conditions, and making periodic inspections. The regulation of non-public education may be delegated to an administrative agency or official; however, in only a few states do the laws delegate these responsibilities to personnel with special competence and training in education.

Educational organization and administration are regulated in part by the policies and practices of voluntary educational accrediting associations. To some extent, therefore, the organizational and administrative patterns of non-public education approximate those found in public education. Typically, education accrediting agencies are private, nonprofit, voluntary associations. Membership in such associations has come to constitute accreditation, however, and withdrawal of membership means the loss of accreditation. In *Parsons College, etc.* v. *North Central Association of Colleges and Secondary Schools, etc.*[48] the court recognized that the loss of accreditation may work "substantial and irreparable harm" to an educational institution. Nevertheless, the court held that it was without jurisdiction to review the membership policies of the Association.

It is difficult to determine from the education cases just what quantity and/or quality of government involvement is sufficient to support a finding of state action in the operations of an educational enterprise. That non-public education serves a public purpose has never been held to be a decisive factor. As indicated above, state laws require private individuals and organizations to procure licenses or comply with corporation laws in order to conduct educational activities, but no cases have been found in which it is held that such government involvement, without more, is sufficient to justify the classification of the activities of such enterprises as state action. In the absence of constitutional prohibitions, non-public education may be supported at least in part from public funds without losing its non-public status. Special problems involved in the use of public funds to support church-related non-public education are discussed in Chapter VI.

The general policy in all states, except Hawaii, under which the overall responsibility for public elementary and secondary education is assumed by states while the responsibility for the financial support, quantity, and quality of such education is shared between state governments and semi-autonomous local school districts, is currently being questioned. The questions, for the most part, have been related to problems of racial segregation in public education. However, they involve the broader issue of a state's responsibilities under the equal protection and due process clauses of the Fourteenth Amendment of the Federal Constitution. May a state, consistent with its constitutional obligations, require its resident pupils to attend schools offering specified programs, provide tax-supported schools that offer such programs, and nevertheless permit the quantity and/or quality of such programs to vary substantially and to be determined, at least in part, by the different local school districts?

In other factual situations discussed in Chapter IV, the U.S. Supreme Court has made it clear that residents of a state have a constitutional right to equal opportunity with respect to any state-supported education. A state violates this right where it classifies its residents on a racial basis and makes the quality of state-supported education available to a resident depend on the resident's race. It is held that it is arbitrary and unreasonable for a state to classify its residents on the basis of race for purposes of education because race is not reasonably related to any proper educational purpose. It does not seem unreasonable to suggest that, if and when the issue is properly before it, the Court may decide that it is arbitrary and unreasonable for a state, through its school district organization, to make the quantity and/or quality of state-supported education available to its residents depend on the school district in which they live. To the extent that the quantity and/or quality of education is determined by the availability of educational resources, a state's statutory scheme for allocating its educational resources between school districts will also be of constitutional relevance.

Educators should be prepared to assist the courts in evaluating school district organizations and school finance statutes. Moreover, they should be considering educationally sound alternatives to present school district organizations and educational finance arrangements which appear to be constitutionally vulnerable.

Notes

1. The Tenth Amendment provides that "The powers not delegated to the United States by the Constitution, nor prohibited by it to the States, are reserved to the States respectively or to the people."

   Although the Federal Constitution makes no express grant of power over education to the Federal Government, in the exercise of their constitutional powers the legislative and judicial branches of the Federal Government have produced a substantial amount of education law which is discussed in Chapter VII.

2. See the conflicting views of different federal district judges in *Guillory* v. *Administrators of Tulane University of Louisiana*, 212 F.Supp. 674 (La. 1962); also see *Hammond* v. *University of Tampa*, 344 F.2d 951 (Fla.1965) holding that the action of an educational institution operating on and with public property is "state action."

   It is reported that in the United States in 1964 there were a total of 77,294 public elementary schools and 26,729 public secondary schools; 14,762 non-public elementary schools and 4,451 non-public secondary schools. (See *Statistical Abstract of U.S.—1966*, U.S. Department of Commerce, Washington, D.C.: Bureau of Census, 1966.) In addition, there were 803 public institutions of higher education and 1,380 non-public institutions of higher education. (See *Digest of Educational Statistics*, 1965 edition, Washington, D.C.: U.S. Office of Education.)

3. It is reported that seventeen states have a two-level structure, thirty-two have a three-level structure, and only Hawaii is completely centralized with the state education agency being responsible for direct administration of all public schools in the state. (See *Journal on State School Systems Development*, 1967, National Education Association.)

4. See *ibid.*, p. 9, reporting that all states but Illinois and Wisconsin have a state board of education ranging in size from twenty-three in Ohio to three in Mississippi.

5. See Morphet, Johns, and Reller, *Educational Administration Concepts, Practices and Issues* (Englewood Cliffs, N.J.: Prentice-Hall, Inc., 1959), pp. 190–212, and Robert R. Hamilton and Paul R. Mort, *The Law and Public Education* (Brooklyn: Foundation Press, Inc., 1959, 2nd ed.), pp. 83–115.

6. 141 N.W.2d 395 (N.D.1966).

7. See *Lewis Consolidated School District of Cass County* v. *Johnson*, 127 N.W.2d 118 (Iowa 1964) and *School District No. 39 of Washington County* v. *Decker*, 68 N.W.2d 354 (Neb.1955). Also see *High School Board in*

Department of Education v. *Board of Education of Roundhead Local School District*, 122 N.E.2d 192 (Ohio 1953) where a statute was annulled because it furnished no guidelines but empowered the state superintendent of public instruction to revoke high school charters upon the recommendation of his advisory board.

8. 86 N.W.2d 231 (Iowa 1957).

9. See Kenneth Culp Davis, *Administrative Law Treatise*, I, Section 1.01, p. 1 and 73 C.J.S. 295, 300.

10. 65 N.Y.S.2d 513 (1945).

11. 286 S.W. 497 (Texas 1926), reh. den. 1926.

12. See Morphet, Johns, and Reller, *op. cit.*, pp. 223–226, for a statement on the development and functions of intermediate agencies.

13. *Journal on State School Systems Development, op. cit.*, p. 27.

14. 133 N.W.2d 903 (Iowa 1965).

15. See *Nethery et al.* v. *McMullen et al.*, 230 S.W.2d 79 (Ky.1950).

16. In *Sunnywood Common School District No. 46 of Minnehaha County* v. *County Board of Education of Minnehaha County*, 131 N.W.2d 105 (S.D.1964) a county board was vested with statutory power "to make minor boundary changes of any school district within its county without a vote of any electors. . . ." It was held improper for the county board to make a boundary change under which a school district lost thirty-one percent of its land area and twenty-one percent of its assessed valuation. In *Sugar Grove School District No. 19* v. *Booneville Special School District No. 65*, 187 S.W.2d 339 (Ark.1945) a school district consolidation was invalidated because the county board did not publish the notice of hearing at least once in each of two weeks as required by statute. In *Board of Education of Wellington Community Unit School District No. 7 of Iroquois County et al.* v. *County Board of School Trustees of Vermilion County et al.*, 142 N.E.2d 742 (Ill.1957) an annexation was invalidated because the county board did not swear in the witnesses and permit cross-examination at the hearing.

17. See *Attorney General of the State of Michigan ex rel. Kies* v. *Lowrey*, 199 U.S. 233, 50 L.Ed. 167, 26 S.Ct. 27 (1905). In this case the legislature by statute reorganized certain school districts that had been established by statute twenty years before. It was contended that residents of the old districts had vested rights in the old districts and that their interests could not be altered without their consent. See also *Wheeler School District No. 152 of Grant County et al.* v. *Hawley*, 137 P.2d 1010 (Wash.1943) holding that a reorganization of school districts was proper even though a majority of the residents of one of the affected districts voted against the reorganization.

18. 189 N.W. 1002 (Mich.1922).

19. *City of Bloomfield* v. *Davis County Community School District*, 119 N.W.2d 909 (Iowa 1963).

20. *Borough of Wilkensburg* v. *School District of Wilkensburg, et al.*, 74 A.2d 138 (Pa.1950).

21. 207 A.2d 864 (Pa.1965).

22. *Southwest Delaware County Municipal Authority* v. *Township of Aston,* 198 A.2d 867 (Pa.1964).

23. *Kansas City* v. *School District of Kansas City,* 201 S.W.2d 930 (Mo.1947), reh. den. 1947.

24. In the *Journal on State School Systems Development, op. cit.,* p. 17, it is reported that the number of school districts throughout the nation had decreased from 100,223 in 1945–46 to 21,753 by the Fall of 1966; a 78.3 percent decrease in twenty years.

25. See *Wall* v. *County Board of Education of Johnson County et al.,* note 8.

26. 203 A.2d 734 (Me.1964).

27. Article 1, Section 10 of the Federal Constitution provides in part that "No state shall . . . pass any . . . law impairing the obligation of contracts. . . ."

     The same conclusion was reached in *Board of Education of City of Lincoln Park* v. *Board of Education of City of Detroit,* 222 N.W. 763 (Mich.1929) where it was held that a district which receives territory by way of annexation is liable for its share of the interest on bonds for which the annexed territory was liable even though the reorganization statute provided that the remaining property should be liable for all such indebtedness.

28. 83 N.W.2d 724 (Wis.1957). For a similar holding, see *Independent Consolidated School District No. 66 et al.* v. *Big Stone County et al.,* 67 N.W.2d 903 (Minn.1954).

29. *Joint School District No. 10 of Towns of Chimney Rock and Burnside et al.* v. *Sosalla et al.,* 88 N.W.2d 357 (Wis.1958), reh. den. 1958. And see *People ex rel. Community Unit School District No. 5* v. *Decatur School District No. 61,* 203 N.E.2d 423 (Ill.1964), reh. den. 1965, where three "islands" were created. But compare *State ex rel. Brown* v. *Community School District of St. Ansgar,* 91 N.W.2d 571 (Iowa 1958) where the court upheld a reorganization which resulted in the creation of one "island" completely surrounded by the reorganized district.

30. 419 P.2d 194 (Wyo.1966). The admitted purpose of the attempted annexation was to increase the district's tax base by adding valuable oil land some forty-five miles away from the district. This case should be compared with *Chicago, B. & Q. Ry. Co.* v. *Byron School District No. 1 et al.,* 260 P. 537 (Wyo.1927) in which the court held that it was not arbitrary for a district to annex a strip of territory four miles wide and twenty miles long in order to add assessable railroad property seventeen miles away from the district.

31. 215 A.2d 35 (N.J.1965).

32. 133 So.2d 351 (La.1961), reh. den. 1961.

33. *Commonwealth of Kentucky ex rel. Breckenridge* v. *Collins,* 379 S.W.2d 436 (Ky.1964), reh. den. 1964. See also *People* v. *Becker,* 246 P.2d 103 (Calif.1952), reh. den. 1952, upholding the removal of a board member who, as an insurance broker along with two other brokers, wrote a policy

of indemnity insurance for a transportation company that had a contract
with the school board for the transportation of school children.

34. 111 S.E.2d 17 (W.Va.1959).

35. 347 U.S. 483, 98 L.Ed.873, 74 S.Ct. 686 (1954) and 349 U.S. 294, 99 L.Ed.
1083, 75 S.Ct. 753 (1955).

36. See *Education Directory, 1964–65* (Washington, D.C.: U.S. Department of
Health, Education and Welfare, 1965), pp. 10, 11.

37. In *State ex rel. University of Minnesota et al.* v. *Chase*, 220 N.W. 951
(Minn.1928) the university was created by Laws of the Territory which
provided that the "government of this university shall be vested in a
board of twelve regents" and, with the coming of statehood, the state
constitution provided that "all the rights, immunities, franchises and en-
dowments heretofore granted" were "perpetuated unto the said university."
It was held that the university was not subject to a commission of administration and finance established by the legislature to have jurisdiction
tion over all "departments and all officials and agencies of the state
government."

In *University of Utah* v. *Board of Examiners of State of Utah*, 295 P.2d
348 (Utah 1956) with the coming of statehood the state constitution provided that "(t)he location and establishment by existing laws of the University of Utah . . . are hereby confirmed, and all the rights, immunities,
franchises . . . heretofore granted or conferred are hereby perpetuated
unto said University. . . ." It was held that the University was subject to a
legislatively created state board of examiners with respect to its purposes
and government.

In *King* v. *Board of Regents of University of Nevada*, 200 P.2d 221
(Nevada 1948) the state constitution provided that "the legislature shall
provide for the establishment of a state university . . . to be controlled
by a board of regents, whose duties shall be prescribed by law." Thereafter the legislature created an advisory board of regents with rights and
privileges of elected regents but with no determining vote on matters
under the control of the elected board. It was held improper to create
such an advisory board.

38. See *Sterling* v. *Regents of the University of Michigan*, 68 N.W. 253
(Mich.1896).

39. 132 N.W. 1037 (Mich.1911).

40. 30 N.W.2d 854 (Mich.1948).

41. 145 N.W.2d 860 (Mich.1966).

42. The Fifth Amendment provides that "No person shall . . . be deprived of
life, liberty, or property, without due process of law; . . ." and is a limitation on Federal Government regulations. The Fourteenth Amendment
provides ". . . nor shall any State deprive any person of life, liberty, or
property, without due process of law; . . ." and is a limitation on state
government regulations.

43. 268 U.S. 510, 69 L.Ed. 1071, 45 S.Ct. 571 (1925).

44. See *Betty–June School Inc.* v. *Young*, 201 N.Y.S.2d 692 (1960) where
municipal regulations directed at all non-public schools were enforced

only against private non-sectarian schools and required such schools to make extensive alterations. The court found no justification for the regulations and questioned whether a municipality could legislate in "purely educational matters" over which the state has regulatory powers. See also *Roman Catholic Welfare Corporation of San Francisco* v. *City of Piedmont*, 289 P.2d 438 (Calif.1955) holding that a city may not constitutionally prevent the building and operation of non-public schools in an area where it permits the building and operation of public schools.

45. 339 P.2d 914 (Calif.1959), reh. den. 1959. In this case the ordinance provided that "conditional permits" could be issued for the building of churches, schools, etc., in residential areas. A permit was granted to construct a non-public school in a residential area and suit was brought to have the permit annulled.

46. For a discussion of cases dealing with the general problem, see "Churches and Zoning," 70 *Harvard Law Review* 1420 (1957).

47. See *Kraft* v. *Board of Education for the District of Columbia,* 247 F.Supp. 21 (D.C.1965) and *Institute of the Metropolis* v. *University of the State of New York et al.,* 289 N.Y.S. 660 (1936), affirmed 291 N.Y.S. 893 (1936).

48. 271 F.Supp. 65 (Ill.1967).

CHAPTER III

The Employment, and Rights and Responsibilities
of Administrative and Teaching Personnel

THE employment of educational personnel is accomplished by agreements entered into between the governing bodies of schools or educational institutions on the one hand, and prospective employees on the other. These agreements or employment contracts, as a general rule, are also the point of reference for determining the rights and responsibilities of education personnel. In addition to the terms and conditions expressly provided in the employment contract, other conditions or requirements may be implied from the express conditions and from the nature of the contract, and still other conditions and requirements may be imposed by relevant statutes which are incorporated into the employment contract by operation of law.

The statutes and court decisions in this area include matters relating to employment in elementary, secondary, and higher education, both public and non-public. A high percentage of the litigated cases are disposed of by applying the principles of the law of employment contracts, but in many of the decisions the constitutional rights of teachers are also at issue.

Public Educational Systems and Institutions

PUBLIC ELEMENTARY AND SECONDARY EDUCATION

Typically, laws in each of the fifty states provide conditions precedent, such as certification, to the creation of an enforceable contract in the employment of professional personnel in public elementary and secondary educational systems. While education laws vary from state to state, in many respects they are substantially similar.

THE SUPERINTENDENT

Laws in all states except Hawaii[1] provide for semi-autonomous local school districts which, as a general rule, are authorized to employ a school superintendent who is the chief administrative officer for the district. Normally, the superintendent is required by law to possess certain minimum academic qualifications. It is generally held that he is an employee of the local school district, and it has been held that he is not a "public officer."[2] As a general rule, the duties of the local school superintendent are provided for in his contract with the local school board, although some of his duties may be provided for in statutes. It has been held that in the absence of express authorization a superintendent may not execute contracts on behalf of the school board.[3] Statutes frequently authorize school boards to employ superintendents for a specific period of time, and it has been held that a contract between the board and a superintendent for a term longer than that authorized by statute is not binding on the board.[4] Where a school board executes an employment contract with a superintendent for a term authorized by statute, it has been held that the board has no authority to execute a new contract for a term to begin before the existing contract has expired.[5]

Where a board does not attempt to change the term of an existing contract but executes a new contract for a term to begin after a change in board membership, courts have had more difficulty in upholding such action. Typically, local school boards are established as corporate entities with powers to act (as a body) without regard to changes in membership. This legal principle has been applied in determining whether a school board is bound by a long-term contract executed by a predecessor board for the employment of a superintendent. In some cases the courts have held that the principle does not apply where there is an unreasonable length of time between the execution of the new contract and the beginning of the superintendent's new term. In *Funchess* v. *Lindsay*[6] a board of education elected a superintendent for a four-year term to begin after a change in board membership. The newly constituted board attempted to rescind the action of the predecessor board, and the superintendent brought suit to compel the recognition of his employment contract. The court granted the superintendent the relief he requested, pointing out that the board is a corporate body which "continues always the same" regardless of a change in the individuals composing it. It is to be noted, however, that the appointment made by the predecessor board was to commence six months after the contract was executed, and the court held that this was not an unreasonable length of time. In *State ex rel. Russell* v. *Richardson*[7] the predecessor board elected a superintendent for a four-year term, and then one year before this term expired and shortly before a change in board membership, the predecessor board re-elected the superintendent to another four-year term to commence one year from the date of re-election and after a change in board membership. The successor board rescinded the action of the predecessor board in re-electing the superintendent and elected another person to serve as superintendent. In upholding the action of the successor board, the court stated that "While it may be true that a school board is a continuous body because of the overlapping terms of its various . . . members, that fact does not authorize the board to elect or appoint a . . . superintendent so far in advance of his term as was done in this case. If this were permitted, the board could elect or appoint a . . . superintendent at any time the majority of its members saw fit to do so, and thereby perpetuate a favored person in office. We think a better practice would be, and one more in consonance with the purpose of the law, to impose this duty of timely electing or appointing a . . . superintendent upon the school board as constituted just prior to the beginning of the new term." In view of the role of school boards in the education process and the legal requirements for periodic changes in board memberships, there is merit to the view that the power of such boards to bind their successors should be limited. However, where a state legislature has made a school board a corporate entity and has not limited its power to bind its successors, there may be some question whether courts should impose limitations by *judicial legislation*.

As a general rule, the decisions of the majority of the members of the governing body of a corporation are binding on the minority and become the decisions of the governing body, unless the by-laws of the corporation or the provisions of an applicable statute provide otherwise. A recent New Jersey decision is not easy to reconcile with this principle of corporation law or with the principles of the law of contracts. In *Thomas* v. *Board of Education of Morris Township*[8] the majority of a predecessor school board, with the superintendent's consent, rescinded his two-year probationary contract and gave him a three-year contract with tenure status. Thereafter, a successor board unilaterally rescinded the three-year tenure contract and, exercising its right under the two-year probationary contract, gave the superintendent a thirty-day notice of termination. The court upheld the successor board's action on the ground that the action of the majority of the predecessor board in participating in the rescission of the two-year probationary contract and executing the three-year tenure contract over the protest of the minority of the predecessor board, was, among other things, contrary to public policy.

Capable superintendents are often in short supply, and some school boards have found it advisable to increase their salaries during their contract periods to prevent them from being attracted away by higher salaries. It is not uncommon, however, for state laws to prohibit increasing the salaries of public employees during their contract periods. Principles of the law of contracts permit the parties to a contract to terminate it by mutual consent and, thereafter, enter into a new contract. In effect, this was done with judicial approval in *Stewart* v. *Eaves*.[9] A superintendent resigned and, thereafter, was reappointed at a higher salary. In *Johnston et al.* v. *Rapp*[10] a clause in the contract reserving the board's right to increase the superintendent's salary received court approval.

As a general rule, the rights of a superintendent who is illegally dismissed during his contract period are not different from those of other employees who are illegally dismissed. Such dismissals constitute a breach of contract; the traditional remedy is a suit for damages. The right to specific performance and injunctive relief are not ordinarily available to an employee for breach of a personal service or employment contract. In some states a superintendent is permitted to acquire tenure,[11] and where tenure is acquired, he is, of course, entitled to the remedies provided for illegal dismissals in the tenure laws.

PUBLIC SCHOOL TEACHERS

U.S. Office of Education statistics indicate that in 1964 a total of 1,667,000 teachers were employed in public elementary and secondary education systems throughout the nation, and that an additional 235,000 were employed in non-public elementary and secondary systems.[12] In general, the public school teachers had employment contracts with local boards of education; these contracts are the primary source of their rights and responsibilities. Relevant education laws are considered as being incorporated into these contracts whether or not they are specifically referred to in the individual contracts.

Certification. The possession of a valid certificate is a prerequisite to employment. It is evidence of academic competence to teach, but its issuance does not create a contract of employment.[13] In many states, certification responsibilities are delegated to the central education agency or official, but the discretion allowed this agency or official varies greatly from state to state. Some state laws make specific provision for several different types of certificates, while in other states, the details are left to the education agency. As a general rule, an applicant for a teacher's certificate may meet the required academic qualifications by presenting evidence of successful completion of studies in an accredited educational institution, or passage of an examination, or both. Some large cities are authorized to give their own examinations and to develop eligibility lists on which prospective teachers are rated according to their examination scores and other criteria.[14] In some states an applicant is required to sign a loyalty oath as a condition to receiving a certificate.[15] It is uniformly held that a certificate, even a "life certificate," may be suspended for adequate cause.[16] In view of the importance of certification to members of the education profession who wish to teach, it would seem that teachers should have more assurance—than existing education laws now provide—that the authority to issue, suspend, and revoke a certificate is vested in agencies and officials qualified to make any required professional decisions.

Employment. As a general rule, local school boards are authorized to employ teachers by executing employment contracts with them in the manner provided by law. All states have statutes of some kind relating to the employment of public school teachers, and these statutes, together with the general principles of contract law not inconsistent with statutory law, determine the requirements for an enforceable teacher's employment contract. Some oral contracts are enforceable under the general principles of contract law, but statutes requiring teacher's contracts to be in writing prevail over such general principles. In general, statutes require a teacher to possess a valid certificate or license to be eligible for employment. Whether a teacher must have the certificate when the contract is executed or at the time actual employment begins depends on the language of the relevant statute or on the court's interpretation of the statute where the legislative intent is not clear from the language used. (In interpreting statutes, courts attempt, at least theoretically, to ascertain the intent of the legislature in enacting the law.)[17] A similar situation is presented where a statute provides that a teacher must have reached a certain age (usually eighteen) to be eligible to teach.[18]

Some courts hold that a contract entered into by a teacher who is ineligible to enter into the contract is a void contract and cannot be ratified by the school board's acceptance of the teacher's services. The position taken in the *Restatement of Contracts* is that there is no contract where one of the parties to an agreement is ineligible to enter into the contract. A contract which can be ratified is a voidable contract under the *Restatement*.[19] It is often difficult to determine whether a legislature intended a statutory requirement for a teacher's contract to be essential to the creation of the contract. If a court determines that the legislature did not intend a particular statutory requirement to be essential to the formation of a teacher's employment contract, the court may hold that failure to comply with the statutory requirement results in a voidable contract which may be ratified.[20] Under the principles of contract law, an offer by a qualified offeror and acceptance by a qualified offeree are essential to the creation of a valid contract,[21] and it has been held that informal negotiations with members of a school board are legally insufficient to constitute a valid offer.[22]

Under some state statutes, the superintendent is responsible for recommending to the board the persons to be employed as teachers. It has been held that where such a statute exists, an appointment by the board without the recommendation of the superintendent is invalid.[23]

As a general rule, a school board may adopt reasonable regulations with respect to the employment of teachers, but such regulations may not conflict with overriding constitutional or statutory provisions. Courts are constantly called upon to determine whether a legislative enactment, an agency regulation, or the conduct of a person is reasonable and, therefore, valid, or unreasonable and, therefore, invalid. In reaching their decisions courts must take several factors into consideration. Thus, in 1939 and in 1940 courts upheld a regulation against the employment of married women as teachers[24] and a regulation requiring teachers to live in the district where they were employed.[25] It must be remembered, however, that what was considered reasonable a quarter of a century ago might not be considered reasonable today. Improved means of transportation, the increased mobility of people generally, the increase in the number of men in the teaching profession, the general preference for competence in teaching without regard to marital status, and other factors would be relevant today in deciding the reasonableness of the regulations held to be reasonable in 1939 and 1940.

Rights and Responsibilities After Employment. In the absence of a statute providing otherwise, the rights and responsibilities of the parties to an employment contract are determined by the express or implied terms of the contract. Almost all states have some type of legislation relating to the contracts of public school teachers.[26] To the extent that they are relevant, these statutes are uniformly held to be part of teachers' contracts whether or not they are expressly incorporated therein. Several states have adopted uniform contract forms which are either mandatory or recommended.[27] An essential element in a teacher's contract is its duration, which may be for one or more school years (i.e., a term contract) or for an indefinite period (e.g., a tenure contract). However, not all contracts for an indefinite period are genuine tenure contracts.[28] Under the general principles of contract law, a school board as an employer has no legal right to terminate a teacher's contract by dismissal before the end of the contract period except for a cause that amounts to a material breach of contract on the part of the teacher. A teacher who has been dismissed without sufficient justification or cause may recover damages in a suit for breach of contract. In determining the amount of damages, the general contract rule is that an employee who has been wrongfully dismissed may recover the total amount which would have been received under the employment contract if it had not been breached, less any sum which he has earned or could have earned by reasonable effort in other suitable and similar employment for which he is qualified. This obligation to mitigate damages has been applied where public school teachers have been wrongfully dismissed.[29]

Of course, under the general principles of contract law a school board has no legal obligation to re-employ a teacher after the end of the contract period. State laws relating to the employment of teachers in public education may provide rights and obligations different from those existing under the general principles of contract law. Such statutes may provide that a teacher may be dismissed before the end of the contract period only for certain specific causes. They may provide that dismissals for cause may be made only after timely notice to the teacher and opportunity to be heard. They may provide for automatic renewal unless a notice of nonrenewal is given to the teacher before a certain date. A statute may qualify as a genuine tenure statute if it provides that (1) a teacher's contract is automatically renewed, normally after serving a certain number of years called a probationary period; (2) dismissals thereafter may be made only for specific causes which must be established by timely notice and opportunity to be heard; and (3) a teacher who has been wrongfully dismissed is entitled to reinstatement and is not limited to damages.

TEACHER TENURE LAWS

Discussions of the employment rights and responsibilities of public school teachers usually distinguish between statutes under which teachers must be given timely notice of specific charges, and an opportunity to be heard thereon before dismissal, on the one hand, and statutes under which the school board is obligated only to give a teacher timely notice of nonrenewal, on the other. The statutes of the former type are classified as genuine tenure statutes.[30]

It is uniformly held that a state legislature, in the exercise of its plenary power over public education, may enact teacher tenure laws and thereafter amend or repeal such laws. This is true *unless* the intent of the legislature, as shown by the language used in the original enactment, was to waive or limit its right to amend or repeal that enactment. Where the legislative intent is not clear from the language used in the statute, the interpretation of the statute by the state's courts is frequently controlling. However, where a federal question is involved and the case is properly before the U.S. Supreme Court, that Court is not bound by the state courts' interpretation of a statute. In *Phelps* v. *Board of Education of West New York et al.*[31] and *State of Indiana ex rel. Anderson* v. *Brand*,[32] the U.S. Supreme Court was called upon to decide whether legislative amendments to teacher tenure laws of New Jersey and Indiana respectively impaired "the obligation of contracts" in violation of Article I, Section 10 of the Federal Constitution.[33] In the *Phelps* case, a New Jersey teacher tenure law passed in 1909 prohibited school boards from reducing the salaries of tenure teachers, but a 1933 amendment removed this prohibition and authorized school boards "to fix and determine salaries" of school board employees "notwithstanding any such person be under tenure." Thereafter, a school board reduced the salaries of its employees including its teachers, and a teacher who had acquired tenure under the 1909 statute brought suit to have the board action set aside and the 1933 amendment declared unconstitutional on the ground that it impaired the obligation of a contract created by the 1909 statute. In the *Brand* case, an Indiana teacher tenure law, passed in 1927, prohibited the dismissal of tenure teachers except for specified causes and in the manner provided in the 1927 tenure law. A 1933 amendment reduced the coverage of the 1927 law by omitting teachers in township schools. Thereafter, a teacher in a township school who had acquired tenure under the 1927 law was dismissed without the tenure procedures required by the 1927 law, and she sued to compel her reinstatement.

The *Phelps* and *Brand* cases are distinguishable in several respects. The tenure statutes were different. The specific relief sought by the teachers was different, but there are some important similarities in relation to ascertaining the intention of the legislatures in enacting the tenure laws. In both cases the state courts interpreted the respective tenure laws as noncontractual, and in both cases the U.S. Supreme Court, while asserting that it was not bound by state court interpretations, also recognized that such interpretations are weighty and entitled to careful consideration. In the *Phelps* case, the U.S. Supreme Court accepted the holding of the New Jersey courts, "that the Act of 1909 did not amount to a legislative contract with the teachers of the state and did not become a term of the contracts entered into with the employees by boards of education." With respect to the views of state courts, the U.S. Supreme Court went so far as to say that it *should* accept them unless they "are palpably erroneous." Thus, it was held that the 1933 amendment authorizing school boards to reduce salaries did not impair the obligation of contracts, because the provision in the 1909 law prohibiting reduction of salaries by school boards "was but a regulation of the conduct of the board and not a term of continuing contract of indefinite duration with the individual teacher . . . ." However, in the *Brand* case, decided only one year after the *Phelps* case, the U.S. Supreme Court refused to accept the holding of the state court that the 1927 law did not amount to a legislative contract. In this case the Supreme Court did not consider itself limited to a consideration of whether the views of the state court were "palpably erroneous." The Supreme Court's responsibility for keeping the "impairment of the obligation of contracts" clause of Article I, Section 10, Clause 1 of the Federal Constitution from becoming "a dead letter," was said to require that the Supreme Court decide for itself whether a contract has been made and whether the state has, by later legislation, impaired its obligation. In holding that the 1927 Indiana law amounted to a legislative contract, the Supreme Court referred to decisions of the Indiana courts recognizing that the "employment of school teachers was contractual," and to the number of times the word "contract" is found in the 1927 law.[34] It does not appear inappropriate to suggest that the decision in the *Brand* case is not one of the Supreme Court's most logical decisions. A dissenting opinion says, among other things, "Indiana's highest court has said that the *State did not,* and has strongly indicated that the *legislature could not,* make contracts with a *few citizens,* that would take away from *all the citizens,* the continuing power to alter the educational policy for the best interests of Indiana school children. . . ." The immediate effect of the decision in the *Brand* case was to prohibit the dismissal of teachers who had acquired tenure under the 1927 law, except in the manner and for the causes specified in that law. That this may have been a pyrrhic victory is indicated by the decision of the Indiana Supreme Court on remand from the U.S. Supreme Court.[35] The state court again sustained the demurrer of the school officials on the ground that although the U.S. Supreme Court had determined that the teacher's contract rights to tenure status acquired under the 1927 law were protected against impairment, it did not "discuss or pass upon the nature of the remedy available." The state court then went on to hold that the teacher's mandamus action was not proper, because it incorrectly assumed that the school officials still had a statutory duty to reinstate her even though the statute creating such a duty had been repealed.[36]

The *Brand* case demonstrates that it is possible for a legislature to draft a tenure statute creating rights and obligations which cannot be changed or annulled by subsequent legislation. Few, if any, state tenure laws are subject to this interpretation and there appears to be no sound basis for such an interpretation. After all, new developments may make it educationally advisable to change tenure laws in a manner which may be of benefit to all teachers.

The legality of teacher tenure laws is no longer open to question, but during the period of their development, they were challenged at times on the ground that their primary purpose was to benefit public school teachers. In general, these challenges have been unsuccessful. The almost uniform judicial position is that the legislative purpose in enacting teacher tenure laws is to strengthen the state's system of public education by giving teachers security against arbitrary dismissals, thus stabilizing the teaching force.[37]

Acquisition of Tenure—the Probationary Period. Most, but not all, tenure laws require a teacher to complete a probationary period ranging from one to five years in order to qualify for tenure status.[38] The general purpose of the probationary period is to give the school board or local school superintendent opportunity to determine whether the teacher is competent to perform the duties for which she or he has been employed. There is evidence that some school boards have attempted to use the probationary period for other purposes.[39]

The rights and responsibilities of probationary teachers vary from state to state, but, in general, statutory provisions relating to probationary periods are strictly construed.[40]

Dismissals for Cause. Under common law principles of employment contracts, an employer has no legal right to dismiss an employee with whom he has a valid contract before the end of the contract period, except for causes amounting to a material breach of contract on the part of the employee. A dismissal without cause during the contract is a breach of contract on the part of the employer, for which the employee may recover damages in a suit brought for that purpose. Whether an employee's action or non-action is cause for dismissal may be determined by the express or implied provisions of the particular contract. State statutes relating to the employment of public school teachers are, in general, part of a public school teacher's contract whether or not they are specifically incorporated therein. As a general rule, the reasonable rules and regulations of a school board are also held to be part of the teacher's contract, and it has been held that a teacher's failure or refusal to comply with such rules and regulations is cause for dismissal even though the evidence shows that the teacher was not aware of the rule.[41] A question can be raised as to the soundness of the view that school board rules and regulations are part of a teacher's contract whether or not the teacher is aware of them. Such a view puts a heavy burden on teachers and permits the existence of a variety of causes for dismissal within a single state without any apparent reason. It should not be too difficult to provide for substantially the same causes for dismissal for all public school teachers within a particular state. The dismissal of a teacher before the end of the contract period is a serious matter, and the opportunities for arbitrary dismissal of academically qualified teachers should be reduced to a minimum.[42]

The general principles of contract law do not require an employer to give an employee a hearing before a dismissal for cause during the contract period. If a dismissed employee believes his dismissal is not justified and is a breach of contract on the part of the employer, he may sue the employer, who will then be required to defend the dismissal by evidence of the employee's failure to perform his contractual obligations. Thus, an employee can get a judicial hearing and determination of the legality of his dismissal and damages for an illegal dismissal. However, local boards of education are state agencies, and their actions are state actions, subject to limitations on state action in the Federal Constitution. One such limitation is the *due process clause* of the Fourteenth Amendment. It has been held that even though there is no statutory requirement, a nontenure teacher is entitled to notice of the charges and a fair hearing before an impartial board before his dismissal for cause.[43] In view of the current judicial concern about *procedural due process* with respect to the dismissal of students in public education, it is not unreasonable to assume that there will be similar concern with respect to the dismissal of teachers in public education.

Typically, while tenure laws recognize the right of school boards and/or superintendents to transfer and reassign tenure teachers, they classify demotions and reductions in salary as equivalent to dismissals which may not be made without timely notice and hearing. Whether a particular change is a bona fide transfer or is, in fact, a demotion has arisen in a number of cases. The judicial answer frequently turns on the language in the particular statute. It has been held that the transfer of a superintendent to a teaching position was a dismissal, but the transfer of a principal to a teaching position was not.[44] In a recent New York case[45] the court upheld the transfer of a tenure teacher from her position as classroom teacher to a non-teaching position in the headquarters of the board. Headquarters duty was held to be within the scope of the teacher's license. From the facts recited in the court's opinion, it is not unreasonable to imply that the teacher's insubordination was adequate cause to support the teacher's dismissal, but the board preferred the transfer procedure to the dismissal procedure required by the tenure law. Assertions that tenure laws make it practically impossible to dismiss a tenure teacher are not uncommon. Members of the teaching profession should be concerned about the merits of such assertions. They have a professional obligation to develop and sponsor whatever changes in tenure laws are needed to prevent them from being used as shields for incompetent teachers, and at the same time provide protection against arbitrary dismissals by school boards.

There is considerable variation in the statutory causes for dismissal. In some statutes specific causes are listed; in others the specific causes are followed by a "catch-all" such as, reasonable and just cause, good and just cause, due and sufficient cause, or simply, cause. In a few tenure laws only a catch-all cause is listed. Many states have laws with respect to loyalty and subversive associations in which certain activities by public school teachers are made causes for dismissal.

Where the list of specific causes for dismissal is followed by a general or catch-all cause, it has been held that the general cause is limited by the specific causes.[46] It has also been held that where a statute lists specific causes for dismissal, they are exclusive, and a teacher may not be dismissed for causes not specified.[47]

Some of the specific causes for dismissal listed in several different tenure laws are incompetence, insubordination, immorality or immoral conduct, neglect of duty, and refusal to obey orders of superiors. Court decisions construing the scope of these specific causes indicate a real need for the development of causes for dismissal that are both educationally and legally sound. An examination of court decisions concerning the specific causes referred to above indicates some of the difficulties.

Incompetence. There is little uniformity in the court decisions interpreting the meaning of incompetence when relied upon as a cause for the dismissal of a tenure teacher. It has not been limited to academic competence. For example, incompetence has been held to include a teacher's persistent refusal to permit his superiors to enter his classroom for the purpose of supervising his work,[48] although insubordination would seem to be a more appropriate cause.

Insubordination. This statutory cause is provided in different forms. In some statutes the language used is "willful and persistent insubordination," in others it is "persistent violation of or refusal to obey school laws or regulations of the board." As already stated, there may be some question whether school board rules and regulations should be given the same status as statutes and considered as part of a teacher's employment contract. Where the statutory cause of "willful" insubordination is used as the basis for a teacher's dismissal, it would seem that proof that a teacher violated a board rule is inadequate unless there is evidence that the teacher had actual knowledge of the rule alleged to be violated. Where a teacher's refusal to obey an order or directive of which he is actually aware is used to support a charge of insubordination, the general rule is that the order or directive must be reasonable. A teacher's refusal to obey a superintendent's *suggestion* that the teacher take over the teaching of certain classes for the twenty-seven days remaining in the school year was upheld on the grounds that the superintendent's suggestion was unreasonable under the circumstances.[49] On the other hand, it has been held to be insubordination and cause for dismissal that a teacher refused to attend an "Open House" conducted in the school to which she was assigned, after being told by the superintendent that she was required to attend the event.[50]

Immorality or Immoral Conduct. It has been reported that this is the most common specific cause for the dismissal of tenure teachers.[51] Court decisions defining the scope of immorality as a cause for the dismissal of teachers indicate judicial reluctance to give the term a narrow construction.[52] In *Watts* v. *Seward School Board*[53] a statute defined immorality as conduct tending to bring a teacher or the teaching profession into public disgrace or disrespect. Two public school teachers were dismissed on grounds of statutory immorality because allegedly they had solicited the support of other teachers to remove certain school administrators, and one of them had made a speech before a local labor union in which he stated that they were "going to get rid of the board." In sustaining the dismissals, the state's highest court held that the teachers' conduct "had a tendency to bring (the teachers) and the teaching profession into public disgrace and disrespect." On appeal to the U.S. Supreme Court, certiorari was granted, but in the interim the state legislature enacted a law establishing the right of public teachers to criticize their superiors to the same extent as other citizens. Thereafter, the U.S. Supreme Court remanded the case back to the Alaska Supreme Court for reconsideration in light of this new legislation.[54] Upon remand, the state Supreme Court, with one dissent, reaffirmed the dismissals. The Court held that board regulations which were part of the teachers' contracts provided grievance procedures which the teachers were contractually obligated to use. That the teachers did not use these procedures was, in itself, held to be a cause for dismissal. The dissenting Justice was of the opinion that the grievance procedure did not prohibit the public airing of grievances, and the teachers' failure to use it was not "sufficient cause for their non-retention."[55] It should be noted, however, the U.S. Supreme Court again granted certiorari, and a decision is now pending.[56]

In some respects the issues in the *Watts* case are similar to those in *Board of Trustees of the Lassen Union High School District* v. *Owens*,[57] where a tenure teacher manifested his dissatisfaction with the educational practices in the school district in which he was employed by establishing and directing a "Public Forum," and conducting a letter-writing campaign to the local newspaper. The teacher's letters were critical of what he termed the "do nothing" attitude of certain board members and certain professional associations. The letters were not vituperative and contained no personal attacks on any person. He did report on the efforts of some board members to stop the letter-writing. His last letter urged all citizens to "elect the maximum number of new board members" at the next election. The teacher's dismissal on the ground of *unprofessional conduct* was upheld by the trial court. However, the appellate court, with one dissent, invalidated the dismissal. It was held that the teacher violated no board rule in publicly airing his grievances, he was not precluded from joining in public debate because of his status as a teacher, and his public behavior had not affected his classroom effectiveness. The dissent argued "that a teacher . . . owes it to the school that is employing him to endeavor to advance the interest of the school and the students," and that the teacher's conduct in this case was a breach of this obligation. The *Watts* and *Owens* decisions involve questions concerning the extent to which public school teachers can be restricted in the exercise of their constitutional rights of freedom of speech. These questions are discussed later under *The Federal Constitutional Rights of Teachers with Respect to Employment.*

Neglect of Duty. In decisions in which a court has been required to determine the scope of this cause for dismissal, it is generally given a liberal construction. It has been held, for instance, that a teacher who directed a vulgar remark at his principal can be dismissed for willful neglect of duty and incompetence.[58]

Refusal to Obey Orders of Superiors. In one form or another, this cause is found in several statutes. In general, the conduct of teachers covered by this cause is also covered by the causes of insubordination or neglect of duty. The initial question here is whether an order given by a superior is consistent with the teacher's contractual obligations, i.e., whether the teacher refused to do something which his contract expressly or impliedly obligated him to do. As previously noted, the general rule is that relevant statutes and board regulations are impliedly a part of a

public school teacher's contract.⁵⁹ Of course, the basic question is
whether the order or directive which the teacher refused to obey
or follow is reasonable.

There is some conflict in the decisions as to the reasonableness
of a regulation, directive, or order requiring a teacher to supervise
after-school pupil activities. Court decisions indicate that the issue
centers around a consideration of whether the activities are a part
of or related to the school's educational program.⁶⁰ There may be
some question whether, and if so, to what extent courts should
read agreements into, or imply terms in teachers' contracts when
called upon to interpret them. There are probably a great many
teachers' contracts in which no reference is made to the teacher's
duty to supervise or otherwise participate in after-school pupil
activities. Such supervision and participation seem educationally
sound, but it does not follow that it is not necessary to make
specific provision for it in teachers' contracts. It has been suggested
that school boards should consider including in the contracts of
teachers a general provision that the teachers agree to perform
such other reasonable duties as the board may indicate, in addition to the general statement of the subjects they are to teach and
the salary to be received.⁶¹ There is evidence that the assignment
of teachers to participate in or supervise after-school pupil activities is regarded by teachers as a negotiable item in professional
negotiation and collective bargaining, which is discussed in
Appendix II.

In some court decisions involving the legality of the dismissal of
a teacher, the issue as framed by the court is whether the charge
or charges are included in specific statutory causes provided by
legislation. It has been held proper for a board to dismiss a tenure
teacher who pleaded guilty to being intoxicated, attempting to
fight, and displaying a gun.⁶² Where members of the community
complain about the manner in which a teacher conducts her class
but the complaints in no way reflect upon the teacher's moral
fitness to teach, it has been held that, even though these complaints have made the teacher "the center of controversy," they do
not constitute good cause for dismissal as the term "good cause"
is used in the tenure law.⁶³

Statutes in a few states provide that the board must give
teachers a warning notice and an opportunity to correct remediable causes before notice of dismissal, and it has been held that the

board's decision that a cause is not remediable and, therefore, does not require a warning notice, is subject to judicial review.[64] The warning notice requirement is educationally sound, and if the decision as to whether a cause is remediable is to be made by the board consisting of laymen or by a court, a court may be more objective. Of course, it would be preferable to vest the decision-making authority in a person or persons with the professional competence to determine whether the teacher has the potential "to make a good teacher."

DISMISSALS AND REFUSALS TO RE-EMPLOY BECAUSE OF RACE AND/OR CIVIL RIGHTS ACTIVITIES

The desegregation of public schools in compliance with the mandate of the U.S. Supreme Court in its *Brown* v. *Board of Education of Topeka, Kansas*[65] decisions of 1954 and 1955 has resulted in the dismissal or refusal to re-employ many Negro teachers formerly employed to teach in public schools maintained for Negro students. On other occasions it has been alleged that Negro teachers have been dismissed or denied re-employment because they exercised their constitutional rights to participate in civil rights activities.

In *Franklin* v. *County School Board of Giles County*[66] a lower court held that certain Negro teachers had been improperly discharged and ordered the board to notify the teachers of any vacancy for which they were qualified and give them an opportunity to apply and be considered along with other eligibles. On appeal, it was held that the relief granted by the lower court was inadequate and that the teachers were entitled to re-employment in any vacancy for which they were qualified. However, in the earlier case of *Brooks et al.* v. *School District of City of Moberly, Missouri et al.*,[67] the court upheld the denial of re-employment to all of the eleven teachers in a formerly Negro school which was closed upon integration, although some of them had a greater number of college credits and more teaching experience than some of the white teachers who were re-employed. The teachers who were re-employed were recommended by the superintendent and appointed by the board of education. In making his recommendations, the superintendent took into consideration such intangible factors as personality and ability to fulfill the requirements of the position. It was conceded by the court that the result was "unusual and somewhat startling" but held that the evidence was insufficient to support the allegation of bad faith on the part of the superintendent or the board.

Recent decisions of the U.S. Court of Appeals for the Fifth Circuit make it clear that the *Brown* decisions require the integration of teaching staffs where dual public school systems were formerly maintained.[68] In suits brought by or on behalf of students seeking compliance with the *Brown* decisions it has been frequently contended that teaching staffs should be integrated. Occasionally this issue has been postponed.[69] However, in *Bradley et al.* v. *School Board of the City of Richmond et al.* and *Gilliam* v. *School Board of City of Hopewell, Virginia et al.*,[70] the U.S. Supreme Court held that district courts, in passing upon school desegregation plans, must consider faculty allocation without regard to race.

In a number of cases the refusal to re-employ Negro teachers has been challenged on the ground that the refusal was based upon the teacher's participation in civil rights activity. In *Johnson* v. *Branch et al.*[71] a Negro teacher after twelve years of successful teaching was charged with some minor rule infractions and refused re-employment. She explained all the charges and alleged that the real reason for the failure to re-employ her was the principal's objection to her civil rights activities. She convinced the court, which ordered her contract renewed and awarded her damages.[72] In other cases Negro teachers have not succeeded in sustaining the burden of proving that the real reason for refusing them re-employment was their civil rights activities.[73]

The problems faced by many Negro teachers, especially in states that have maintained separate public school systems for Negro and white students, should be a matter of serious concern to members of the teaching profession. Before racial segregation in public education was outlawed, Negro students were the principal victims of unqualified teachers, and there is evidence of laxity on the part of school boards in the staffing of public schools maintained for Negro students. Some of the cases discussed above show that it is possible for well-qualified Negro teachers to obtain legal redress for illegal dismissals or refusals to re-employ even in the absence of tenure laws. However, the *Brooks* case demonstrates some of the problems involved in the reduction of teaching staff brought about by the integration of formerly separate schools. One may question whether a superintendent should be permitted to recommend teachers on the basis of intangible factors that override academic qualifications and teaching experience. Position papers by such organizations as the National Education Association and the American Federation of Teachers might aid the courts in arriving at educationally sound conclusions in cases similar to the *Brooks* case. Teachers with minimal or inadequate academic training present a more difficult problem. In view of the national shortage of qualified teachers, it might be money well spent to provide government subsidies for their additional training.

THE FEDERAL CONSTITUTIONAL RIGHTS OF TEACHERS WITH RESPECT TO EMPLOYMENT

State legislatures, governing bodies of public educational systems and institutions, and other administrative agencies and officials vested with powers and duties with respect to public education are state agencies. Their actions must conform to the requirements and limitations on state action imposed by provisions of the Federal Constitution. In addition to the constitutional prohibition against impairing the obligation of contracts referred to earlier, provisions of the First, Fifth, and Fourteenth Amendments have been invoked by teachers and other personnel in public education as protections against state action in relation to their employment. The actions which have been challenged as unconstitutional fall mainly within three areas: loyalty oath requirements, actions relating to invocation of the Fifth Amendment, and actions relating to freedom of speech and freedom of association.

It is generally agreed that the individual rights protected by the First, Fifth, and Fourteenth Amendments are not absolute and are subject to reasonable governmental limitation and regulation. When governmental action, either legislative or administrative, in the three areas set out above is challenged and the controversy is properly before a court, the court in most cases must determine whether the governmental action is reasonable. Because the applicability of one or more provisions of the Federal Constitution is at issue, the U.S. Supreme Court is the final arbiter. In examining education laws relating to the constitutionally protected rights of public school teachers, it seems appropriate to inquire whether there is a logical basis for imposing special limitations on public employees because they are public (as distinguished from private) employees, and also, whether there are unique aspects of public education which justify special limitations on the constitutionally protected rights of public school teachers because they are public school teachers.

The decision of the U.S. Supreme Court in *Brown* v. *Board of Education of Topeka, Kansas*[74] has been interpreted as giving minority group school teachers rights to employment without regard to their minority group status. The cases providing this interpretation are discussed in Appendix I, "Before and After *Brown* v. *Board of Education of Topeka, Kansas*."

Loyalty Oaths. The federal constitutional issues in loyalty oath and subversive organization cases are the same whether the teachers involved are in public elementary and secondary schools or in public institutions of higher education. Accordingly, this discussion will include court decisions relating to teachers at all levels of public education.

One of the early decisions of the U.S. Supreme Court involving loyalty oaths is *Wieman* v. *Updegraff*,[75] one of the Court's few loyalty oath cases in which the decision was unanimous, although several Justices wrote separate concurring opinions. This was a taxpayer's suit to enjoin the payment of salaries to certain members of the faculty of a public institution of higher education who had refused to subscribe to a statutory loyalty oath. Among other things, the statute required public employees, including teachers, to subscribe to an oath affirming that they were not affiliated with, and during the past five years had not been a member of, any organization determined by the U.S. Attorney General to be "subversive." The statute was upheld by the state courts, but the U.S. Supreme Court held that the statute violated the due process clause of the Federal Constitution, because it was not limited to public employees who joined or were affiliated with "subversive" organizations *knowing* them to be subversive. The Court reviewed its earlier loyalty oath decisions[76] and observed that in all the loyalty oath statutes which had been upheld, *scienter,* or knowledge of the facts, was required either by implication or by state court interpretation. The legal principle to be drawn from *Updegraff*, and the decisions referred to therein, is that in the interest of protecting its public schools from subversive influence, a state may not exclude from public school employment persons who are or who have been members or affiliates of subversive organizations, but it may exclude them if, after notice and opportunity to be heard, it is determined that the organizations are subversive and such persons *knew* they were subversive.

In *Adler* v. *Board of Education of City of New York*,[77] New York's Feinberg law was upheld in a six-to-three decision. This law required, among other things, that the state board of regents make a list of organizations found to be subversive, after giving such organizations notice and opportunity to be heard. The board of regents was required to provide by regulation that membership in these organizations would be *prima facie* evidence of disqualification for employment in the public schools. New York courts had construed the legislation as requiring teachers to have knowledge of the subversive nature of the organizations before the regulation could apply. In his dissenting opinion, in which Mr. Justice Black concurred, Mr. Justice Douglas contended that the Feinberg law "proceeds on a principle repugnant to our society—guilt by association."

Fifteen years after the *Adler* decision, New York's Feinberg law was again before the U.S. Supreme Court in *Keyishian et al.* v. *Board of Regents of the University of the State of New York et al.*,[78] where certain employees of one of New York's public institutions of higher education refused to sign the certificate required by the law and brought suit for declaratory and injunctive relief. In a five-to-four decision it was held that the Feinberg law is invalid insofar as it penalizes "mere knowing membership without any showing of specific intent to further the unlawful aims" of subversive organizations. Aware of the *Adler* decision upholding the Feinberg law, the Court majority held that "the constitutional doctrine which has emerged since (Adler) . . . has rejected its major premise . . . that public employment, including academic employment, may be conditioned upon the surrender of constitutional rights which could not be abridged by direct governmental action." The dissenters felt, among other things, that the cases since *Adler* showed no emergence of a constitutional doctrine rejecting *Adler's* premise. In their opinion, the narrow issue was whether a state may provide that one "... who wilfully and deliberately becomes a member of an organization that advocates the overthrow of government by force or violence is *prima facie* disqualified from teaching in the state's public educational institutions...." The dissenters' answer was unequivocally, yes.

In *Baggett et al.* v. *Bullitt et al.*[79] the U.S. Supreme Court, in a seven-to-two decision, held that two state loyalty oath statutes were unconstitutionally vague and violated due process, because the language was too uncertain and broad. The majority were concerned that conscientious teachers would "steer far wider of the unlawful zone" than if the boundaries of the forbidden zone were clearly marked and, thus, their freedom of speech would be unreasonably inhibited because of the indefinite language of the statutes. The statutes were held to be too vague notwithstanding the term *subversive person* was defined with considerable specificity.[80] This decision seems to require more specificity than was required under the *Adler* decision and earlier Supreme Court holdings. In *Adler,* knowing membership in a subversive organization was said to be sufficiently specific, but the decision in *Keyishian* has now virtually overruled *Adler.* In *Keyishian* the majority held that to avoid the charge of vagueness, a state loyalty oath must be limited to those teachers who not only knowingly associate with or belong to subversive organizations, but who knowingly support the subversive purposes of such organizations.[81]

One of the cases decided by the U.S. Supreme Court between the *Adler* and *Keyishian* decisions was *Elfbrandt* v. *Russell et al.,*[82] where the challenged statute, in addition to requiring public school teachers to sign a loyalty oath, provided that any person who signed the oath and thereafter became affiliated with the Communist Party, or "any other organization" having for "one of its purposes" the overthrow of the state government, would become subject to dismissal and prosecution for perjury. The law also provided that a public employee "... shall not be entitled to compensation unless and until ..." he or she "does take and subscribe to the form of the oath." A teacher refused to sign the oath, alleging that it was too vague, and subsequently brought suit for declaratory relief. The state Supreme Court upheld the constitutionality of the law,[83] but the U.S. Supreme Court, after granting certiorari, remanded the case back to the state's Supreme Court for further consideration[84] in light of the U.S. Supreme Court's decision in *Baggett et al.* v. *Bullitt et al.*[85] Upon remand, the state Supreme Court,[86] purporting to apply the *Baggett* v. *Bullitt* test of vagueness, again upheld the constitutionality of the statute. The U.S. Supreme Court again granted certiorari.[87] Thereafter, in a five-to-four decision, the statute was held to be unconstitutionally vague,[88] because it was not restricted only to those who join subversive organizations with the specific intent of furthering the organization's subversive purposes. Mr. Justice White, writing for the dissenters, referred to the Court's previous decisions in which states were upheld in denying public employment to persons who are members of organizations which they know to have subversive purposes, even though the persons may not be in sympathy with or have specific intent to further the subversive purposes of the organization.

The legal principle to be drawn from the *Elfbrandt* and *Keyishian* cases is that a state, in the interest of protecting its public schools from subversive influence, may not exclude from public school employment persons who have been or who are members of organizations known to such persons to have subversive aims or purposes, unless it is shown that it is the specific intent of such persons to further the subversive aims of the organizations.

Pleading the Fifth Amendment. Closely related to the problems arising out of loyalty oaths and subversive organizations are the problems incident to the exercise by teachers of their constitutional right to plead the Fifth Amendment. This Amendment provides in part that "No person ... shall be compelled in any criminal case to be a witness against himself ...." This constitutional privilege against self-incrimination has been judicially construed to extend to hearings before official bodies such as federal and state legislative committees.[89] Although it has been consistently held that no inference is to be drawn from the exercise of this privilege, there is a widespread tendency to interpret the plea of the Fifth Amendment as a confession of guilt.

Statutes in several states provide for the automatic dismissal of public employees, including teachers, who exercise this constitutional privilege and refuse to answer questions put to them in hearings before federal or state investigating committees. Prior to 1956 there was a conflict in lower federal court and state court decisions as to the legality of summary dismissals of public employees for invoking the Fifth Amendment before official investigating committees.[90] In several decisions upholding dismissals for exercising the privilege against self-incrimination, teachers have contended that such dismissals violate their constitutional privilege to remain silent. The courts have answered by saying that a teacher has a constitutional privilege to refuse to answer but not a constitutional right to remain a teacher in public education. This half-truth is misleading, because the issue is not whether a teacher has a constitutional right to teach in a public educational institution, but rather whether a teacher has a constitutional right not to be dismissed from, or denied employment in, a public educational institution solely on the ground that he has exercised his constitutional privilege against self-incrimination. This issue is both legal and educational. The legal issue has been resolved, at least in part.

Slochower v. *Board of Higher Education of City of New York*[91] involved the constitutionality of a New York City charter provision requiring the automatic dismissal of any public employee who invoked the Fifth Amendment to avoid answering questions related to his official conduct. A tenure teacher in a public college invoked the Fifth Amendment when called before a subcommittee of the U.S. Senate, and shortly thereafter, was dismissed from employment in the college without a hearing. The New York Court of Appeals upheld the dismissal, but the U.S. Supreme Court, in a five-to-four decision, held that the dismissal violated the teacher's rights under the "due process clause" of the Fourteenth Amendment of the Federal Constitution. The majority opinion conceded that a state has broad powers in the selection and dismissal of its employees, but held, in effect, that due process requires that the dismissal of a public employee must be based on some act or event from which an inference can be drawn as to fitness of the employee to perform the tasks for which he is employed. On the other hand, the dissenters contended that New York City, as a public employer, had a right to decide that it did not want the kind of employees who claim the constitutional privilege against self-incrimination; it was not, in their opinion, a denial of due process to make the claim of the privilege grounds for dismissal.

Two years after its decision in the *Slochower* case, the Court handed down another five-to-four decision in *Beilan* v. *Board of Education, School District of Philadelphia*.[92] This case also involved the legality of the dismissal of a tenure teacher, but the facts were somewhat different from those in the *Slochower* case, and the split was due in large part to the views of the Justices with respect to the materiality of these differences. In the *Beilan* case the teacher was first called before the superintendent of schools in June, 1952, at which time he refused to answer questions concerning his associations with subversive organizations in 1944. In October, 1952, he again refused to answer the superintendent's questions about his activities in 1944 and was warned that his refusal "might lead to his dismissal." The teacher was retained and rated "satisfactory" until November, 1953, when the board instituted dismissal proceedings against him five days after he had invoked the Fifth Amendment before a congressional investigating committee. In the dismissal proceedings the teacher was charged with *incompetence,* and after proper notice and hearing was dismissed in January, 1954. When the case reached the U.S. Supreme Court, the majority held that the "only question ... is whether the Federal Constitution prohibits petitioner's (the teacher's) discharge for statutory 'incompetence' based on his refusal to answer the Superintendent's questions." The Court majority found that the superintendent's questions which the teacher refused to answer were "relevant to the issue of (the teacher's) fitness and suitability to serve as a teacher" and that nothing in the Federal Constitution requires "that a teacher's classroom conduct be the sole basis for determining his fitness." The majority noted that the state's courts had given the term incompetency a broad interpretation.[93] There is also an inference to be drawn from the majority opinion that implied in a public school teacher's contract is the obligation on the part of the teacher to be frank, candid, and cooperative in dealing with his superiors.[94] The majority distinguished the *Slochower* case by pointing out that the discharge in that case was based entirely on events that took place in a hearing before a federal committee, and the questions which the teacher refused to answer were admittedly asked "for a purpose wholly unrelated to (the teacher's) college functions." The dissenters in *Beilan* were of the view that the legality of Beilan's dismissal could not be determined without reference to his exercise of the constitutional privilege against self-incrimination five days before dismissal proceedings against him were initiated.[95]

The present state of the law as represented by the *Slochower* and *Beilan* cases is that a public school teacher may not be dis-

missed solely because he exercises his constitutional privilege of
refusing to answer questions put to him by a federal or state legislative committee, at least where the questions are not related to
his fitness to teach in public schools or institutions. However, it is
ground for dismissal for such a teacher to refuse to answer similar
questions when put to him by his school superintendent or to
refuse to explain to the superintendent why he exercised his
constitutional privilege before the governmental legislative committee. It is said that the refusal to answer his superintendent is a
violation of his obligation to be frank, candid, and cooperative
with his educational superiors in matters relating to his fitness and
loyalty as a teacher in public schools or institutions. Public employment is a privilege, not a right, and governments (federal,
state, and local) have the right to limit public employment to
persons who sign loyalty oaths affirming loyalty to federal and state
governments. However, it is only in a broad sense, if at all, that
such oaths are effective in screening out persons who are unfit or
incompetent to perform the specific assignments they seek or for
which they are employed. One can agree with the majority
opinion in *Beilan* that there is no constitutional requirement
"that a teacher's classroom conduct be the sole basis for determining his fitness." It does not follow from this, however, that a
teacher's invocation of the privilege against self-incrimination
when called before a legislative committee and his subsequent
refusal to discuss such invocation or his beliefs and associations
with his superintendent, is relevant to his fitness to teach in a
public educational system or institution.

The validity of the majority conclusion in *Beilan,* that teachers
as public employees have an obligation to be frank, candid, and
cooperative with their superiors with respect to matters relating
to their fitness and loyalty to teach, has been made doubtful by
two recent U.S. Supreme Court decisions not involving teachers.
Garrity et al. v. *State of New Jersey*[96] and *Spevack* v. *Klain*[97] both
involved the right of persons to remain silent under threat of loss
of employment. In *Garrity* police officers were threatened with
removal from office if they did not discuss questions relating to
their official conduct put to them by state officers who presumably
were their superiors. In *Spevack* a lawyer was threatened with dis-
barment if he did not produce records requested of him in a proceeding against him for professional misconduct. In both cases

the Court majority held that the right to remain silent under threat of loss of employment or the right to practice law are rights protected by the Fifth Amendment guarantee against self-incrimination.

Freedom of Speech and Association. The rights of teachers in public education to freedom of speech and its concomitants have been involved in some of the court decisions already discussed. Moreover, in *Rackley* v. *School District No. 5, Orangeburg County, South Carolina*[98] and *Williams* v. *Sumter School District Number 2*,[99] it was held that participation by teachers in civil rights activities is protected by the First Amendment guarantee of freedom of speech and assembly, and, accordingly, teachers may not be dismissed for such activity.

It is contended by one writer that some members of the Supreme Court have adopted a *balance of interest* approach in First Amendment freedoms cases.[100] It is said that this approach "rests on the theory that it is the Court's function in the case before it when it finds public interests served by legislation on the one hand, and First Amendment freedoms affected by it on the other, to balance the one against the other and to arrive at a judgment where the greater weight shall be placed." Assuming this to be the approach acceptable to a majority of the U.S. Supreme Court in deciding cases involving the freedom of speech of teachers in public education, several questions can be raised. In *Barenblatt* v. *United States of America*,[101] where an educator was called to testify before a legislative committee, the Court majority held that the threat to national security posed by dissemination of communist tenets, and the public interest fostered by the committee's investigations, made the educator's right to privacy and academic freedom subsidiary and not entitled to protection. Recalling the decision of the Alaska Supreme Court reaffirming the teacher's dismissal after remand by the U.S. Supreme Court,[102] raises the following question: Would the U.S. Supreme Court hold that the teachers' constitutionally protected right to criticize their superiors and advocate their ouster is subsidiary to the school board's interest in requiring teachers to use established grievance procedures to criticize their superiors and advocate their ouster? Apparently the dissenting judge on the Alaska Court did not think so.[103] The decision in the *Owens* case[104] suggests that the time, place,

and manner in which teachers exercise their freedom to criticize
their superiors may be the critical factor in "weighting the scales."
It is not unreasonable to conclude that in using the balance of
interest approach, much more weight is given by the U.S. Supreme
Court to the public interest served by the governmental action
complained of where loyalty and subversive associations are involved than in other cases, but one cannot be sure. In *Sweezy* v.
New Hampshire,[105] decided three years before *Barenblatt,* the
Court majority held that questions asked a university professor
about his associations with the Progressive Party and the contents
of a lecture he had given at the university violated his constitutionally protected freedoms of thought and association and reversed his conviction for contempt.

In a series of cases the U.S. Supreme Court has recognized that
under some circumstances, an organization, on behalf of its members, has a constitutionally protected right of associational privacy
under which it may refuse to supply a list of its members. The
Court has held that a state law penalizing an organization for
refusing to furnish such a list deprived the organization's members
of their freedom of association protected by the due process clause
of the Fourteenth Amendment.[106] The circumstances upon which
the Court majority relied were community hostility toward the
organization (even though its operations were legitimate) and the
possibility that disclosure of the membership list would expose the
members to community sanctions and reprisals. In *Bates* v. *City of
Little Rock et al.*[107] it was held that a municipal ordinance requiring organizations doing local business to pay a license tax and
disclose their membership list was unconstitutional as applied to
the local branch of the National Association for the Advancement
of Colored People (NAACP). It was held that the disclosure of
the organization's membership was not relevant to the municipality's interest in regulating and taxing nonprofit organizations.
In both of these cases it was not seriously contended that the
NAACP was subversive. The organization was, however, and still
is, unpopular in many communities, and the real purpose of the
state action was rather obvious. The constitutional right to be a
member of a legitimate but unpopular organization and to participate in its legitimate but unpopular activities is impaired when
federal or state action requires membership disclosure. If the court
uses the balance of interests approach, it must determine whether

the federal, state, or local interest outweighs the interest in associational privacy. The state's interest in the Alabama case and the municipality's interest in the Little Rock case were not very substantial. Where the government's interest relates to national security against subversive activity, the U.S. Supreme Court may be expected to attach great weight to it. In *Gibson* v. *Florida Legislative Investigation Committee*[108] a state committee was empowered to investigate allegations of subversive activity in a state unit of the NAACP, and the issue was whether a witness was justified in refusing to produce the membership list of the state unit of the NAACP. The U.S. Supreme Court was sharply divided, but the majority held that the witness was justified in his refusal because the evidence did not establish a sufficient connection between the Communist Party and the state unit of the NAACP.[109]

The freedom of association about which Justices of the U.S. Supreme Court have spoken in the cases just discussed does not involve a constitutional right to be a member of an organization and participate in its legitimate activities without governmental interference, as the phrase might suggest. It refers only to associational privacy or the right to refuse to disclose the membership list of an organization under a limited set of circumstances. It does not refer to the right of teachers to academic freedom, although it is intimated in a few cases that teachers have such a right. In the *Barenblatt* case[110] the Court, using the balance of interests approach, concluded that the teacher's interest represented by his right to privacy and academic freedom was out-weighed by the government's interest in national security. In the *Sweezy* case[111] the Court said the due process clause protected the teacher's freedom of thought and association from impairment by governmental action. In *Shelton* v. *Tucker*[112] the Court majority held that a state law requiring all teachers in public education, as a condition of employment, to file an affidavit listing every organization to which they had belonged or contributed within the preceding five years violated the teachers' freedom of association which is protected against impairment by the due process clause of the Fourteenth Amendment. The majority conceded that the state's interest in the character and fitness of its teachers in public education justified a partial impairment of the teachers' constitutionally protected right to associational privacy, but only to the extent that the required disclosures have some bearing on the teachers' fitness and competence. The majority held that the sweeping disclosures required by the law might result in public pressures that would tend to discourage teachers from exercising their guaranteed freedoms of thought and association. The dissenters, on the other hand, felt that all of a teacher's affiliations have a bearing on his performance, character, and fitness, and that under the statute as construed by the state court, the disclosures would not be made public.

Except for the express reference in the *Barenblatt* case[113] and the inference that may be drawn from the Court's reference to the teacher's freedoms of thought and association in *Shelton* v. *Tucker*,[114] judicial concern for academic freedom, as that term is understood in academic circles on an international scale, is the exception[115] rather than the rule.

In some of the cases discussed in this chapter where the issue has been the teacher's fitness to teach in a public school or public institution of higher education, the Court's decision should be a matter of serious concern to members of the education profession. One can agree that the determination of fitness to teach should not be limited to a teacher's classroom performance, but it does not follow that proof of any unorthodox conduct is *pro tanto* proof of unfitness to teach in public schools or institutions.

In recent years a number of state legislatures have enacted laws specifically authorizing public school teachers to form or join teachers' organizations and requiring school boards to negotiate or bargain collectively with representatives of teachers' organizations. None of these new statutes authorizes public school teachers to strike. On the contrary, these new statutes typically prohibit strikes. Because of the importance of these developments and the education laws they are spawning, a special discussion of collective negotiations in public education is included as Appendix II.[116]

Public Higher Education

As a general rule, state constitutional or statutory provisions authorizing the establishment of public institutions of higher education delegate to the governing bodies of such institutions the authority to appoint a president or chief administrative officer.

Typically, the institution's governing body is also empowered to appoint or employ additional administrative personnel and the necessary academic personnel. In the absence of contrary statutory provisions or regulations of governing bodies, the rights and responsibilities of administrative and academic personnel appointed by governing bodies are determined by applying the principles of the law of employment contracts.

THE PRESIDENT OR CHIEF ADMINISTRATIVE OFFICER

The chief administrative officer normally is not covered by tenure or civil service laws or regulations, and serves *at the pleasure of* the governing body responsible for his or her appointment. In *Eyring* v. *Board of Regents of New Mexico Normal University at Las Vegas*[117] the governing body of the institution summarily dismissed the president, but later, to comply with a statutory requirement of notice and hearing, written charges were sent to the president and a hearing was scheduled. The president came to the hearing but did not remain; the governing body sustained the charges and dismissed him. In a tort action for malicious breach of contract, the court upheld the dismissal.

TEACHERS IN PUBLIC HIGHER EDUCATION

Teachers in public higher education, like their counterparts in elementary and secondary education, are public employees. As employees, their rights and responsibilities are governed in large part by contract principles, and as public employees, they enjoy some of the same protections and are subject to some of the same restrictions as other public employees. Thus, in *Sittler* v. *Board of Control of Michigan College of Mining and Technology*,[118] it was held that under contract principles the governing body of an institution and not a department head is empowered to consummate employment contracts. Accordingly, an assistant professor who accepted an offer of appointment from a department chairman had no valid employment contract, at least where it was not shown that the governing body authorized or subsequently ratified the acts of the department head. Under the principles of employment contracts, a valid contract may be consummated by a person who has been authorized to negotiate contracts, as where a governing body with the express authority to make appointments delegates this authority to others. However, in public education, there may be some question whether the power to make appointments may be delegated.[119] Typically, the president and/or deans and/or department heads in public institutions of higher education are delegated authority to make appointments of teaching personnel, subject to the confirmation or ratification of the governing body of the institution.[120]

In general, teacher tenure statutes do not apply to teachers in higher education. However, many institutions of higher education have adopted tenure regulations either of their own making or by formal acceptance of the Statement of Tenure Principles of the American Association of University Professors. Even where a tenure statute is applicable to teachers in higher education and it provides that appointments after the probationary period should be permanent, it has been held that tenure can only be conferred by the institution's governing body. Accordingly, it was held in *Application of Fallon*[121] that the failure of the university president to give timely notice of non-reappointment did not constitute a tenure appointment.

A special problem has arisen in a few states where it has been contended that the governing body of an institution is vested with the statutory duty to appoint and discharge teaching staff when *in the judgment of the governing body* such action is in the best interest of the institution, and that this authority cannot be delegated by adoption of tenure regulations. This position was taken by the court in *Worzella* v. *Board of Regents of Education of the State.*[122] This decision has been criticized and its educational soundness questioned.[123]

Non-Public Educational Systems and Institutions

TEACHERS IN NON-PUBLIC EDUCATIONAL SYSTEMS AND INSTITUTIONS

The rights and responsibilities of teachers in non-public educational institutions are governed to a large extent by the principles of the law of contracts. Where a state statute relates specifically to contracts of employment, its provisions prevail over conflicting common law contract principles. It has already been noted that the due process clause of the Fourteenth Amendment of the Federal Constitution has been construed as a prohibition against arbitrary or unreasonable state action with respect to teachers in non-public schools.[124] However, it is uniformly held that where parents enroll their children in a non-public school in compliance with compulsory attendance laws, it is not unreasonable for the state to require the teachers in such a non-public school to possess certain academic qualifications.[125] Generally speaking, state laws setting forth the manner in which the employment contracts of public school teachers must be executed do not apply to teachers in non-public schools. The essential elements of an enforceable employment contract under the general principles of contract law have already been described.[126] These principles are applicable in determining the validity of a teacher's contract to teach in a non-public school or institution.

Preliminary negotiations, even actual offers from persons who are not qualified to make offers, normally do not give rise to actionable rights and obligations, i.e., a binding contract. Under certain circumstances, a court may hold that although the person making the offer had no authority to make it, the school or institution had clothed him with sufficient indicia of authority to constitute implied authority to execute employment contracts. Also, the school or institution may permit a person to execute employment contracts openly, and a prospective teacher, in reasonable reliance upon such apparent authority and in good faith, may accept the offer of employment. In such a situation a court may hold that the school or institution is estopped from denying that the person making the offer had no authority to make it. Courts, however, are reluctant to apply this doctrine of estoppel. In *Braden* v. *Trustees of Phillips Academy*[127] the comptroller of a non-public educational institution offered Braden the position of assistant comptroller, saying that the institution was not "offering him any temporary position . . . (and) that the job would last him the rest of his life if he behaved himself." Braden accepted the position, but was dismissed after two years. He sued to recover damages for the breach of contract for lifetime employment. In upholding the dismissal the court said, among other things, that "the record contains no intimation of conduct on the part of the academy which, reasonably interpreted, could have caused (Braden) . . . to believe that it consented to have the comptroller enter into a lifetime contract on its behalf."

Under the principles of the law of employment contracts, an employer is under no legal obligation to re-employ an employee after the end of his contract term, but statutes in some states provide that if the parties continue the relation of employer and employee after the expiration of the contract term, they are presumed to have renewed the contract. Such a statute was involved in *McLaughlin* v. *Hammond Hall et al.*,[128] where a non-public school employed a headmaster for a school year. Nothing was said at the end of the school year; the headmaster worked for one month in the second school year when he was dismissed and paid for the month he had worked. The court upheld his claim for damages for breach of an implied contract for the second year.

In the absence of a controlling statute, it is uniformly held that an employee hired for a definite term may be dismissed before the end of the contract term only for a cause amounting to a material breach of contract. In two early cases the issue was whether the refusal of a teacher employed by a non-public educational institution to obey a rule or regulation promulgated by the institution was sufficient cause for dismissal. In *Koons* v. *Langum*[129] a non-public business school promulgated a rule prohibiting teachers from visiting any saloon in the vicinity of the school. A teacher was dismissed for violating this rule and brought suit for breach of contract. The court held that the rule was reasonable "as a matter of law" whether or not it was promulgated before he was employed, and the dismissal was sustained. However, in *Hall–Moody Institute* v. *Copass*,[130] the trustees of a non-public school advised a teacher that she could not see men on weekday evenings and that she must retire by half past ten each night. She was also told to speak to the students about keeping better order in the study hall which she supervised. Because she did not speak to her class as requested and was out until midnight on one occasion, she was dismissed. When she sued for breach of contract, the court on appeal upheld the trial court's judgment in her favor. It was held that the rules and regulations "would be regarded in law, as arbitrary, unreasonable and oppressive," and that she had a right to ignore them. As indicated earlier, what is reasonable depends on many factors, including time!

Notes

1. "While Hawaii is divided into seven . . . districts, they are not autonomous. The entire state is under a single Board of Education, which employs a single superintendent. All school funds come from the State Legislature, with the usual federal augmentation." (From an unpublished letter from the Dean of the College of Education, University of Hawaii.)

2. See *Board of Education of Graves County* v. *De Weese,* 343 S.W.2d 598 (Ky.1961); *Main* v. *Claremont Unified School District,* 326 P.2d 573 (Calif.1958); and *Stewart* v. *Eaves,* 257 P.917 (Calif.1927).

3. *State Board of Education* v. *Elbert County Board of Education,* 146 S.E.2d 344 (Ga.1965), reh. den. 1965.

4. In *Sullivan* v. *School Committee of Revere,* 202 N.E.2d 612 (Mass.1964) the statute provided that a superintendent shall be elected annually by the school board, and it was held that the execution of a three-year contract did not prevent the board from terminating the contract at the end of one school year.

5. In *Board of Education of Pendleton County* v. *Gulick,* 398 S.W.2d 483 (Ky.1966) the statute authorized the board to appoint a superintendent for a term of one, two, three or four years, and the board appointed a superintendent to a four-year term. One year before the expiration of this term and a few months before a school board election and possible change in board membership, the board appointed the superintendent to another four-year term to take effect immediately. In an action brought by the newly elected board challenging the validity of the second appointment, the court held that "once the length of the term had been fixed, the board loses control over the term thus created," and held further that the predecessor board had no power to "change a . . . term after it has been established under legislative authority."

6. 133 So.2d 351 (La.1961), reh. den. 1961.

7. 152 So.2d 748 (La.1934).

8. 215 A.2d 35 (N.J.1965).

9. See note 2.

10. 229 P.2d 414 (Calif.1951).

11. See *McNely* v. *Board of Education of Community Unit School District No. 7,* 137 N.E.2d 63 (Ill.1956); *Le Masters* v. *Willman,* 281 S.W.2d 580 (Mo.1955). However, see *Irish et al.* v. *Collins et al.,* 107 A.2d 455 (R.I. 1954) where a state board and the state commissioner of education ruled that a superintendent was included within the provisions of the teacher tenure law, but on appeal to the court it was held that "a superintendent . . . is not a teacher in the ordinary usage of the term . . . and

would not come within the provisions of the teacher tenure act unless the legislative intent is clearly and expressly stated therein."

12. Kenneth A. Simon and W. Vance Grant (eds.), *Digest of Educational Statistics for 1965* (Washington, D.C.: U.S. Department of Health, Education and Welfare, Office of Education, Bulletin OE-10024-65, Bulletin 1965, No. 4).

13. See for example, *Council* v. *Donovan*, 244 N.Y.S.2d 199 (1963) holding that a license to teach does not vest a teacher "with the right of having the Board of Education employ him, but only afford(s) him an expectancy of such employment as and when same (is) made available to him. . . ."

14. See *Weinberg* v. *Fields et al.*, 114 N.Y.S.2d 238 (1952) construing provisions of New York's law.

15. For example, see *Michigan Statutes Annotated* (M.S.A.), Section 15.3851.

16. See *Council* v. *Donovan*, note 13; *Vogulkin* v. *State Board of Education*, 15 Cal. Rptr. 335 (1961), hearing den. 1961; and *Hodge* v. *Stegall*, 242 P.2d 720 (Okla.1952).

17. In *Johnson* v. *School District No. 3 of Clay County*, 96 N.W.2d 623 (Neb.1959) a statute requiring a certificate at the time of contract was later amended to require a certificate prior to commencement of teaching. It was held that there was a valid contract where the teacher had a certificate before beginning to teach even though she had none at the time the contract was entered into. In *Buchanan* v. *School District No. 134, Elk County*, 54 P.2d 930 (Kans.1936) the contract signed by the teacher recited that the teacher was "the holder of a county certificate, this day in force. . . ." Although the board and the teacher knew that the teacher had no certificate at the time, the contract was signed; the court held the contract void.

18. In *Floyd Co. Board of Education* v. *Sloane*, 307 S.W.2d 912 (Ky.1957) a teacher was assigned to teach although she had not reached the eligibility age of eighteen and had no certificate. The court denied her suit to recover salary for teaching services rendered before she reached the age of eighteen. It was held that the teacher was a volunteer because she was ineligible to enter into a valid contract to teach.

19. The *Restatement of Contracts*, Vol. I, Section 1, defines a contract as ". . . a promise or a set of promises for the breach of which the law gives a remedy, or the performance of which the law in some way recognizes a duty." Acceptance of this definition has the effect of making a *void contract* a contradiction of terms. In recognition of the fact that some contracts are not enforceable unless ratified, the *Restatement* uses the term *voidable contract*, which is defined in Vol. I, Section 13, as ". . . one where one or more parties thereto have the power, by a manifestation of election to do so, to avoid the legal relations created by the contract; or by ratification of the contract to distinguish the power of avoidance."

20. In *Ryan* v. *Humphries*, 150 P.1106 (Okla.1915), two members of a three-member board met and "employed" two teachers. The third member was not notified of the meeting and did not attend. However, all three

members attended a subsequent meeting where salaries for the two
teachers were voted and allowed. The court held that this action was a
ratification of the voidable contract. In *Spicer* v. *Anchorage Independent
School District*, 410 P.2d 995 (Alaska 1966), the statute required teachers'
contracts to be signed by at least two members of the school board. An
offer of employment was sent to a prospective teacher by an assistant
superintendent of schools with a request that acceptance be indicated by
letter to the superintendent, and this was done. Thereafter, the superintendent advised the prospective teacher that the offer had been
rescinded. In a suit by the prospective teacher for breach of contract, the
court held in effect that the assistant superintendent was not authorized
to make the offer and, therefore, there was no valid contract.

21. *Restatement of Contracts, op. cit.*, Section 19.
22. See *Thomas* v. *Bagwell et al.*, 226 P.2d 563 (Colo.1950) where a teacher
    carried on negotiations with two members of a three-member board and
    it was held that there never was a contract because there was no evidence
    that the board had ever acted.
23. *Beverly et al.* v. *Highfield*, 209 S.W.2d 739 (Ky.1948), reh. den. 1948. Also
    see *Cochran* v. *Trussler*, 89 S.E.2d 306 (W.Va.1955).
24. *Houghton* v. *School Committee of Somerville*, 28 N.E.2d 1001 (Mass.
    1940).
25. *Jones* v. *School District of Borough of Kulpmont*, 3 A.2d 914 (Pa.1939).
26. Research Monograph 1959–M3, "The Teacher and the Law" (Research
    Division, National Education Association, September, 1959), p. 30, re-
    ports that only South Carolina, Vermont, and Wyoming have no state
    laws concerning teachers' contracts.
27. *Ibid.*, pp. 42–44.
28. *Ibid.*, pp. 30–32.
29. See *Mullen* v. *Board of Education of Township of Jefferson*, 195 A.2d 195
    (N.J.1963). See also *Wyatt* v. *School District No. 104, Fergus County*, 417
    P.2d 221 (Mont.1966) where the value of the housing provided for the
    teacher as part of her contract was included as part of the money amount
    she would have received under the contract.
30. It is reported that as of November, 1965, twenty-eight states had tenure
    laws applicable throughout the state. An additional nine states had
    tenure laws of limited application, ten states had laws requiring timely
    notice of nonrenewal, and three states had no laws relating to the length
    of the contract term. See publication of the N.E.A. Research Division,
    "School Law Summaries, Tenure and Contracts," November, 1965
    (revised).
31. 300 U.S. 319, 81 L.Ed. 674, 57 S.Ct. 483 (1937).
32. 303 U.S. 95, 82 L.Ed. 685, 58 S.Ct. 443 (1938), reh. den. 303 U.S. 667, 82
    L.Ed. 1123, 58 S.Ct. 641.
33. This Section provides in part that, "no State shall . . . pass any . . . law
    impairing the obligation of contracts. . . ."
34. The opinion states, "The title of the Act is couched in terms of contract.
    It speaks of the making and canceling of indefinite contracts. In the

body the word 'contract' appears ten times in Section 1, . . . 11 times in Section 2, . . . and four times in Section 4, ... The tenor of the Act indicates that the word 'contracts' was not used inadvertently or in other than its usual legal meaning."

35. *State ex rel. Anderson* v. *Brand,* 13 N.E.2d 955 (Ind.1938).

36. The position of the state court was that the U.S. Supreme Court held that the 1933 legislation (which repealed that portion of the 1927 law permitting teachers in township schools to acquire tenure status) was ineffectual to destroy contractual tenure rights of such teachers acquired under the 1927 law, but that the repeal of the 1927 law was otherwise valid. Thus, the school officials had no *statutory* duty to reinstate the teacher. However, the teacher had a *contractual* right to tenure dismissal procedures which she could have enforced by bringing a civil action in her own name.

37. See *Ehret* v. *School District of Borough of Kulpmont,* 5 A.2d 188 (Pa. 1939) and *McSherry* v. *City of St. Paul,* 277 N.W. 541 (Minn. 1938) for a judicial analysis of the history and purposes of teacher tenure legislation.

38. In the N.E.A. Research Monograph 1959–M3, "The Teacher and the Law," *op. cit.,* p. 32, it is reported that four tenure laws do not provide for any probationary period.

39. See *Briney* v. *Santa Ana High School District et al.,* 21 P.2d 610 (Calif. 1933) where, in keeping with board practice, a teacher's contract for her third year contained the following statement: "You have been classified by this board as a permanent employee." Toward the end of her third year, the teacher was advised that she would not be re-employed for a fourth year; one of the reasons given was the board's decision not to place any teacher on permanent tenure at that time. The court held that as the teacher had accepted the contract with the statement that she had been classified as a tenure teacher and had rendered services for the year in question, the board was "estopped from denying that she was classified as a permanent employee." See also *Hosford* v. *Board of Education of City of Minneapolis,* 275 N.W. 81 (Minn.1937) where the statute provided for a three-year probationary period and provided also that employment after the probationary period establishes tenure rights. At the beginning of her third year a teacher was requested to submit her resignation which was to be held by the superintendent and submitted to the board in the event that she did not "make good" during her third year. No resignation was submitted at that time, but she did submit one at the end of her third year upon being told that the city's financial condition purportedly did not allow "so many girls to go on tenure." She was told, however, not to get excited about teaching in the coming year without a contract. For the next two years she was employed as a substitute teacher, but shortly before the end of her second year of substitute teaching, she was dismissed by the board. The court held that the acceptance of the resignation without any intention of terminating the teacher's employment and upon a definite promise of re-employment, was ineffectual and void as an attempt to circumvent the tenure statute.

40. In *State ex rel. Brubaker* v. *Hardy*, 214 N.E.2d 79 (Ohio 1966) a teacher resigned at the end of a three-year statutory probationary period. The board accepted his resignation and thereafter employed him on a one-year contract, but during the year notified him that he would not be re-employed. No charges were made, and no hearing was requested or given. It was held that by allowing his resignation to stand and voluntarily entering into a one-year contract, the teacher waived his right to a tenure contract.

In *Elder* v. *Board of Education of School District Number 127½, Cook County*, 208 N.E.2d 423 (Ill.1965) the statute required a teacher to serve a probationary period of two years, and a board resolution provided that the continued service of a teacher would not be affected by a temporary illness, defined as an incapacity of not more than three-months duration. A teacher was absent from work for a period in excess of three months. Upon her return, she was given another one-year contract but was dismissed after serving a total of two and one-half years. Her demand for a hearing was denied. In sustaining the dismissal, the court held that the statutory requirement of "two consecutive years is not satisfied by serving the equivalent of two years over a three year period."

In *State ex rel. King* v. *North Gallia Local Board of Education et al.*, 198 N.E.2d 786 (Ohio 1963) the statute required a three-year probationary period and a recommendation by the superintendent in order to acquire tenure. After serving the probationary period, a teacher was not recommended by the superintendent but was offered, and accepted, one-year contracts for four years during which period the statute was amended so as to eliminate the superintendent's recommendation as a condition to tenure status. It was held that the statute as it read when the teacher began his probationary period determined the teacher's right to tenure status.

In *Wilson* v. *Board of Education of the City of Flint*, 106 N.W.2d 136 (Mich.1960) the statutory probationary period was two years, but it provided that "a third year of probation may be granted by the controlling board upon notice to the tenure commission." It was held that this proviso did not authorize a school board to adopt a policy of requiring all new teachers to serve a three-year probationary period.

41. See *Romeike* v. *Houston Independent School District*, 368 S.W.2d 895 (Texas 1963) where a board rule prohibited teachers from engaging in the liquor business, and a teacher was dismissed for refusing to give up his interest in and connection with a liquor store. In upholding the dismissal, the court held that the teacher knew or should have known of the existence of the board rule.

In *Arlington Independent School District* v. *Weekley, et vir.*, 313 S.W.2d 929 (Texas 1958) a board rule required a teacher to withdraw from school upon becoming pregnant. The evidence showed that a teacher who was forced to withdraw was not aware of the rule, but her suit to recover the balance due on her contract was unsuccessful.

42. Of course, it is assumed here that certification procedures have screened out teachers who are not academically qualified.

43. See *Kuehn* v. *School District No. 70, Goodhue County*, 22 N.W.2d 220 (Minn.1946).

44. See *McCartin* v. *School Committee of Lowell et al., Sullivan* v. *Same*, 79 N.E.2d 192 (Mass.1948), but see *School City of Peru et al.* v. *State ex rel. Youngblood*, 7 N.E.2d 176 (Ind.1937) where the transfer of a tenure teacher from a superintendency to a principalship at a lower salary was upheld. The court held that the board had "full authority to either promote or demote any teacher . . . in the absence of a specific statutory restriction."

45. *Application of Munter*, 225 N.Y.S.2d 1008 (1962).

46. In *Madison County Board of Education* v. *Miles*, 173 So.2d 425 (Miss. 1965) the statutory causes were "incompetence, neglect of duty, immoral conduct, intemperance, brutal treatment of a pupil or other good cause." A school board dismissed a principal under general charges including *impugning the integrity* of a board employee. The court held that the principal was not guilty of any of the statutory causes or the general cause because of the "well recognized rule of law that where in a statute general words follow a designation of particular charges, the meaning of the general words will be presumed to be restricted by the particular designation, and to include only things of the same kind, class, or nature as those specifically enumerated, unless there is a clear manifestation of a contrary purpose . . . ." This rule of law, called *ejusdem generis*, was also applied by the court in *School District of Wildwood* v. *State Board of Education et al.*, 185 A.664 (N.J.1936) where a school board was unsuccessful in relying upon "other just cause" as the basis for dismissing a teacher because she got married.

47. In *Spencer* v. *Laconia School District*, 218 A.2d 437 (N.H.1966) a statute provided that a teacher may not be dismissed before the end of the contract period except for immorality, incompetence, or acting in conflict with prescribed regulations. A teacher on a three-year contract was notified after teaching one year that her position was being abolished because of lack of funds. Subsequently the position was partially restored and other teachers hired. In an action for wrongful dismissal, it was held, among other things, that the legislative purpose in enacting the statute was to "limit the authority of school boards with respect to the dismissal of teachers to the grounds specified."

48. *Tichenor* v. *Orleans Parish School Board*, 144 So.2d 603 (La.1962). The same year, in *Herbert* v. *Lafayette Parish School Board*, 146 So.2d 848 (La.1962), the court held, with one dissent, that where a teacher was transferred to an assignment in adult education from an assignment in vocational agriculture which he had held for three years without a charge of incompetence, evidence of his incompetence in the previous vocational agriculture assignment did not support a charge of incompetence in his later assignment in adult education.

49. *Shockley* v. *Board of Education, Laurel Special School District*, 149 A.2d

331 (Dela.1959). In this case there was question whether the superintendent's suggestion constituted an order, but it was held that even if it was an order, there was no emergency requiring it, and it would have been "unfair to the school children in the classes involved."

50. *Johnson* v. *United School District Joint School Board*, 191 A.2d 897 (Pa. 1963). In this case there was evidence that the teacher was advised when she was interviewed that the "Open House" was an important part of the school's program and gave parents of pupils an opportunity to talk with teachers about the work of their children. The lower court held that the teacher's refusal was "indiscreet" but not a sufficient cause for dismissal. See also *State ex rel. Williams* v. *Avoyelles Parish School Board*, 147 So.2d 729 (La.1962) where it was held that it was ground for dismissal for an industrial arts teacher to refuse to have his class construct wooden forms for concrete sidewalks as a teaching demonstration, even though the pouring of the concrete was to be performed by an outside contractor.

51. N.E.A. Research Monograph 1959–M3, "The Teacher and the Law," *op. cit.*, p. 36.

52. In *DiGenova* v. *State Board of Education et al.*, 367 P.2d 865 (Calif. 1962), it was held that a statute requiring the dismissal of a teacher upon conviction of a sex crime could not be applied retroactively to justify the dismissal of a tenure teacher in the elementary schools, where his conviction occurred before the enactment of the statute. There were two dissents in which it was contended that the language of the statute did not imply that it should not be applied retroactively, and in the interest of school children it should be given retroactive application.

53. 395 P.2d 372 (Alaska 1964).

54. 381 U.S. 126, 14 L.Ed.2d 261, 85 S.Ct. 1321 (1965).

55. 421 P.2d 586 (Alaska 1967).

56. 389 U.S. 818, 19 L.Ed 2d68, 855. Ct.84 (1967).

57. 23 Cal. Rptr. 710 (1962).

58. See *Moffett* v. *Calcasieu Parish School Board*, 179 So.2d 537 (La.1965), reh. den. 1965, where the court upheld a dismissal for neglect of duty and incompetence upon evidence showing that the teacher made a vulgar remark during a heated discussion with his principal. The court agreed that the teacher had reason to be upset, but held that "it was the board's judgment that such vulgarity and flagrant disrespect, if left unpunished, would cause a serious breakdown in the disciplinary control of the principal over the teachers and of the principal and teachers over the children."

59. See for example, *School City of East Chicago* v. *Sigler*, 36 N.E.2d 760 (Ind.1941) where the contract expressly provided that the teacher would "observe all rules and regulations of the ... school authorities," and the court said that "all rules" meant existing rules and also rules subsequently adopted. However, by way of dictum, the court said that "without such provision we think this agreement would be read into the contract." See also *Romeike* v. *Houston Independent School District*,

Arlington Independent School District v. *Weekley, et vir.*, note 41, and *Backie* v. *Cromwell Consolidated School District No. 13*, 242 N.W. 389 (Minn.1932).

60. In *Pease* v. *Millcreek Township School District*, 195 A.2d 104 (Pa.1963), reh. den. 1963, a statute authorized a school board to "assign any school employee to serve in any capacity in connection with any" activity relating to the school program. A high school teacher was assigned to serve as sponsor of a boys' bowling group which met one day a week after regular school hours. The bowling program was entirely voluntary, and the school paid none of the expenses. The teacher refused the assignment, was dismissed for incompetence after notice and hearing, and appealed to the state superintendent, who ordered his reinstatement. The board appealed to the court, which affirmed the teacher's dismissal. The teacher then carried the case to the appellate court which reversed the decision of the trial court. The appellate court held that "schools have no duty to supervise students in their play after school and off school premises when such play is not genuinely connected with the school program."

In *McGrath* v. *Burkhard*, 280 P.2d 864 (Calif.1955), the statute provided that a board of education "shall fix and prescribe the duties to be performed by all persons in public school service." A high school teacher was assigned to supervise three football games and three basketball games during the school year. Other teachers were also assigned to supervise such games. The teacher brought suit for declaratory relief to determine whether these assignments were within the scope of teachers' duties. The court upheld the board's assignment and ruled that "a teacher's duties and obligations to students and the community are not satisfied by closing the classroom door at the conclusion of a class . . . . Supervising . . . at school athletic and social activities, conducted under the name and auspices of the school, is within the scope of the contract and . . . are proper duties so long as they are distributed impartially, . . . are reasonable in number and hours of duty, and each teacher has his share of such duty."

See also *Council* v. *Donovan*, 244 N.Y.S.2d 199 (1963) where, pursuant to a directive of the state civil defense commission, a superintendent of schools ordered all public schools to hold two shelter drills within a two-week period. It was held that a teacher's refusal to participate in such drills after notice and hearing, was ground for revoking his teacher's license, even though the teacher's refusal was on the ground of conscience.

61. Robert R. Hamilton and Paul R. Mort, *The Law and Public Education* (Brooklyn: Foundation Press, Inc., 1959, 2nd ed.), p. 368.

62. *Williams* v. *School District No. 40 of Gila County*, 417 P.2d 376 (Ariz. 1966), reh. den. 1966, review den. 1966, involved a board regulation which obligated teachers to adhere to any reasonable pattern of behavior accepted by the community for professional persons. In sustaining the dismissal, the court held that "the statutory power of a school board to discharge teachers is always freely construed, and good cause has been

held to include any ground put forward by the board, in good faith, which is not arbitrary, irrational, unreasonable, or irrelevant to the board's task."

63. *Kersey* v. *Maine Consolidated School District No. 10,* 394 P.2d 201 (Ariz. 1964). See also *Board of Directors of Kennewick School District No. 17 of Benton County* v. *Coates,* 287 P.2d 102 (Wash.1955), reh. den. 1955, where the court held that the dismissal of a junior high school principal for "gross insubordination and unprofessional conduct," evidenced by the principal's intemperate conduct, was improper where the facts showed that the intemperate conduct was provoked by actions of the school board.

64. In *Miller* v. *Board of Education of School District No. 132, Cook County,* 200 N.E.2d 838 (Ill.1964) the causes belatedly given to the teacher's attorney were: (1) using profanity, (2) inflicting corporal punishment, (3) ungovernable temper, and (4) best interest of the school. The court said the law requires the board to make a determination on the issue of remediability and courts have jurisdiction to review such determinations for possible abuse of discretion.

65. 347 U.S. 483, 98 L.Ed. 873, 74 S.Ct. 686 (1954) and 349 U.S. 294, 99 L.Ed. 1083, 75 S.Ct. 753 (1955).

66. 242 F.Supp. 371 (Va.1965), on appeal 360 F.2d 325 (Va.1966).

67. 267 F.2d 733 (Mo.1959). Here there were ninety-eight teachers in the white schools of the district and eleven teachers in the Negro school. In the integration plan that was adopted the Negro school was closed and the eleven Negro teachers and four white teachers were denied re-employment.

68. See *United States* v. *Jefferson County Board of Education et al.,* 372 F.2d 836 (Ala.1966).

69. See *Vick* v. *County Board of Education of Obion County, Tennessee,* 205 F.Supp. 436 (Tenn.1962) and *Bush et al.* v. *Orleans Parish School Board et al.,* 230 F.Supp. 509 (La.1963).

70. 382 U.S. 103, 15 L.Ed.2d 187, 86 S.Ct. 224 (1965). Also see *Mapp et al.* v. *Board of Education of City of Chattanooga, Hamilton County, Tennessee et al.,* 373 F.2d 75 (Tenn.1967).

71. 364 F.2d 177 (N.C.1966), cert. den. 385 U.S. 1003, 17 L.Ed.2d 542, 87 S.Ct. 706 (1967).

72. See also *Williams* v. *Sumter School District No. 2,* 255 F.Supp. 397 (S.C. 1966) where a Negro teacher with a ten-year record of excellent teaching was denied re-employment because of her civil rights activities. It was contended that since the state had no tenure law, the board was under no obligation to re-employ any teacher. Nevertheless, the court held that the refusal to re-employ the teacher was an arbitrary deprivation of her rights and granted an injunction. Also, see *Rackley* v. *School District No. 5, Orangeburg County, South Carolina,* 258 F.Supp. 676 (S.C.1966).

73. See *Henry* v. *Coahoma County Board of Education et al.,* 246 F.Supp. 517 (Miss.1963), where a Negro teacher with eleven years of teaching experience was denied re-employment. She alleged that the denial was be-

cause she and her husband participated in civil rights activities. The school superintendent alleged that the denial was because of the husband's immoral and illegal conduct. The court held that the teacher failed to sustain the burden of proving that the denial of re-employment was because of her civil rights activity. See also *Bradford* v. *School District No. 20, Charleston, South Carolina,* 364 F.2d 185 (S.C. 1966) upholding the suspension of a Negro teacher after his conviction for disorderly conduct in connection with his entering a white barber-shop to get a haircut.

74. See note 65.

75. 344 U.S. 183, 97 L.Ed. 216, 73 S.Ct. 215 (1952).

76. *Adler* v. *Board of Education of City of New York,* 342 U.S. 485, 96 L.Ed. 517, 72 S.Ct. 380 (1952); *Garner et al.* v. *Board of Public Works of City of Los Angeles et al.,* 341 U.S. 716, 95 L.Ed. 1317, 71 S.Ct. 909 (1951); and *Gerende* v. *Board of Supervisors of Elections of Baltimore City,* 341 U.S. 56, 95 L.Ed. 745, 71 S.Ct. 565 (1951), reh.den. 341 U.S. 923, 95 L.Ed. 1356, 71 S.Ct. 741 .

77. See note 76.

78. 385 U.S. 589, 17 L.Ed.2d 629, 87 S.Ct. 675 (1967).

79. 377 U.S. 360, 12 L.Ed.2d 377, 84 S.Ct. 1316 (1964). This was a class action by teachers in a public institution of higher education challenging the constitutionality of two loyalty oath statutes. One statute required teachers to, among other things, swear or affirm that they would by precept and example promote respect for the flag and reverence for law and order. The other statute required teachers to, among other things, swear or affirm that they were not subversive persons or knowingly members of a subversive organization. Both statutes contained penalties for perjury.

80. The statute provided that a subversive person is one who commits an act, or who advocates, abets, advises, or teaches anyone to commit or aid in the commission of any act intended to destroy or alter the form of government by revolution, force, or violence.

81. The statute ". . . is invalid insofar as it sanctions . . . mere knowing membership without any showing of specific intent to further the unlawful aims of the Communist Party . . . ."

82. 384 U.S. 11, 16 L.Ed.2d 321, 86 S.Ct. 1238 (1966).

83. 381 P.2d 554 (Ariz.1963), reh. den. 1963.

84. 378 U.S. 127, 12 L.Ed.2d 744, 84 S.Ct. 1658 (1964).

85. See note 79.

86. 397 P.2d 944 (Ariz.1965), reh. den. 1965.

87. 382 U.S. 810, 15 L.Ed.2d 59, 86 S.Ct. 116 (1965).

88. See note 82.

89. *McCarthy* v. *Arndstein,* 266 U.S. 34, 69 L.Ed. 158, 45 S.Ct. 16 (1924); *Brown* v. *Walker,* 161 U.S. 591, 40 L.Ed. 819, 16 S.Ct. 644 (1896); *Counselman* v. *Hitchcock,* 142 U.S. 547, 35 L.Ed. 1110, 12 S.Ct. 195 (1892); *Boyd* v. *United States,* 116 U.S. 616, 29 L.Ed. 746, 6 S.Ct. 524 (1886); see also Corwin, "The Supreme Court's Construction of the Self-Incrimination Clause," 29 *Michigan Law Review* 1–27, 195–207 (1930).

90. See *Board of Education of City of Los Angeles* v. *Eisenberg*, 277 P.2d 943 (Calif.1954), hearing den. 1955, upholding the dismissals; *Faxon* v. *School Committee of Boston*, 120 N.E.2d 772 (Mass.1954) upholding the dismissals; *Goldway* v. *Board of Higher Education*, 37 N.Y.S.2d 34 (1942) upholding the dismissals.

On the other hand, in *Board of Education of the San Francisco Unified School District et al.* v. *Mass*, 304 P.2d 1015 (Calif.1956) a statute provided that any school employee who invokes the Fifth Amendment before a legislative committee is guilty of insubordination and shall be dismissed *in the manner provided by law*. In a split decision, the court majority held that a teacher who invokes the Fifth Amendment before a legislative committee cannot be dismissed without a full hearing and a determination that his reasons for invoking the Fifth Amendment are not sufficient, and in *Laba* v. *Board of Education of Newark*, 129 A.2d 273 (N.J.1957) it was held that invoking the Fifth Amendment, in and of itself, does not constitute just cause for dismissal. However, the court did hold that if, after a meaningful hearing, it were determined that the teacher's reasons for invoking the Fifth Amendment were "patently frivolous or contumnacious," dismissal would be justified.

91. 350 U.S. 551, 100 L.Ed. 692, 76 S.Ct. 637 (1956), reh. den. 1956.

92. 357 U.S. 399, 409, 2 L.Ed.2d 1414, 1433, 78 S.Ct. 1317, 1324 (1958).

93. The opinion reads: "The Pennsylvania statute, unlike those of many other States, contains no catch-all phrase, such as 'conduct unbecoming a teacher,' to cover disqualifying conduct not included within the more specific provisions. Consequently, the Pennsylvania courts have given 'incompetency' a broad interpretation."

94. The opinion reads: "By engaging in teaching in the public schools, petitioner (the teacher) did not give up his right to freedom of belief, speech or association. He did, however, undertake obligations of frankness, candor and cooperation in answering inquiries made of him by his employing board examining into his fitness to serve it as a public school teacher . . . ."

95. Chief Justice Warren pointed to the fact that the teacher was continued in employment and was rated satisfactory for thirteen months after his refusal to answer the superintendent's questions. Mr. Justice Douglas, with Mr. Justice Black concurring, expressed the view that even if the teacher's frankness is the issue, "Government has no business penalizing a citizen merely for his beliefs or associations . . . ." Mr. Justice Brennan stated unequivocally that, ". . . in reality, Beilan was not dismissed (because of his refusal to answer his superior's questions related to his fitness to continue in his position) for he received satisfactory ratings for a full year after his refusal to answer the superintendent's questions; he was dismissed only after invoking the Fifth Amendment before a legislative subcommittee."

96. 385 U.S. 493, 17 L.Ed.2d 562, 87 S.Ct. 616 (1967).

97. 385 U.S. 511, 17 L.Ed.2d 574, 87 S.Ct. 625 (1967).

98. 258 F.Supp. 676 (S.C.1966).

99. 255 F.Supp. 397 (S.C.1966).
100. See Paul G. Kauper, *Civil Liberties and the Constitution* (Ann Arbor: The University of Michigan Press, Ann Arbor Paperbacks, 1966), p. 112 et seq.
101. 360 U.S. 109, 3 L.Ed.2d 1115, 79 S.Ct. 1081 (1959). The principal issue in this case was whether a former college instructor had been sufficiently advised of the relevancy of questions asked by a congressional investigating committee to the committee's investigatory authority. The Court majority held that the educator had been sufficiently advised, while the dissenters contended, among other things, that compelling the educator to answer questions about his Communist Party affiliations was a violation of the educator's First Amendment freedoms, not supportable by the requirements of national security.
102. See note 55.
103. See note 55 and text preceding note.
104. See note 57.
105. 354 U.S. 234, 1 L.Ed.2d 1311, 77 S.Ct. 1203 (1957). This case is somewhat similar to *Barenblatt* except that the investigation into subversive associations was by a state official instead of a congressional committee. However, here, as in *Barenblatt*, the educator challenged the relevance of the questions asked. He testified that he had never been a member of the Communist Party but refused to answer questions concerning his associations with the Progressive Party or concerning a lecture he had given at the university.
106. See *NAACP v. Alabama*, 357 U.S. 449, 2 L.Ed.2d 1488, 78 S.Ct. 1163 (1958) where the state law required all organizations doing business in the state to disclose their membership lists. See also 360 U.S. 240, 3 L.Ed.2d 1205, 79 S.Ct. 1001 (1959) and 377 U.S. 288, 12 L.Ed.2d 325, 84 S.Ct. 1302 (1964).
107. 361 U.S. 516, 4 L.Ed.2d 480, 80 S.Ct. 412 (1960).
108. 372 U.S. 539, 9 L.Ed.2d 929, 83 S.Ct. 889 (1963).
109. Mr. Justice Douglas, concurring in the majority opinion, said that the constitutional right of privacy of an admittedly legitimate organization cannot be invaded merely because some Communists may have joined it.
    For the dissenters, it was argued that the request for the membership list was proper when the witness was asked to produce membership records, not for the purpose of wholesale divulgence, as was true in the Alabama and Little Rock cases, but only to refresh his recollection.
110. See note 101.
111. See note 105.
112. 364 U.S. 479, 5 L.Ed.2d 231, 81 S.Ct. 247 (1960).
113. See note 101.
114. See note 112.
115. The following excerpts indicate the views of some members of the U.S. Supreme Court as to the proper role of teachers and reasons for protecting their academic freedom:
    In his separate concurring opinion in the *Updegraff* case (see note 74)

Mr. Justice Frankfurter said, "To regard teachers—in our entire educational system, from the primary grades to the university—as the priests of our democracy is therefore not to indulge in hyperbole. It is the special task of teachers to foster those habits of open-mindedness and critical inquiry which alone make for responsible citizens . . . . They must be free to sift evanescent doctrine, qualified by time and circumstance, from the restless, enduring process of extending the bounds of understanding and wisdom, to assure which the freedoms of thought, of speech, of inquiry, of worship, are guaranteed by the Constitution of the United States against infraction by national or State government . . . ."

In the *Sweezy* case (see note 105) Mr. Chief Justice Warren said, "The essentiality of freedom in a community of American universities is almost self-evident. No one should under-estimate the vital role in a democracy that is played by those who guide and train our youth. To impose any strait jacket upon the intellectual leaders in our colleges and universities would imperil the future of our Nation. No field of education is so thoroughly comprehended by man that new discoveries cannot yet be made. Particularly is that true in the social sciences, where few, if any, principles are accepted as absolutes. Scholarship cannot flourish in an atmosphere of suspicion and distrust. Teachers and students must always remain free to inquire, to study and to evaluate, to gain new maturity and understanding; otherwise our civilization will stagnate and die."

116. For a detailed discussion of this subject, see Myron Lieberman and Michael H. Moskow, *Collective Negotiations for Teachers—An Approach to School Administration* (Chicago: Rand McNally & Company, 1966).

117. 277 P.2d 550 (N.M.1954). See also *Application of Lee,* 223 N.Y.S.2d 417 (1962) upholding the summary dismissal of the president of a state university. It was held that he was in the unclassified service and, therefore, not protected by civil service legislation.

118. 53 N.W.2d 681 (Mich.1952). In this case a department chairman offered and an assistant professor accepted the offer of an appointment and entered upon his duties. When he was later summarily dismissed, he sued for breach of contract, but the court held that he never had a valid contract. See also *Finch* v. *City of New York,* 205 N.Y.S.2d 308 (1960) where it was held, among other things, that negotiations with an *agent* of an institution do not constitute a valid contract.

119. In the *Sittler* case the court said, "Public officers have and can exercise only such powers as are conferred on them by law, and a state is not bound by contracts made in its behalf by its officers or agents without previous authority conferred by *statute* or the *constitution*." (Emphasis supplied.)

120. See Thomas Edward Blackwell, *College Law—A Guide for Administrators* (Washington, D.C.: American Council on Education, 1961), pp. 59–62, for a discussion of implied contracts and equitable estoppel.

121. 178 N.Y.S.2d 459 (1958), confirmed on reargument 192 N.Y.S.2d 239 (1959). See also *Trilling* v. *Board of Higher Education of City of New York et al.,* 67 N.Y.S.2d 572 (1946) where a teacher alleged that the

president of the institution promised him tenure, but the court held that such action could not estop the governing body from denying that the teacher had acquired tenure.

122. 93 N.W.2d 411 (S.D.1958). For a similar holding, see *Posin v. State Board of Higher Education*, 86 N.W.2d 31 (N.D.1957).

123. See Clark Byse, "Academic Freedom, Tenure, and the Law: A Comment on Worzella v. Board of Regents," 73 *Harvard Law Review*, 304–322 (1959).

124. In *Meyer v. State of Nebraska*, 262 U.S. 390, 67 L.Ed. 1042, 43 S.Ct. 625 (1923) a teacher of the German language was arrested for teaching German to a child enrolled in a non-public school. A statute made it a criminal offense to teach a child who had not passed the eighth grade certain modern languages, including German, in any school. It was held that the statute as applied to the teacher of German was unreasonable and violative of due process. See also *Farrington v. Tokushige*, 273 U.S. 284, 71 L.Ed. 646, 47 S.Ct. 406 (1927), in which the Court enjoined enforcement of an act of the Territory of Hawaii which prohibited maintenance of foreign-language schools except upon written permit and payment of a fee based upon attendance.

125. In *Pierce v. Society of Sisters of the Holy Names of Jesus and Mary* and *Pierce v. Hill Academy*, 268 U.S. 510, 69 L.Ed. 1071, 45 S.Ct. 571 (1925), the U.S. Supreme Court observed that "no question is raised concerning the power of the State . . . to require that teachers shall be of good moral character and patriotic disposition."

126. See note 19.

127. 71 N.E.2d 765 (Mass.1947).

128. 61 P.2d 1219 (Calif.1936).

129. 101 N.W. 490 (Minn.1904). See also *Story v. San Rafael Military Academy*, 3 Cal. Rptr. 847 (1960), where the court affirmed the dismissal of a teacher who was employed by a non-public educational institution to teach and supervise a school dormitory. The facts show that a few months after his employment, the teacher announced that he would no longer supervise the dormitory. The court held that this announcement constituted an anticipatory breach of contract, justifying the dismissal.

130. 69 S.W. 327 (Tenn.1902).

CHAPTER IV

The Admission, and Rights and Responsibilities of Students[1]

ONE of the purposes of education in a democratic society is to provide opportunity for a certain level of learning for all who participate in the democratic process. In accordance with this purpose, the American society imposes an obligation on those legally responsible for minor children between certain ages to enroll such children in institutions of public education or to provide them with the equivalent educational opportunity. Education at this level is commonly referred to as elementary and secondary education. In addition to education at these levels, however, the American society, as most modern societies, affords the student an opportunity to continue his education beyond the elementary and secondary levels. As a result, increasing numbers of students today are seeking higher education.[2]

The relations between the governing bodies of educational systems and institutions, on the one hand, and students and their parents or guardians, on the other, are regulated in large part by laws.[3] These laws form a significant part of the total body of education law.

Laws relating to the rights of students with respect to education fall into two general categories: those relating to public education and those relating to non-public or private education. As already indicated, the line between these two categories is not always easy to draw. A distinction is also made between elementary and secondary education, both of which as a general rule are free and compulsory, and post-secondary or higher education, which is neither free nor compulsory.

Public Education

STUDENTS IN ELEMENTARY AND SECONDARY EDUCATION

Consistent with the belief that an educated citizenry is of paramount importance to a democratic society, almost all the state constitutions make some provision for a system of free tax-supported elementary and secondary schools. In general, state legislatures have wide discretion in providing for education and, typically, as already indicated in Chapter II, they delegate to semi-autonomous local school districts the actual responsibility for the management of public elementary and secondary public schools.

Right of Students to Admission. Because states generally impose a legal obligation, with criminal sanctions, upon parents and guardians to provide their children or wards between certain ages (e.g., six to seventeen) with specific learning experiences (i.e., elementary and secondary education), states have the reciprocal legal obligation to provide the necessary facilities and personnel and to admit such children to the facilities, or to permit them to acquire comparable educational experience elsewhere, subject to reasonable regulations.[4] Local school boards have express or implied powers to promulgate regulations for the admission of children of the requisite ages into the public schools established in their respective school districts. Of course, local school board regulations must not be in conflict with relevant state legislation. As a general rule, a child of school age who is a resident of a school district has a legal right to admission to a school in that district unless otherwise provided by law. However, he has no legal right to admission to a particular school within the district of his residence. Normally regulations limit admissions to certain times during the school year. The legality of cut-off dates has been challenged, but they are usually upheld.[5]

Compulsory Attendance. State statutes, as has been mentioned, generally impose a legal obligation on parents or guardians of children between certain ages to send those children or wards to a public school or provide equivalent educational opportunity. It has been uniformly held that compulsory school attendance statutes are proper exercises of the police power of the several states. In one form or another, courts have affirmed that the object of compulsory attendance laws is to provide an educated citizenry.[6] In *Pierce* v. *Society of Sisters of the Holy Names of Jesus and Mary* and *Pierce* v. *Hill Academy*,[7] the U.S. Supreme Court conceded that states may constitutionally enact compulsory school attendance laws, but held that a state may not, consistent with due process, compel parents or guardians to send their children or wards to *public* schools. The Court also conceded that states may impose reasonable regulations on non-public schools to insure that they provide educational opportunities equivalent to those offered in the states' public schools.

The compulsory attendance statutes in many states contain a number of exceptions, but in the absence of a statutory exception, it has been held that a parent must send her child to school every weekday even though one of the weekdays is considered a day of worship by the religious sect to which the parent belongs.[8] A school board's refusal to furnish transportation has been held to be no legal justification for non-compliance with a compulsory attendance law,[9] although some statutes make an exception where the school is more than a specified distance from where the pupil resides.[10]

Residence Requirements. Where compulsory attendance laws are to be satisfied by enrollment in public schools, the general rule is that students are eligible to enroll in schools located in the school district in which they reside, and the residence of a minor student is considered to be that of his or her parent or guardian. Attendance at a public school in a district other than that of a student's residence normally requires the payment of tuition by either the parent or guardian or by the district of the student's residence. Whether the alleged residence of the student for school attendance purposes is the bona fide residence of the parent or guardian is a question to be determined by the facts of each case.[11] It should be noted, however, that, pursuant to its plenary power over education, a state legislature may require a school district to accept as residents for school attendance purposes students whom the school district does not consider residents.[12]

Compulsory Vaccination. In the early case of *Jacobson* v. *Massachusetts*,[13] the general principle was laid down that a government may constitutionally impose restraints on the liberty of citizens "to secure the general comfort, health and prosperity of the state." It is uniformly held that a state may require that students be vaccinated as a prerequisite to enrollment in school. In some early cases it was held that compulsory vaccination was not justified in the absence of a threatened epidemic.[14] In more recent cases, however, compulsory vaccination has been upheld even though there is no threatened epidemic.[15] Parents sometimes challenge compulsory vaccination statutes on religious grounds, but, in general, these challenges are unsuccessful unless the relevant statute makes an exception on religious grounds.[16]

In the recent case of *State ex rel. Mack* v. *Board of Education of Covington*,[17] the statute provided that no pupil would be admitted to school unless he first received certain immunizations, presented evidence that he was in the process of receiving such immunizations, or presented a written statement of his parents' objection to immunizations. The statute also provided that no other provision of the statute should limit or impair the right of the school board to make and enforce regulations concerning immunizations. A school board refused to admit a student who presented a written statement of his parents' objection to immunizations; the court upheld the action of the board, and refused to issue a writ of mandamus compelling the student's admission. This decision relates to the limited function of the writ of mandamus which, as a general rule, will not be granted except to compel the performance of a clear duty.[18] As the court construed the statute, the board was not compelled to admit a student merely because he had complied with one of the two possible alternatives in the immunization statute. The student, in the court's opinion, was required to comply with the particular regulation adopted by the board.

School Attendance Zones or Areas Within a District. Where two or more schools with the same grade levels are maintained in a single school district, the school board of the district has wide discretion in adopting regulations for the distribution of pupils to the several schools. A school board is responsible for making educationally sound decisions in establishing school attendance zones, and several different factors may be involved. As small children are a factor in elementary education, distances and travel hazards must be considered. The *neighborhood school* concept or doctrine recognizes many of the relevant factors and is generally accepted as an educationally sound basis for the distribution of elementary and even secondary school pupils. Under this doctrine, pupils are assigned to schools in or near the neighborhoods in which they reside. However, in many situations, especially in sparsely settled areas, it has always been necessary to transport pupils considerable distances. While the actions of school boards in fixing boundaries for attendance zones are often challenged as being arbitrary and, thus, an abuse of board discretion, it has been held that an increase in travel hazards caused by a change in attendance boundaries does not necessarily show arbitrariness.[19]

Prior to the Supreme Court's decision in *Brown* v. *Board of Education of Topeka, Kansas*,[20] it was the policy in many states to assign pupils to schools on the basis of race, without regard to educational soundness or the neighborhood school doctrine. In *Gonzales et al.* v. *Sheely*,[21] however, which was decided three years before *Brown* v. *Board of Education of Topeka, Kansas*, it was held that a policy of denying the admission of three hundred pupils of Mexican and Latin descent to a school attended by white pupils was arbitrary and unreasonable. A full discussion of the impact of the *Brown* decision on the area of pupil assignment in the public schools is found in Appendix I, "Before and After *Brown* v. *Board of Education of Topeka, Kansas*."

Curriculum Requirements. One of the most serious problems in modern American public education at the elementary and secondary school levels relates to the laws under which the power to determine curriculum content is vested in and delegated to various agencies and officials. Except for federal constitutional prohibitions, such as those provided by the *establishment* and *free exercise* clauses of the First Amendment, states through their constitutions and legislative enactments have plenary power over curriculum content in public educational systems. Typically, state legislatures require the teaching of certain subjects such as American history, civics, and hygiene. In some states, the central agency or state board of education is vested with curriculum control, but, as a general rule, local school boards have wide discretion in determining curriculum content.[22] It has been asserted that "it is safe to say that local districts and boards are free to include in the school curriculum any non-sectarian subject not expressly prohibited by the constitution of the state or by statute."[23] There is a serious question as to whether the present state of the law, under which the decision-making power to determine curriculum content is vested in lay school boards, produces educationally sound results. In apparent justification of this condition, it has been pointed out that "different people develop widely different beliefs and sets of values," and "if values held by many are ignored, there is bound to be criticism of some of the things the schools are trying to do. Because of this situation . . . in America lay citizens cannot be left out of the basic processes of curriculum development."[24]

A leading critic of American public education takes the position that "our entire society" does have the final responsibility for determining the *broad purposes* of education, but the *choice of means* for achieving these broad purposes "is one for the teaching profession to decide." It is submitted that there is merit to this critic's conclusion that curriculum content is a professional matter that should be left to professionally trained education personnel.[25] There is reason to believe that public school teachers should assert their right to make professional decisions on curriculum matters as they exercise their rights—which are receiving recognition in an increasing number of states—to engage in professional negotiations with school boards with respect to matters within their professional competence.

Public participation in curriculum development through state constitutional and statutory provision is also open to question because of the time-consuming necessity of changing the constitution or statutes to correct what are later felt to be mistakes. An historic example of this procedure is to be found in the notorious case of *Scopes* v. *State*.[26] The unfavorable publicity which the state received was widespread, and it is reported that the court urged the Attorney General of the state to drop the case. The statute under which the case was prosecuted, however, was not repealed until 1967—forty years later! As a general rule, school boards are vested with authority over curriculum development for their respective districts, and except as otherwise provided in recently enacted collective bargaining statutes, teacher participation in the process of curriculum development is not a question of law but a matter left to the educational policy of each school board. Accordingly, the court decisions in this area are concerned for the most part with the exercise of this authority by school boards.[27]

Parents on occasions have challenged school board requirements that students must enroll in certain specified courses. In such cases courts often appear to make an educational judgment as to the importance of the required course in the circumstances of each case. If the court considers the course educationally important the requirement will be upheld as reasonable, but if the court considers the course relatively unimportant under the circumstances the requirement will be annulled as unreasonable.[28]

In *Meyer* v. *State of Nebraska*,[29] discussed later under non-public elementary and secondary education, the U.S. Supreme Court implied that a state could constitutionally prohibit the teaching of any foreign language in public elementary schools.[30] (Of course, it is familiar law that courts are concerned with the power to legislate and not with the wisdom of the legislation which a state has the power to enact.) One of the concerns here is the wisdom and educational soundness of laws which allocate the power over curriculum development to lay persons and agencies. For example, the patriotic zeal of a lay group might prompt the prohibition of foreign-language teaching in public schools, although most educators today regard the development of competence in at least one foreign language as an important part of a student's education, unrelated to patriotism.

Where a parent objects on religious grounds to a requirement that his child enroll in a particular course, the constitutional right to religious freedom must be considered. Thus, in the *Hardwich* case[31] it was held unreasonable to expel a student who refused to participate in dancing as part of a physical education course. On the other hand, in the recent case of *Mitchell* v. *McCall*,[32] where the state had repealed its compulsory attendance law, it was held that a writ of mandate could not be issued to compel a school board to admit a student who refused on religious grounds to enroll in a required physical education course. The court could properly hold that there was no requirement that the student attend the public schools.[33]

Scholastic Performance. Typically, the responsibility for setting up standards of performance is delegated to the local school boards and, in general, it is both legally reasonable and educationally sound to establish minimum standards of scholastic performance which must be met in order for a student to continue in school. Compulsory attendance laws do not as a rule make any exception for students between the compulsory attendance ages who do not maintain the minimum scholastic requirements. No case has been found where this point was in issue. In *Barnard* v. *Shelbourne*[34] the court implied that some provision for continued education should be made even where scholastic performance is below the required standard. The statute provided for demotion, but the only issue was whether the student was properly dismissed from the first-year class in high school, and the court held that his dismissal was proper.

Discipline for Non-Scholastic Causes. Included in its general responsibility for the management of the schools in a district, is the local school board's express or implied authority to control the conduct of students. As a practical matter, much of this authority is delegated to the principals and classroom teachers. In exercising their responsibility for controlling student conduct, school boards may promulgate reasonable rules and regulations and may punish students for violating such rules or regulations by corporal punishment, suspension, or expulsion. The basis for this authority is the much criticized doctrine of *in loco parentis*,[35] which has not lost its vitality in elementary education.

The statutes of some states prohibit *corporal punishment*,[36] and even where there is no statewide prohibition, it may be prohibited in specific districts by regulations of the local school board. Where corporal punishment is not prohibited, its administration must be appropriate to the cause and reasonable in its application. Whether its application is appropriate and reasonable is, in general, a question of fact to be determined in each case. The decided cases indicate that relevant facts and circumstances include: (1) the severity of the punishment as determined by the extent, if any, to which the student is injured, (2) the age and size of the student, (3) the student's reaction to the punishment, (4) the nature of the student's conduct for which the punishment is administered, and (5) the motive of the person administering the punishment.

It is sometimes said that the nature of the instrument, if any, that is used in administering the punishment is a relevant fact.

Cases which have been decided indicate that no one fact is determinative. It has been held not unreasonable for a teacher to spank a student with a ping-pong paddle or apple-crate slat for insubordination and scuffling in the halls, at least where the student suffered no permanent injury and the punishment was not administered in anger.[37] On the other hand, it was held unreasonable for a teacher to continue to slap a student on the head after the student was subdued and promised not to misbehave again, and where the student's eardrum was ruptured by the slapping and partial loss of hearing resulted.[38] In *Calway* v. *Williamson*,[39] it was held, with one dissent,[40] that it was unreasonable for a school principal who was 5'7" tall and weighed one hundred and ninety pounds to push an eighty-nine-pound, ten-year-old student to the floor and hold him there with his knee on the student's abdomen. It also appeared that the student suffered an abrasion on his back during this treatment, which resulted in a fairly severe infection. The court's conclusion, that the student was justified in trying to escape from the unreasonable force, seems inconsistent with the conclusion of the court in the *Tinkham* case just referred to, where the fact that the student offered no resistance was emphasized. It is to be noted that in the *Tinkham* and *Calway* cases there was discernible injury resulting from the infliction of corporal punishment held to be unreasonable.

Corporal punishment is prohibited by law in the District of Columbia and New Jersey. It is also prohibited by school board regulations in several school districts.[41] It has been observed that in recent years there has been a decrease in the number of corporal punishment cases that reach the courts of last resort.[42]

In general, it is held that a school board, in exercising its managerial authority over public schools, may provide for the *suspension or expulsion* of students who violate rules and regulations for student behavior. The authority to suspend students is sometimes delegated to superintendents, principals, and teachers, but normally the authority to expel is not delegated.

In the early case of *State ex rel. Bowe* v. *Board of Education of City of Fond du Lac*,[43] it was held that a school board rule which required each student coming in from the recess period to bring in a stick of wood for the classroom stove was not necessary for the government, good order, and efficiency of the school and, therefore, a student could not be suspended for refusing to obey such a rule. Later cases uphold as reasonable regulations covering a wide range of activities related to the management of schools and the control of students. Suspensions and expulsions have been upheld for the violation of regulations prohibiting the wearing of cosmetics at school;[44] prohibiting the wearing of metal heel plates on shoes;[45] prohibiting unusual haircuts;[46] and restricting the use of automobiles by students during the lunch hour.[47]

An important legal issue in these cases is the extent to which school board regulations can infringe upon the rights of parents to control their children's activities and grooming. As a general rule, the position of the courts is that the rights of parents must give way to school board restrictions reasonably related to management of the schools, which, of course, includes the control of student conduct. Given this reasonable relationship, the courts do not concern themselves with the wisdom of the regulations. This position was made clear in the *Pugsley* case, decided in 1923, involving the use of cosmetics by students,[48] and also in the *Leonard* case, decided forty-two years later, involving the hairstyling of students.[49] It does not follow, however, that members of the education profession do not have a responsibility to determine the educational soundness of such regulations, although, at present, there seems to be little agreement on this matter among educators.[50]

In two recent cases the U.S. Court of Appeals for the Fifth Circuit has held that the validity of regulations against the wearing of "civil rights buttons" depends on the extent to which the administration of the school is disrupted thereby. In one case the wearing of the buttons was accompanied by considerable disturbance in the school; efforts were made to forcibly pin the buttons on unwilling students. The regulation was upheld as a reasonable restriction on freedom of speech.[51] In the other case, similar buttons were worn by approximately forty students, but there was no evidence of any commotion or disruption of classes. The regulation prohibiting the wearing of the buttons on pain of suspension was held to be unreasonable because "the legitimate interests of the state have not been threatened."[52]

Student's Right to Counsel in Disciplinary Proceedings. In the recent case of *Madera* v. *Board of Education of City of New York* a federal district court had ruled that a school board regulation

barring attorneys from a "guidance conference" convened to determine a student's future status in the educational system, was a
denial of due process of law.[53] This decision was reversed by the
U.S. Court of Appeals,[54] which held that the guidance conference
was only a preliminary proceeding. It was held that any serious
consequences which might flow from the guidance conference
would have to be effectuated in later proceedings in which "the
full panoply of due process safeguards" would apply.

Restrictions Relating to Married Students. School boards have
been faced with special problems relating to students, usually high
school students, who marry and continue or seek to remain in
school. As a general rule, it is held that married persons are not
subject to compulsory attendance laws even though they are
within the compulsory attendance age limits.[55] The reasons for
this judicial exemption differ, as seen in the two cases cited, but it
may be significant that in both of these cases the girls in question
were not interested in continuing their schooling. In this connection, the position of the court in *Nutt* v. *Board of Education of
City of Goodland, Sherman County et al.*[56] may shed some light.
In that case a high school sophomore girl got married and six
months thereafter gave birth to a child. A short time later she
separated from her husband and attempted to enroll in the high
school for her junior year. She was denied admission and petitioned for a writ of mandamus to compel the school board to
readmit her. In granting her relief, the court stated that the fact
that the girl conceived a child out of wedlock was not in itself
sufficient indication of character so immoral as to warrant expulsion from school, especially where there are factors indicating
that the student is of good character and *wants* to return to school.

Where school boards have adopted regulations restricting the
activities of married students, such regulations are generally
upheld. It has been held reasonable for a school board to provide
that married students shall not be eligible to participate in athletic
activities and such extracurricular activities as band, glee club,
class offices, cheerleading, and class plays.[57] To the extent that
marriage while in school contributes to the drop-out problem and
interferes with the administration of school affairs, restrictions
designed to discourage such marriages may be educationally
sound. On the other hand, it is not easy to understand how the

"harmful effects" of the forced association of married students with allegedly impressionable and unmarried ones will be prevented substantially by such restrictions. Out-of-school contacts, motion pictures, television spectaculars, and other news media provide all the information such restrictions seek to avoid.

Membership in Secret Student Organizations. Related in some respects to regulations about married students are the regulations designed to discourage student membership in secret organizations by restricting the school activities of such students. In the early case of *Wayland* v. *Board of School Directors of District No. 1 of Seattle et al.,*[58] the court upheld a school board rule providing that any student who is a member or pledge of a secret society will not be permitted to engage in any activity offered by the high school, save attendance in classes. In support of the rule, the court concluded that the evidence "overwhelmingly establishes the fact that such fraternities do have a marked influence on the school, tending to destroy good order, discipline and scholarship. . . ." There is some conflict in the decisions from other states.[59] In *Hughes et al.* v. *Caddo Parish School Board et al.*[60] the U.S. Supreme Court affirmed *per curiam* a lower federal court opinion[61] holding that it was not a violation of the Fourteenth Amendment of the Federal Constitution for a school board, acting pursuant to a state statute, to adopt a resolution abolishing high school fraternities and sororities and authorizing the suspension or expulsion of students who are or remain members of such organizations. The lower federal court adopted the principles laid down by the U.S. Supreme Court in the early *Waugh* case, involving the University of Mississippi, which is discussed later under *Students in Higher Education—Disciplinary Action Because of Membership in Organizations.*

Any consideration of the educational soundness of regulations restricting the activities of students who are members of secret organizations must take into account the vigor with which parents in several of the cases stoutly defended their children's right to belong to such organizations. Some of these parents no doubt were members of fraternities or sororities during their college days and defended the alleged rights of their children with a feeling of nostalgia. On the other hand, there is a serious question whether, at least at the high school level, it is educationally sound to encourage the somewhat superficial group loyalties and divisive tendencies that characterize most Greek letter organizations.

STUDENTS IN HIGHER EDUCATION

In contrast with students in elementary and secondary education, students in higher education are not required to conform to compulsory attendance laws. Governing bodies of public institutions of higher education have considerable discretion in the development of policies relating to the admission of students and their discipline after admission. As state agencies, however, these governing bodies are subject to the requirements and limitations of the Federal Constitution with respect to state action.

Admissions. In the development of admissions policies, the governing bodies of public institutions are not prohibited from making reasonable classifications of students applying for admission. Whether a particular classification is reasonable is a legal question which, in the final analysis, is for the U.S. Supreme Court to decide. When a statute divides persons within the state's jurisdiction into different classes, such as in-state students and out-of-state students, the statute may be challenged as a violation of the due process and the equal protection clauses of the Fourteenth Amendment. The Supreme Court has pointed out that the two clauses overlap, but the spheres of protection they offer are not coterminous. It has been held that the due process clause "tends to secure equality of the law in the sense that it makes a required minimum of protection for everyone's right of life, liberty, and property, which the Congress or the legislature may not withhold. . . . The guaranty (of equal protection) was aimed at undue favor and individual class privilege on the one hand, and at hostile discrimination or the oppression of inequality, on the other."[62]

The judicial position with respect to the legality of statutes and regulations classifying resident and non-resident students for tuition purposes is revealed in three rather recent decisions: *Newman* v. *Graham*,[63] *Landwehr* v. *The Regents of the University of Colorado*,[64] and *Clark* v. *Redeker*.[65] In each of these cases a regulation of the governing body of a public institution of higher education classified students as out-of-state for tuition purposes if such students had not resided in the state for a specified length of time prior to their initial enrollment. In each case the student had enrolled initially as an out-of-state student. The basic issue involved in all three cases was whether a state statute or regulation of the governing body of a public institution of higher education is prohibited (1) from classifying all students who have not been residents of the state for a specific length of time, e.g., six months, as out-of-state students for tuition purposes, and (2) from providing that such students retain their out-of-state status as long as they are continuously enrolled in the institution, even though the time spent in the state by such students qualifies them as residents for voting and other purposes.

In *Newman* it was stipulated, among other things, that subsequent to his enrollment, the student had voted in the state election and had "complied with all of the requirements for the establishment of residence in the state of Idaho, by both intent and actual residence, for all purposes except to qualify as a resident student" under the regulations of the state Board of Education. The court held that the legislature had no power to delegate to the institution's governing body "the right to fix residence in this manner"; it held that the regulation was arbitrary because it did not give the student an "opportunity to show a change of residential or domiciliary status," and was a denial of equal opportunity to persons of the same class similarly situated.

In *Landwehr* an out-of-state student alleged that, for the four years of his attendance at a state university, he was a "resident and domiciliary of the state." The court held that the classification of students as "in-state" and "out-of-state" was "not arbitrary or unreasonable and is not so lacking in a foundation as to contravene the constitutional provisions" upon which the student relied.

In *Clark* a male student married a life-long resident of the state after his third year of attendance as an out-of-state student at the institution. The court held that the classification was not arbitrary because it was not absolute, in that any decision of the institution's governing body could be appealed to a review board. The court indicated, however, that, although the classification was not arbitrary, it could be administered in an arbitrary fashion[66] unless the opportunity existed for a student to overcome the presumption of non-residence "by an appropriate showing of change of circumstances." The case was remanded to the review board for reconsideration in light of the court's opinion.

In view of the federal district court's opinion in the *Clark* case, it is not unreasonable to assume that the U.S. Supreme Court would accept the view taken in that case, which, while inconsistent with the court's position in *Landwehr*, is consistent with the decision in *Newman*. Briefly stated, the view here suggested is that a regulation promulgated by the governing body of a state institution of higher education which classifies students as out-of-state or non-resident for tuition purposes must make provision for such students to demonstrate that their conduct justifies re-classification as in-state or resident students.

These three cases deal with the applicability of the due process and equal protection clauses of the Fourteenth Amendment which also provides that "(n)o State shall make or enforce any law which shall abridge the privileges or immunities of citizens of the United States." It might be argued that attending a public institution of higher education in any state is a privilege of U.S. citizens and that the differential treatment by any state of non-resident students is an unconstitutional abridgement of that privilege. However, practically no support for this argument is to be found in the decided cases. It has been stated that "(u)nique among the constitutional provisions, the privileges and immunities clause of the Fourteenth Amendment enjoys the distinction of having been rendered a 'practical nullity' by a single decision of the Supreme Court rendered within five years after its ratification."[67] The decision referred to is that of a narrow Court majority in *The Slaughter House Cases*[68] limiting the coverage of the clause to those privileges and immunities "which owe their existence to the Federal Government, its National Character, its Constitution, or its laws." Under this interpretation a state may make reasonable distinctions between residents and non-residents with respect to a variety of state privileges as distinguished from national privileges. On occasions the U.S. Supreme Court has enumerated some of the privileges that are national in character but none appear to be similar to the privilege of attending a state institution of higher education.[69] On the other hand, many state laws distinguishing between residents and non-residents have been held not to violate the privileges and immunities clause, such as the privilege of voting in state as distinguished from federal elections,[70] taxation,[71]

and marriage.[72] The list of privileges that are national in character
has been expanded from time to time but as yet it has not been
expanded to include the privilege of attending state-supported
institutions of higher education.

Individual states may classify persons temporarily within their
borders for a variety of purposes, such as voting, taxation,
marriage, and divorce. The special treatment may be to encourage
or discourage such persons from becoming domiciliaries. One
purpose of charging higher tuition to non-resident students who
enroll in a state's tax-supported colleges and universities is to
equalize the cost of public education between resident and non-
resident students, the assumption being that the tax burden for
education is greater for residents than for non-residents. The
necessity of distributing the cost of higher education aside, the
educational soundness of requiring non-residents to pay higher
tuition may depend on the educational policy of the particular
state or institution. A policy of encouraging the intermingling of
non-resident and resident students would dictate the elimination of
tuition differentials. The portion of the cost of public higher
education that is recovered in tuitions is so inconsequential that it
is not unreasonable to assume that increased tuition charges for
non-resident students are politically rather than financially or educationally motivated.

Classification for Admission on the Basis of Sex. Most state-
supported institutions of higher education admit both male and
female students, but in *Heaton et al.* v. *Bristol et al.*[73] the court
reversed a decision of the trial court which had granted a writ of
mandamus to compel the governing body of a public all-male
college to admit female students.[74] The U.S. Supreme Court dismissed an appeal and denied certiorari.[75] There is merit to the
trial court's assertion that the classification of males and females
is unrelated to any educational purpose, but the state court of
appeals thought otherwise in light of the existence of sixteen
public coeducational institutions. It should be noted again that no
significance is to be attached to the U.S. Supreme Court's denial of
certiorari or dismissal of an appeal.

Classification for Admission on the Basis of Race. The U.S.
Supreme Court began its piecemeal repudiation of the "separate

but equal doctrine" in public higher education in 1938, sixteen years before the judicial basis for the doctrine was destroyed when *Plessy* v. *Ferguson*[76] was squarely overruled in the *Brown* decision.[77] In that year the Court held in *Missouri ex rel. Gaines* v. *Canada, Registrar of the University of Missouri et al.*[78] that a state may not constitutionally satisfy its obligation under the equal protection clause of the Fourteenth Amendment by paying the expenses of a Negro resident applicant to obtain higher education outside the state, if such education is made available to white applicants within the state. The *Gaines* case was followed by *Sweatt* v. *Painter*[79] and *McLaurin* v. *Oklahoma State Regents for Higher Education.*[80] In the *Sweatt* case the Court again stressed the *equality* part of the separate but equal doctrine and held that the separate law school for Negroes provided by the state at considerable expense was not equal to the law school provided for white students because it lacked "those qualities which are incapable of objective measurement but which make for greatness in a law school." Thus, while the Court did not expressly repudiate the separate but equal doctrine, "it raised the standard of equality to such a level as to make it virtually impossible for any scheme of segregation to meet the test of constitutionality."[81] In the *McLaurin* case the Court held that, even after a Negro student has been admitted into a public institution of higher education which formerly accepted white students only, it is a denial of equal protection of the laws to segregate such a student from his white classmates in the institution's classrooms, library, and dining room solely because of his race.[82]

Scholastic Performance. It is familiar law that the governing body of a public institution of higher education may adopt minimum standards of scholarship which students must maintain in order to remain in the institution; the only legal requirement is that the standards must be reasonable. This was the holding of the court in *Foley* v. *Benedict et al.*[83] It has been held that a student who fails to receive a degree because of poor scholarship cannot recover his tuition from the institution on the theory that the institution is contractually obligated to ensure that the student learns.[84] It has also been held that a state-supported university does not violate any contractual rights of a student by utilizing an examination prepared by a national board of examiners as a method of evaluating the student's scholastic performance.[85] However, it was recently held that due process requires that the grade that is given a student must be a fair appraisal of his scholastic performance.[86] The court observed that, while it could not pass on the issue of whether a student should have received a passing grade, it did have a duty to decide the question of arbitrariness when properly presented.

Disciplinary Action for Non-Scholastic Causes. At the higher education level the usual academic sanctions for student misconduct are suspension and expulsion. Recorded reprimand is sometimes imposed. During the past decade there has been an increase in the number of challenges to the imposition of academic sanctions by public institutions of higher education to reach the courts of record. In a substantial number of these cases the challenge is based on the ground that the student has been denied due process of law in contravention of the Fourteenth Amendment of the U.S. Constitution. State action, it will be remembered, must be consistent with procedural and substantive due process as those terms have been construed by the U.S. Supreme Court.

Procedural due process in student disciplinary cases requires, as a minimum, that a student must be given timely advance notice of the charges against him and an opportunity to be heard before academic sanctions are imposed. *Substantive due process* requires that the charges of misconduct be of such nature that academic sanctions may properly be imposed.[87] Most of the cases decided thus far have been concerned with procedural due process. As late as 1956 a state's highest court upheld the suspension of a student from a public university, even though she had not been given prior notice of the charges against her and had not been given the opportunity to face her accusers and cross-examine them.[88] This decision has been severely criticized,[89] and it is worth noting that the criticism is quoted approvingly by the court in *Dixon* v. *Alabama State Board of Education et al.*,[90] wherein it is held that due process requires prior notice and some opportunity for hearing *before* a student at a tax-supported college is expelled for misconduct.

In the *Dixon* case six Negro students who were enrolled in a state institution of higher education participated in off-campus sit-in demonstrations and were ordered out by the police. The incident was publicized, and the institution's governing body, acting through the institution's president, expelled the students without notice or hearing. The students brought suit alleging denial of due process. Relying on a regulation appearing in the institution's catalog which stated that "the college may at any time decline to continue to accept responsibility for the supervision and service to any student with whom the relationship becomes unpleasant and difficult," the university contended that the students had waived any rights to notice and hearing prior to expulsion. The trial court upheld the expulsions, and the students appealed. In reversing the university's action because of its denial of due process to the students involved, the appellate court relied in part on Professor Seavey's criticism of the *Bluett* decision, using the following quotation:

> At this time when many are worried about dismissal from public service, when only because of the overriding need to protect the public safety is identity of informers kept secret, when we proudly contrast the full hearings before our courts with those in the benighted countries which have no due process protection, when many of our courts are so careful in the protection of those charged with crimes that they will not permit the use of evidence illegally obtained, our sense of justice should be outraged by denial to students of the normal safeguards. It is shocking that the officials of a state education institution, which can function properly only if our freedoms are preserved, should not understand the elementary principles of fair play. It is equally shocking to find that a court supports them in denying to a student the protection given to a pickpocket.

The appellate court laid down the following guidelines for the notice and hearing required by due process:

> The notice should contain a statement of the specific charges and grounds which, if proven, would justify expulsion under the regulations of the Board of Education.... The case before us requires something more than an informal interview with an administrative authority of the college.... In such circumstances, a hearing which gives the Board or the administrative authorities of the college an opportunity to hear both sides in considerable detail is best suited to protect the rights of all involved. This is not to imply that a full-dress judicial hearing with the right to cross-examine witnesses is required....

Replying to the contention that the students waived their right to notice and hearing by enrolling with knowledge of the institution's regulation reserving the right to dismiss any student "with whom the relationship becomes unpleasant and difficult," the appellate court declared:

> ... the State cannot condition the granting of even a privilege upon the renunciation of the constitutional right to due process .... Only private associations have the right to obtain a waiver of notice and hearing before depriving a member of a valuable right. And even here, the right to notice and a hearing is so fundamental to the conduct of our society that the waiver must be clear and explicit.

The legal principle laid down in the *Dixon* case has been applied in subsequent cases.[91]

Where a student is given notice and a hearing prior to suspension or expulsion, it has sometimes been contended that the hearing was inadequate or deficient in one or more respects. These contentions have as a rule been unsuccessful, at least where the student had the right of appealing to the institution's governing body. It has been held that due process is satisfied by a hearing before the institution's disciplinary committee, even though the student is neither represented by counsel nor permitted to cross-examine witnesses.[92]

The recent case of *Woody* v. *Burns*[93] involved the University of Florida, a public institution. A student was charged with "altering a record of the University" and not taking a course required by his department head. After a hearing before the Faculty Discipline Committee, the student was found innocent of the specific charge of altering the record but guilty of conduct unbecoming a student. The Committee's recommendation, that the student be placed on probation for the remainder of his undergraduate career, was approved by the institution's President, but the faculty of the department in which the student had been enrolled summarily denied his petition for enrollment. When the student inquired of the institution's President as to the reasons for this action, he was told that the departmental faculty took the position that his failure to take the required course constituted defiance of the college requirements which disqualified him from further attendance because of failure to maintain a satisfactory academic record. At a full hearing before the University's governing body, it was revealed that the student had maintained the required grade average, but that his department did "not wish him to continue as a student." He was denied further enrollment in that department "without prejudice to apply for enrollment in the other colleges of the University." This decision was affirmed by the State Board of Education, and the student petitioned the court for mandamus to compel his readmission. The trial court denied the petition, but this decision was reversed on appeal.

The appellate court held, among other things, that, since there had been no legislative delegation of authority "to faculty members of any college of the higher education system . . . to arbitrarily or capriciously decide who they desire to teach," if a student's behavior meets the standard required of the University students in general, he may not be denied permission to enroll in any department in particular.

One of the cases arising out of the disturbances on the Berkeley campus of the University of California involved the disciplinary action taken against four students for the repeated and public display of obscene language.[94] The court upheld the dismissal of one student and the suspension of three others. This action was taken after several committee hearings during which the students were present and represented by counsel who were allowed to present and cross-examine witnesses. The regulations under which the action was taken were held to be a reasonable restriction on freedom of speech and assembly.

Substantive due process differs from procedural due process in that it is addressed to the law itself rather than the method of its enforcement.[95] When state action in the form of legislation or an agency regulation is challenged as a violation of substantive due process, the basic issue is whether the legislation or regulation bears a reasonable or adequate relation to a legitimate governmental or agency purpose. State action that restricts or interferes with the exercise of First Amendment liberties and freedoms must be justified by showing that the interference is necessary in order to protect a substantial public interest.[96] Regulations of public institutions of higher education restricting students in the exercise of their First Amendment freedoms present substantive due process issues. In the *Knight* case[97] it was held that there was a denial of procedural due process when certain students were summarily dismissed because they had been arrested and convicted of disorderly conduct in connection with their participation in a freedom ride demonstration in a neighboring state. The institution attempted to justify the dismissals on the ground that the students' misconduct brought dishonor and discredit upon the institution. In response to this contention, the court held that a hearing was necessary because *all* personal misconduct on the part of the students does not necessarily reflect dishonorably upon an institution. The court may have had in mind that a hearing could reveal that the students were merely exercising their constitutional right of advocacy and/or protest. If this were the case, then the question would arise as to whether or not their dismissals were justified.[98] First Amendment freedoms, of course, are not absolute. Their exercise may be regulated as to time, place, and manner and, when so regulated, the basic issue will be whether the regulations are reasonable under the circumstances.[99]

Student misconduct that tends to disrupt the administration of an institution is certainly subject to regulation, and academic sanctions for such misconduct are common in most public institutions of higher education. In *Steier* v. *New York State Education Commissioner*[100] a student in a public institution was charged with repeatedly circulating intemperate letters critical of the institution and some of its officers. After a faculty hearing, the student was expelled. He appealed to the State Board of Education, then to the State Commissioner of Education, and, after further hearings, his appeal was dismissed. The student brought suit alleging denial of due process, but the court held that the decision of the Commissioner was neither "arbitrary nor palpably illegal . . . . No constitutional rights of any kind have been violated." It is clear that the student received procedural due process, and the case also stands for the proposition that the academic sanction of dismissal for exercising the right of criticism and protest in the manner in which it was exercised was not a violation of substantive due process, although the court does not address itself to the question of substantive due process. It does not follow, however, that student criticism of institution officials is, in itself, sufficient to justify a dismissal, even though such criticism might cause "public inconvenience, annoyance and unrest." The right of students to freedom of speech, advocacy, criticism, and protest must be balanced against the interest of public institutions in promoting the educational activities for which they exist. Quite apart from what the courts may eventually say about the dismissal of students for off-campus misconduct, there may be some question as to whether or not such misconduct interferes with institutional operations.[101]

In *Cornette et al.* v. *Aldridge*[102] officials of a state university, pursuant to statutory authority, promulgated a regulation which was made a part of the men's dormitory contract, providing in part that "Each man is accountable as an adult citizen who respects the laws of the community, state and nation, both on and off the campus." A student living in a dormitory violated regulations with respect to possessing liquor and driving at excessive speeds on the campus. He was put on probation and prohibited from driving any car on or off campus during the period of probation. Thereafter, he was apprehended for driving at an excessive rate of speed off campus. After a hearing before a university disciplinary committee, he was suspended indefinitely and brought a mandamus suit to compel his reinstatement. The trial court issued the writ, but the appellate court reversed, holding that the regulations were reasonable and known to the student. The appellate court limited its decision to the impropriety of issuing a writ of mandamus to compel the performance of a discretionary act, and the problem of substantive due process was not discussed.[103]

Regulation of Student Organizations. In the 1915 case of *Waugh* v. *Board of Trustees of the University of Mississippi*[104] the U.S. Supreme Court sustained the constitutionality of a statute outlawing fraternities in public education. In 1954 a lower federal court took the same position.[105] In 1966 a lower federal court upheld a board resolution placing on probation any fraternity, social organization, or other student group denying membership to any person because of his race, color, or religion.[106] It was held that the resolution was not an unconstitutional infringement of the right of association.

Non-Public Education

The principles of law relating to the admission, and rights and responsibilities of students in non-public education differ in several important respects from those of students in public education.

These differences stem in large part from the fact that, as a general rule, the actions of non-public educational schools and institutions of higher education are not subject to the federal constitutional limitations on *state action,* as that term is judicially construed.

STUDENTS IN ELEMENTARY AND SECONDARY EDUCATION

State regulations governing non-public elementary and secondary schools are often similar in some respects to those governing public schools. This is the case where attendance in non-public schools is used by parents or guardians to satisfy their legal responsibilities under compulsory attendance laws. State statutes vary in their provisions for satisfying compulsory attendance requirements but, in general, the qualifications of teachers and the quality of the curriculum must be equivalent to those required in public education.

In *People* v. *Harrell*[107] it was held that the enrollment of children in a purportedly non-public school, which was not staffed by certified teachers and did not offer courses required in public schools, did not qualify as a private school under a statute requiring that all children between certain ages attend a public, private, or parochial school. In this case certain parents had withdrawn their children from public school to place them in a school which they themselves undertook to establish. In another case it was held that an arrangement under which children were enrolled in a correspondence course, for which the parents, neither of whom held teaching credentials, served as proctors, did not satisfy the requirements of a private school for purposes of the compulsory attendance law.[108] The statutes of some states recognize home instruction by a qualified teacher as a satisfactory equivalent of compulsory attendance in school. These statutes were examined in *People* v. *Turner et al.,*[109] and the conclusion was reached that one of the conditions which a purportedly private school must meet is the presence of a qualified teacher.

Followers of the Amish faith contend with sincere religious fervor that the education offered in public elementary and secondary schools is more than is necessary for their simple way of life. However, unless a statutory exception is made in their behalf, they are subject to the compulsory attendance laws that are operative in most states. This was held to be the rule in *State* v. *Garber*,[110] where it was maintained that participation in a correspondence course and/or attendance in a non-public school taught by an uncertified teacher and offering neither the amount of instruction nor the courses of instruction required in the public schools, does not constitute attendance in a private or parochial school for the purpose of compliance with compulsory school attendance laws.

Admissions. In the development of their admissions policies, non-public schools are not subject to the limitations of the equal protection clause of the Fourteenth Amendment of the Federal Constitution, but some states have enacted *public accommodation statutes* under which operators of places of public accommodation are prohibited from denying their accommodations solely because of race, creed, color, or national origin. Whether a non-public school is a place of public accommodation under such a statute is a question of statutory interpretation. Such a statute was involved in the recent case of *Fraser* v. *Robin Dee Day Camp*,[111] and the court held that a "day camp, private school, or nursery school" which publicly advertises its facilities and invites applications for enrollment from the public is prohibited by the statute from refusing admission to an applicant solely on the basis of his race. It has been unsuccessfully contended that state legislation prohibiting discrimination by non-public organizations is an unlawful interference with the right of such organizations to choose whom they wish to accommodate.[112] However, in the absence of prohibitory state legislation, the legal right of a non-public school to maintain a discriminatory admission policy is clear. The educational soundness of admissions policies in non-public education based upon race, color, or national origin is difficult to support in view of the purposes of education in a democratic society. To be sure, there may be controversy over the most appropriate statement of the broad purposes of American education, but it is submitted that there is merit and logic to the contention that "the American people are in substantial agreement that the purposes of education are the development of critical thinking, effective communication, creative skills, and social, civic, and occupational competence."[113] It would appear that the use of a student's race, color, or national origin for admissions purposes has no educational relevance or social value in the heterogeneous American society.

The admissions policies of non-public schools which are based upon creed or religion are justified on religious grounds and supported by the provisions of the First Amendment protecting the free exercise of religion. It has been held, however, that a state statute requiring the vaccination of all children before their attendance in public or private schools is valid when applied to a student attending a non-public parochial school, even though that school does not require vaccination as a condition for admission, and even though the student's parents adhere to a religion which teaches that vaccination is against the will of God.[114]

Curriculum Requirements. It has already been observed that the U.S. Supreme Court in *Pierce* v. *Society of Sisters of the Holy Names of Jesus and Mary,*[115] while holding that a state may not prohibit parents from sending their children to non-public schools, conceded that states may require certain non-public schools to conform to the standards which it promulgates with respect to curriculum and teacher qualifications. The standards must be reasonable, however, and related to an educational purpose within the police power of the state. In *Meyer* v. *State of Nebraska*[116] the Court invalidated a state statute making it a crime to teach German in a non-public school to children who had not successfully passed the eighth grade. It was held that the teaching of German to such children was not harmful to the state and was an arbitrary restriction "without any reasonable relation to any end within the competency of the state." This decision in effect permits non-public schools to include any subjects in their curricula not shown to be harmful to the students or the state. In this respect, non-public schools enjoy an educational advantage over public schools, which are subject to legislative judgment with respect to curriculum content.

The Rights and Responsibilities of Students in Non-Public Schools After Admission. No legal problems comparable to those involving students in public schools exist in this area. The few litigated cases that have been discovered have been primarily concerned with the recovery of the stipulated tuition, where for one reason or another a student's attendance is terminated before the end of the school year or some other period. In these cases the courts, as a rule, dispose of the issues by applying general contract principles. In *Missouri Military Academy* v. *McCollum*[117] a father applied for the admission of his son to the military academy and agreed to pay a stipulated tuition fee for the school year. The application for admission provided, among other things, that, in the event a student left the school before the end of the school year, any fees or charges would become due immediately. The son was admitted but voluntarily withdrew a few months after enrollment. The academy brought suit for breach of contract and for recovery of the balance of the tuition. In upholding the academy's right to recover, the court applied the familiar contract principle that a party suing on a contract must allege performance on his part or a good and sufficient excuse for nonperformance. It was held that the student's voluntary withdrawal was sufficient excuse for the nonperformance by the academy of its agreement to provide the student with schooling for the school year.[118] It has also been held that a military academy can recover the unpaid balance of the agreed upon tuition if a student, whose contract provides for the full payment of tuition in the event of his withdrawal, is dismissed from the academy during the school year.[119] The court found in this case mutuality of obligation, although the legal soundness of this finding may be questioned. Where it is understood that a non-public school student may be dismissed for any cause considered sufficient by the school proprietor, and there is an agreement to pay a stipulated tuition in any event, it has been held that the school may recover the unpaid balance of the tuition after dismissal of a student for violating a school rule against staying away from the school overnight without special permission, even where the student stayed overnight in a hotel with her parents.[120]

State constitutions as well as statutes may contain provisions that protect students in non-public schools against certain kinds of regulations. It has been held that a state constitutional provision guaranteeing religious freedom protected a Jewish student against a private school's regulation requiring all students to attend one of the several churches in a nearby village on Sundays.[121]

STUDENTS IN HIGHER EDUCATION

The actions of governing bodies and representatives of non-public institutions of higher education with respect both to applicants for admission and students who have been admitted are, generally speaking, not subject to the limitations of the Federal Constitution on state action. The decided cases indicate, however, that government involvement in the establishment or support of an institution of higher education may be sufficient to cause the court to conclude that actions on behalf of the institution constitute state action and must conform to the requirements of the Federal Constitution. Thus, in *Hammond* v. *University of Tampa*,[122] it was held that an institution of higher education which uses municipal land and facilities for its educational operations is subject to the requirements of the Fourteenth Amendment of the Federal Constitution and may not deny the admission of applicants on the basis of race.

Admissions. Subject to the provisions of its charter and applicable state legislation, a non-public institution of higher education is free to develop any admissions policy it desires. It has been held that the fact that a student meets an institution's specific entrance requirements gives him no legal right to admission.[123] As noted above, some states have so-called *public accommodation statutes,* and whether such statutes restrict the admissions policies of non-public educational enterprises is a question of statutory interpretation. In *Reed* v. *Hollywood Professional School et al.*[124] it was held that the state's public accommodation and amusement statute did not apply to non-public schools.

Rights and Responsibilities of Students After Admission to Non-Public Institutions of Higher Education. Most of the cases under this heading have been decided by applying the principles of the law of contracts, including specific performance, although in many of the cases there is an issue as to whether the writ of mandamus is the proper remedy for the relief sought.

In one of the few recent cases that has been discovered, a third-year medical student in a non-public institution with a marginal scholastic average was dismissed for scholastic reasons after failing a course for the second time. He sued for a writ of mandamus to compel his readmission and for specific performance of his contract with the institution. He was unsuccessful. The court noted that the institution's catalog, the provisions of which are generally regarded as part of the contract, vested the institution's Promotions Committee with final authority over promotions. It was held, among other things, that "mandamus cannot be used to control an exercise of discretion."[125] In the earlier but frequently cited case of *Anthony* v. *Syracuse University*,[126] a student in a non-public institution was dismissed in her fourth year of attendance because, among other things, the institution's authorities felt that she was not a "typical Syracuse girl." Her suit for specific performance was granted by the trial court, but the appellate court reversed, because the student had expressly agreed that the institution could dismiss her at any time for any reason deemed sufficient to it. The court held that the institution had not acted unreasonably.[127]

There is conflict in some of the early cases as to whether mandamus is the proper remedy where a student in a non-public institution seeks readmission after an allegedly wrongful dismissal.[128]

As a general rule, the officials of a non-public educational institution are under no legal obligation to give a student notice and hearing before dismissing him or her on academic or non-academic grounds. Thus, in *DeHaan* v. *Brandeis University*,[129] a student was dismissed without a hearing and sued to enjoin the institution from dismissing him. In upholding the dismissal, the court stated that "while it might be better policy to hold a hearing ... I hold as a matter of law that the (institution) is not required to do so."

The substantial contributions of non-public schools and institutions of higher education in providing the education uniformly regarded as essential to the strength and viability of the American democratic society certainly support the claim that non-public education serves an important public purpose. This and related considerations are sometimes advanced in support of the contention that the legal rights of students in relation to non-public higher education should not be essentially different from the legal rights of students in relation to public higher education. One of the difficulties involved in this contention is that a legal conclusion that a non-public activity or enterprise is *affected with a public interest* may serve to support state legislation restricting the conduct of such an activity or enterprise, but it does not follow that such conduct is state action, subject to the restrictions on state action imposed by the Federal Constitution. The legal rights of students in relation to public education are based on the fact that the conduct of public education is state action, and not on the fact that public education is *affected with a public interest*.[130] State legislation regulating the activities of non-public institutions of higher education has been upheld,[131] and it could reasonably be assumed that state legislation prohibiting non-public institutions from dismissing students for non-academic causes without notice and hearing would be upheld by the courts as reasonable. In the absence of such legislation, there is merit to the contention that the familiar principles of contract law are not adequate to dispose properly of problems involving the rights and responsibilities of students in non-public institutions of higher education.

Several writers have observed that the general principles of contract law have been developed to regulate relations involved in ordinary arm's length transactions in which the rights and responsibilities of the parties are negotiated by the parties, both or all of whom are equally free to accept or reject various proposals and counter-proposals. It has been noted further that the relationship between an institution of higher education and its students is not of this character.[132]

It has been suggested by some that a *fiduciary* relationship exists between an institution of higher education and its students, and that the laws developed with respect to such relationships should be applied by the courts in resolving conflicts between institutions and students.[133] In a fiduciary relationship the parties are not dealing at arm's length and the fiduciary, in this case the institution, is under an obligation to deal fairly and reasonably with the other party, in this case the student. Judicial acceptance of this approach would enable courts to hold that institutions are impliedly obligated to deal reasonably with students, and courts would decide whether the institution's action in a given case was reasonable. No case has been found in which a court has taken this position. It would seem, however, to be educationally sound for the governing bodies of institutions of higher education, both public and non-public, to use the concept of the fiduciary relationship as the basis for developing regulations relating to student discipline. If institutions do this, they may relieve the growing pressure for state judicial or legislative action.[134]

Notes

1. The term *students* as used in this chapter includes pupils enrolled in elementary and secondary schools, as well as those enrolled in higher education.
2. Statistics show an increase in the number of students in higher education, public and non-public, over a ten-year period as follows: 1955—2,679,000; 1965—5,570,000. *Statistical Abstracts of the United States—1966 Edition* (Washington, D.C.: U.S. Department of Commerce, Bureau of Census).
3. These relations are also regulated by such nonlegal norms as religion, custom, and accepted academic practice.
4. Following the U.S. Supreme Court's 1954 and 1955 decisions in *Brown* v. *Board of Education of Topeka, Kansas*, discussed in Appendix I, many of the states directly affected by the decisions amended their laws in an effort to preserve segregation by race in education. These efforts are described in *The Ordeal of Segregation* by Reed Sarratt (New York: Harper and Row, 1966), in particular pp. 28–35.
5. In *State ex rel. Ronish* v. *School District No. 1 of Fergus County*, 348 P. 2d 797 (Mont.1960) the court upheld a school board's refusal to admit a child who reached the minimum age for admission three days after the cut-off date. But, see *Simonson et al.* v. *School District No. 14*, 258 P.2d 1128 (Colo.1953), where a child who missed the November 30 cut-off date for entering school in one district, moved to another state and entered school there. Upon moving back to the original district after the Christmas holidays, he was refused admission by the school board. The court held that the board's action was arbitrary and reversed its decision.
6. See, for example, *Stephens* v. *Bongart et al.*, 189 A. 131 (N.J.1937) holding that the object of the compulsory attendance statute "was to create an enlightened American citizenship in sympathy with our principles and ideals, and to prevent children reared in America from remaining ignorant and illiterate."
7. 268 U.S. 510, 69 L.Ed. 1071, 45 S.Ct. 571 (1925).
8. In *In re Currence*, 248 N.Y.S.2d 251 (1963) the mother belonged to a religious sect in which the Sabbath begins at noon Wednesday and ends at noon Thursday. Proceedings against the mother for refusing to send the child to school during this period were upheld.
9. In *In re Conlin*, 130 N.Y.S.2d 811 (1954) two girls lived with their father 1.8 miles from the public school to which they were assigned. A statute gave school boards discretion to provide transportation for pupils living

within two miles of their assigned school, and the board in question actually operated a bus that passed within two blocks of plaintiff's home. It was held, however, that the board's refusal to provide transportation for plaintiff's daughters was no defense to the charge of non-compliance with the compulsory attendance law.

10. See for example, Michigan's Statute (M.S.A.15, 3732(e)) providing an exception for "children under 9 years of age whose parents do not reside within 2½ miles, by the nearest traveled road, of some public school: . . . ."

11. In *School District No. 16-R, Umatilla County* v. *McCormach*, 392 P.2d 1019 (Ore.1964) a family owned a furnished cabin which they used from time to time, living there for two months on one occasion. The children attended a school in the district in which the cabin was located but lived with their parents on a farm a mile outside the district. The court held that the children were non-residents of the district and that their parents were liable to the district for tuition.

In *Luoma* v. *Union School District of Keene*, 214 A.2d 120 (N.H. 1965) a pupil's father lived in School District A, which maintained no high school, but paid tuition for all resident pupils who attended high school in District B. Because transportation between the father's home and the high school was difficult to arrange, the boy boarded during the week in District B and returned to his father's home in District A over the weekends. District A sought to have the father pay the boy's tuition, claiming that the boy was not properly a resident of District A and, therefore, not entitled to have his tuition paid for by the District. The court held that the boy was a resident of District A for tuition purposes, as he would have lived full-time with his father had there been a high school available to him in District A.

12. See *Child Welfare Society of Flint* v. *Kennedy School District*, 189 N.W. 1002 (Mich.1922), where a school district was required by the state legislature to accept as residents for school attendance purposes students residing in a children's home in the district even though the parents or guardians of the students were not necessarily residents of the district.

13. 197 U.S. 11, 49 L.Ed. 643, 25 S.Ct. 358 (1905).

14. See *People ex rel. Labaugh* v. *Board of Education of District No. 2*, 52 N.E. 850 (Ill.1899) holding that compulsory vaccination in the absence of a threatened epidemic was not a proper use of the state's police power. In the *Jacobson* case (see note 13), the court recognized that there might be circumstances under which vaccination would not be justified because of a person's health.

15. See *Pierce* v. *Board of Education of City of Fulton*, 219 N.Y.S.2d 519 (1961); *Mosier* v. *Barren County Board of Health*, 215 S.W.2d 967 (Ky. 1948); *Commonwealth* v. *Childs*, 12 N.E.2d 814 (Mass.1938); and *People* v. *Ekerold*, 105 N.E. 670 (N.Y.1914).

16. In *State* v. *Miday*, 140 S.E.2d 325 (N.C.1965) the statute exempted those children "who's parent, parents or guardian are bona fide members of a recognized religious organization whose teachings are contrary to the

practices herein required." The court held that where the religious organization in question did not specifically forbid vaccination, but its members were exhorted to rely on faith in God rather than medicine, it was a question for the jury as to whether the exemption applies.

Where there is no statutory exemption on religious grounds, compulsory vaccinations have been upheld against religious objections. See *Mannis* v. *State of Arkansas ex rel. DeWitt School District #1,* 398 S.W. 2d 206 (Ark.1966), reh. den. 1966, and *Cude* v. *The State of Arkansas et al.,* 377 S.W.2d 816 (Ark.1964), where there was a dissent in both cases. In the *Mannis* case the compulsory vaccination requirement was held to apply to children attending parochial schools!

17. 204 N.E.2d 86 (Ohio 1963), reh. den. 1963.

18. In early English law the writ of mandamus was used to compel the performance of a specific duty in cases where the ordinary forms of legal procedure furnished no adequate remedy. Under state laws it is regarded as one of the extraordinary writs sought in a special proceeding. Whether the writ should be issued is within the discretion of the court in which the petition is brought. See 55 C.J.S., pp. 15, 16, 50, 450–451.

19. In *Galston* v. *School District of City of Omaha,* 128 N.E.2d 790 (Neb. 1964), it was held that a board was not arbitrary in fixing new boundaries and refusing to furnish transportation to new schools, although there was evidence that travel hazards were greatly increased. See also *Hiers* v. *Brownell,* 136 N.W.2d 10 (Mich.1965).

20. 347 U.S. 483, 98 L.Ed. 873, 74 S.Ct. 686 (1954) and 349 U.S. 294, 99 L.Ed. 1083, 75 S.Ct. 753 (1955). These two cases are often referred to as the *School Segregation Cases.* Their full legal effect is still the subject of litigation.

21. 96 F.Supp. 1004 (Ariz.1951).

22. See generally: Madaline K. Remmlein, *School Law* (Danville, Ill.: Interstate Printers and Publishers, 1962, 2nd ed.), pp. 246–247; Robert L. Drury and Kenneth C. Ray, *Principles of School Law* (New York: Appleton-Century-Crofts, 1965), p. 44; and Robert R. Hamilton and Paul R. Mort, *The Law and Public Education* (Brooklyn: Foundation Press, Inc., 1959, 2nd ed.), pp. 130–131.

23. Hamilton and Mort, *op. cit.,* p. 131.

24. Edgar L. Morphet, Roe L. Johns, and Theodore L. Reller, *Educational Administration Concepts, Practices and Issues* (Englewood Cliffs, N.J.: Prentice-Hall, Inc., 1959), p. 313.

25. See Myron Lieberman, *The Future of Public Education* (Chicago: University of Chicago Press, 1960, 5th impression), pp. 15–33.

26. 289 S.W. 363 (Tenn.1927). In this case the legislature had enacted a statute prohibiting the teaching of evolution, and a teacher was convicted for violating its provisions. The conviction was reversed on technical grounds.

27. In the early landmark case of *Stuart* v. *School District No. 1 of Village of Kalamazoo,* 30 Mich. 69 (1874) it was held not to be an abuse of board authority to develop a high school curriculum even though no express

authority existed. The state's constitution provided only that free schools be kept in every district three months of the year and that instruction should be conducted in the English language. The constitution also provided for the establishment of a state university. A school board's establishment of a high school curriculum, including a foreign language, was challenged. The court upheld the board on the ground that it was reasonable to assume that "the people" intended that a public school curriculum would be established that would prepare students for the university.

28. See *Crews* v. *Johnson*, 148 P. 77 (Okla.1915) holding that it was reasonable to require students to enroll in a course in grammar. In *Hardwich* v. *Board of School Trustees of Fruitridge School District*, 205 P. 49 (Calif.1921) a school board included dancing as part of a physical education program and dismissed some students who refused, on religious grounds, to participate in dancing. The court held the dismissals unreasonable and ordered the students reinstated.

    In Re Reassignment of Hayes, 135 S.E.2d 645 (N.C.1964) involved a challenge to a school board's refusal to reassign a student back to the school from which she had been transferred. The reassignment was to permit her to complete a language course in preparation for college, which course was available in the school to which reassignment was requested but was not offered at the school to which she had been transferred. The court held that the board's refusal to reassign her was unreasonable and upheld a reversal of the board's action.

    In *State ex rel. Kelley* v. *Ferguson et al.*, 144 N.W. 1039 (Neb.1914) parents instructed their daughter not to attend a class in domestic science conducted a mile from where her other classes were held. The parents asserted that the time spent by their daughter in going to and from the domestic science class could more profitably be spent in private music lessons which they wanted to give her at their own expense. The daughter was expelled for refusing to attend the domestic science classes. The court thought this unreasonable and ordered her reinstatement.

29. See note 116.

30. The opinion states in part: "The power of the state to compel attendance at some school and to make reasonable regulations for all schools, including a requirement that they shall give instructions in English, is not questioned. Nor has challenge been made of the state's power to prescribe a curriculum for institutions which it supports."

31. See note 28.

32. 143 So.2d 629 (Ala.1962).

33. Under Section 256 of the Alabama Constitution as amended, the state is under no obligation to provide public schools and, therefore, the court could say that the student's attendance was purely voluntary.

34. 102 N.E. 1095 (Mass.1913), affirmed on rehearing 109 N.E. 818 (1915). This was a tort action for damages for wrongful dismissal from school where the plaintiff student was dropped from the freshman class in high school for poor scholarship. The court denied the relief.

35. See 79 C.J.S. 493 where it is stated: "As a general rule a school teacher, to a limited extent at least, stands *in loco parentis* to the pupils under his charge and may exercise such powers of control, restraint, and correction over them as may be reasonably necessary to enable him properly to perform his duties as teacher and accomplish the purposes of education, and is subject to such limitations and prohibitions as may be defined by legislative enactment . . . ."

36. New Jersey and District of Columbia.

37. *Suits* v. *Glover*, 71 So.2d 49 (Ala.1954). See also *Drake* v. *Thomas*, 33 N.E.2d 889 (Ill.1941), where a student in a special high school for incorrigibles was struck several times with a paper tube. In upholding the teacher, the court pointed out that there was no evidence of malice on the part of the teacher and no discernible injury to the student resulted.

38. See *Tinkham* v. *Kole*, 110 N.W.2d 258 (Iowa 1961) where a student put on another student's gloves and was slow in removing them after the teacher ordered their removal.

39. 36 A.2d 377 (Conn.1944).

40. The dissenter contended that the majority failed to note that the principal had only one hand free, that the student was very active in trying to escape and that an instantaneous decision was necessary as to whether more control should be applied or whether the discipline should be abandoned altogether. It was also noted that the abrasion on the student's back was caused by the student's own resistance to control.

41. See Remmlein, *School Law, op. cit.*, pp. 267-268, and Drury and Ray, *Principles of School Law, op. cit.*

42. In Hamilton and Mort, *The Law and Public Education, op. cit.*, p. 20, it is said that this decrease ". . . is a commentary on the good sense and understanding of educators that they have devised more effective and humane means of enforcing discipline . . . . it will be surprising if the necessity for corporal punishment does not all but disappear."

43. 23 N.W. 102 (Wis.1885).

44. *Pugsley* v. *Sellmeyer et al.*, 250 S.W. 538 (Ark.1923), reh. den. 1923. The board rule prohibited "the wearing of transparent hosiery, low-necked dresses . . . or the use of face paint or cosmetics . . . ."

45. *Stromberg* v. *French*, 236 N.W. 477 (N.D.1931). The court held that the rule was enacted for the purpose of maintaining more quiet and discipline and preventing undue wear and tear on the school building.

46. In *Ferrell* v. *Dallas Independent School District*, 261 F.Supp. 545 (Texas 1966) a principal had the authority to "determine when attire of students is in good taste." Three high school students who wore extreme Beatle-type haircuts to further their careers as members of a musical group were told to cut their hair before enrolling. They were unsuccessful in an injunction suit to allow them to enroll with their long hair styles. See also *Leonard et al.* v. *School Committee of Attleboro et al.*, 212 N.E.2d 468 (Mass.1965) where the school dress regulation excluded "items which are felt to be detrimental to classroom decorum."

47. *McLean Independent School District et al.* v. *Andrews et al.*, 333 S.W.2d

886 (Texas 1960). In this case the rule provided that "children driving automobiles to school shall park same in the parking lot when they arrive at school and not move same until 3:45 p.m. unless by special permission." The court noted that the regulation was "for the purpose of controlling the conduct of the students to the end that student pedestrians on the streets adjacent to the schools might be safe from student operated automobiles and that better order, decorum and discipline might prevail at the noon recess."

48. See note 44. There the court said, "The question ... is not whether we approve this rule as one we would have made as directors of the district . . . ."

49. See note 46. The court expressly stated that it "will not pass upon the wisdom or desirability of a school regulation."

50. Mary Anne Raywid, "The Great Haircut Crisis of Our Time," *Phi Delta Kappan*, XLVII, No. 4 (December 1966), 150–155.

51. In *Blackwell et al.* v. *Issaquena County Board of Education et al.*, 363 F.2d 749 (Miss.1966) the so-called "freedom buttons" bore the symbol, "SNCC," referring to the Student Nonviolent Coordinating Committee. Some one hundred and fifty students wore the buttons, distributed them in the corridors, and tried to pin them on unwilling students. The principal held several unsuccessful meetings with parents and eventually some three hundred students were suspended for the balance of the school year.

52. *Burnside et al.* v. *Byars et al.*, 363 F.2d 744 (Miss.1966). Here the court held that school officials "cannot infringe on their students' right to free and unrestricted expression as guaranteed to them . . . where the exercise of such rights in the school buildings and school rooms do not materially and substantially interfere with the requirements of appropriate discipline in the operation of the school . . . ."

53. 267 F.Supp. 356 (N.Y.1967). In relation to the juvenile court proceedings this decision is in accord with the decision of the U.S. Supreme Court in *In Matter of Gault,* 387 U.S. 1, 18 L.Ed.2d 527, 87 S.Ct. 1428 (1967), upholding a juvenile's right to due process, including counsel.

54. 386 F.2d 778 (N.Y.1967).

55. See for example, *In re Rogers,* 234 N.Y.S.2d 172 (1962) where it was held that the compulsory attendance law did not apply. One of the reasons given was the possible "harmful effects" of the forced association of a married child with other impressionable and unmarried children, "especially where the former is not disposed to attend school." Also, see *In re State in the Interest of Goodwin,* 39 So.2d 731 (La.1949) where the court, in holding that a fourteen-year-old married girl was no longer subject to the compulsory attendance laws, opined that the girl "having acquired the status of a wife, it is not only her right but also her duty to live with her husband at their matrimonial domicile and to follow him wherever he chooses to reside."

56. 278 P. 1065 (Kans.1929).

57. See, for example, *Board of Directors of Independent School District of Waterloo* v. *Green,* 147 N.W.2d 854 (Iowa 1967) where the board's re-

fusal to permit a student to continue playing basketball after marriage was upheld, and *Cochrane* v. *Board of Education of the Mesick Consolidated School District*, 103 N.W.2d 569 (Mich.1960), where a lower court upheld the school board's refusal to permit two "top flight" students who married during the summer vacation to continue playing football, and the state's highest court split four to four! See also *Kissick* v. *Garland Independent School District*, 330 S.W.2d 708 (Texas 1959), reh. den. 1959, and *State ex rel. Thompson* v. *Marion County Board of Education et al.*, 302 S.W.2d 57 (Tenn.1957), upholding a board regulation providing that any student who marries during the school term shall be automatically expelled for the remainder of the term. This regulation was applied to a high school senior who got married three months before the end of the term and graduation! However, in *Board of Education of Harrodsburg* v. *Bentley*, 383 S.W.2d 677 (Ky.1964), a board regulation providing that any student who marries must withdraw from school at once and may not return for one full year was held unreasonable when applied to a girl student with above average grades.

58. 86 P. 642 (Wash. 1906).

59. In *Burkitt et al.* v. *School District No. 1 Multnomah County et al.*, 246 P.2d 566 (Ore.1952) a state statute declared unlawful the existence of any and all secret societies in the public schools, and school boards were authorized to suspend or expel all students who engage in the organization or maintenance of such societies. Pursuant to this statute a school board adopted a regulation prohibiting the establishment of student clubs which draw their numbers from more than one school. The regulation was upheld.

In *Wilson et al.* v. *Abilene Independent School District et al.*, 190 S.W.2d 406 (Texas 1945) a board regulation required all high school students to sign a pledge not to become a member of any secret organization, and members of such organizations were barred from all school activities save that of attending classes. The court, while upholding the regulation, limited its operation to the school term. The extension of the regulation to cover vacation periods was held to be "an undue invasion of parental authority."

In *Wright et al.* v. *Board of Education of St. Louis*, 246 S.W. 43 (Mo. 1922) a divided court held unreasonable a board regulation forbidding secret organizations and denying all privileges of school attendance save classroom work to students who were members of such organizations. The majority and dissent were in sharp conflict as to whether the evidence supported the conclusion that membership in secret societies was detrimental to the operation and control of the schools.

60. Mem. 323 U.S. 685, 89 L.Ed. 554, 65 S.Ct. 562 (1945).

61. 57 F.Supp. 508 (La.1944).

62. *Truax* v. *Corrigan*, 257 U.S. 312, 66 L.Ed. 254, 42 S.Ct. 124 (1921). For a general discussion, see *Constitution of the United States of America*, Revised and Annotated, 1963, pp. 1279 et seq.

63. 349 P.2d 716 (Idaho 1960).

64. 396 P.2d 451 (Colo.1964).

65. 259 F.Supp. 117 (Iowa 1966).

66. See *Yick Wo* v. *Hopkins*, 118 U.S. 356, 30 L.Ed. 220, 6 S.Ct. 1064 (1886), where a Chinese had been convicted of operating a laundry in violation of a municipal ordinance which made it unlawful to engage in such business except in a building constructed of brick or stone, without the consent of the Board of Supervisors. The evidence showed that the consent had been granted to some eighty persons, but denied to two hundred Chinese carrying on the same business under circumstances similar to the eighty. This discrimination, solely on the basis of nationality, was held to be illegal. The point was made that the unlawful administration of a valid statute constitutes a violation of constitutional rights.

67. *Constitution of the United States,* Revised and Annotated, 1963, pp. 1075–1076.

68. 83 U.S. (16 Wall.) 36 (1873).

69. In *The Slaughter House Cases* the Court listed the right of access to the seat of Government, seaports, subtreasuries, land offices, and courts of justice, the right to demand protection of the Federal Government on the high seas or abroad, the right of assembly and the privilege of the writ of habeas corpus, the right to use the navigable waters of the United States, and rights secured by treaty. In *Twining* v. *New Jersey,* 211 U.S. 78, 53 L.Ed. 97, 29 S.Ct. 14 (1908), the Court recognized that "privileges and immunities" include the right to pass freely from state to state, the right to vote for national officers, and the right to enter public lands. In *Hague* v. *C.I.O.,* 307 U.S. 496, 83 L.Ed. 1423, 59 S.Ct. 954 (1939), the list was expanded to include the freedom to use streets and parks for the dissemination of information.

70. *Pope* v. *Williams,* 193 U.S. 621, 48 L.Ed. 817, 24 S.Ct. 573 (1904).

71. See *Williams* v. *Fears,* 179 U.S. 270, 45 L.Ed. 186, 21 S.Ct. 128 (1900). Also *Kirtland* v. *Hotchkiss,* 100 U.S. 491, 25 L.Ed. 558 (1879).

72. See *Ferry* v. *Spokane P. & S. Ry. Co.,* 258 U.S. 314, 66 L.Ed. 635, 42 S.Ct. 358 (1922).

73. 317 S.W.2d 86 (Texas 1958), reh. den. 1958, cert. den. 359 U.S. 230, 3 L.Ed.2d 765, 79 S.Ct. 802 (1959).

74. The trial court held, among other things, that the classification of males and females for purposes of education was irrational and a violation of the equal protection clause of the Fourteenth Amendment. The state court of appeals pointed out, however, that the state had provided sixteen coeducational institutions and one all-female and one all-male institution, thus giving every student the widest possible choice.

75. Mem. 359 U.S. 230, 3 L.Ed.2d 765, 79 S.Ct. 802 (1959). Petition for rehearing denied, mem. 359 U.S. 999, 3 L.Ed.2d 987, 79 S.Ct. 1123 (1959). Mr. Justice Douglas was of the opinion that a rehearing should be granted.

76. 163 U.S. 537, 41 L.Ed. 256, 16 S.Ct. 1138 (1896).

77. *Brown* v. *Board of Education of Topeka, Kansas,* see note 20.

78. 305 U.S. 337, 83 L.Ed. 208, 59 S.Ct. 232 (1938), reh. den. 305 U.S. 676, 83 L.Ed. 437, 59 S.Ct. 356 (1939).

79. 339 U.S. 629, 94 L.Ed. 1114, 70 S.Ct. 848 (1950).

80. 339 U.S. 637, 94 L.Ed. 1149, 70 S.Ct. 851 (1950).

81. See George W. Spicer, *The Supreme Court and Fundamental Freedoms* (New York: Appleton-Century-Crofts, Inc., 1959), p. 108.

82. The Court recognized that the Negro student's classmates might refuse to associate with him, but the Court said, "There is a vast difference—a constitutional difference—between restrictions imposed by the state which prohibit the intellectual commingling of students, and the refusal of students to commingle where the state presents no such bar."

83. 55 S.W.2d 805 (Texas 1932). The court said, ". . . a student who is unable to maintain and meet the standards of proficiency required is not entitled to continue to attend a state-supported institution, provided the standard required is not unreasonable and arbitrary."

84. See *Trustees of Columbia University* v. *Jacobsen,* 156 A.2d 251 (N.J. 1959), wherein the court observed that learning is a result of several factors and cannot be assumed to be a part of a contract between a student and the institution in which he is enrolled.

85. See *Petition of Johnston,* 114 N.W.2d 255 (Mich.1962) where a senior medical student, along with all others in his class, was required to take an examination sponsored by a national board of medical examiners. He failed certain portions and also failed an oral examination on at least one of the subjects in which he had failed the board examination. The court denied his petition for mandamus to compel the institution to grant him a degree.

86. See *Connelly Jr.* v. *University of Vermont and State Agricultural College,* 244 F.Supp. 156 (Vt.1965) where the court refused to dismiss the complaint of a third-year medical student in which it was alleged that failing grades received by the student were given without proper attention to his academic performance. At the trial, however, several medical school professors testified, and the court ruled that the student's dismissal was not arbitrary or capricious. (Unpublished letter from one of the attorneys in the case.)

87. For a detailed statement of the development of the due process clause, see *Constitution of the United States,* Revised and Annotated, 1963, pp. 1082–1087.

88. See *People ex rel. Bluett* v. *Board of Trustees of University of Illinois,* 134 N.E.2d 635 (Ill.1956), where a student was suspended without notice and hearing for allegedly cheating in an examination. She was not advised of the charge until she appeared before a disciplinary committee some time after her suspension. The court held that the student had no legal right to a hearing and that it would be both ineffective and impractical to require a hearing.

89. See Warren A. Seavey, "Dismissal of Students: 'Due Process,'" 70 *Harvard Law Review* 1406 (April, 1957).

90. 294 F.2d 150 (Ala.1961), cert. den. 368 U.S. 930, 7 L.Ed.2d 193, 82 S.Ct. 368 (1961).

91. See, for example, *Knight et al.* v. *State Board of Education et al.,* 200

F.Supp. 174 (Tenn.1961) where the State Board instructed institutions under its control to promptly suspend any students arrested and convicted on charges of personal misconduct—such misconduct being a reflection of dishonor and discredit upon the institutions. Certain students participated in freedom rides into another state, were arrested and convicted of disorderly conduct, and were suspended without a hearing. In reversing the suspensions, the court held that due process obligates the institution to examine the facts in each case, because *all personal misconduct* does not necessarily reflect dishonorably upon an institution.

92. See *Due* v. *Florida Agricultural and Mechanical University,* 233 F.Supp. 396 (Fla.1963).

93. 188 So.2d 56 (Fla.1966), reh. den. 1966.

94. *Goldberg* v. *Regents of University of California,* 57 Cal.Rptr. 463 (1967).

95. For a general discussion of the development of the concept of substantive due process, see *Constitution of the United States,* Revised and Annotated, 1963, pp. 1082–1087.

96. Since World War I the U.S. Supreme Court has enlarged the meaning of the word *liberty* in the due process clause of the Fourteenth Amendment. State action is often prohibited where it interferes with individual freedom of speech, including advocacy and protest. For a time the Court applied the *clear and present danger test,* under which interference with speech could be justified only by showing that, unless restrained, the speech represented a threat of a clear and present danger to a substantial public interest. Moreover, the danger must rise "far above public inconveniences, annoyance, or unrest." This test was frequently but not consistently applied between 1915 and 1950. Today, freedom of speech and its concomitants are given considerable judicial protection, but it is quite clear that the Court attempts to balance the public interest on the one hand against the individual's interest in freedom of speech on the other.

97. See note 91.

98. For example, see the "Sit-in" Cases: *Peterson* v. *City of Greenville,* 373 U.S. 244, 10 L.Ed.2d 323, 83 S.Ct. 1119 (1963); *Shuttlesworth et al.* v. *City of Birmingham,* 373 U.S. 262, 10 L.Ed.2d 335, 83 S.Ct. 1130 (1963); *Lombard et al.* v. *Louisiana,* 373 U.S. 267, 10 L.Ed.2d 338, 83 S.Ct. 1122 (1963); *Gober* v. *City of Birmingham,* judgments reversed per curiam, 373 U.S. 374, 10 L.Ed.2d 419, 83 S.Ct. 1311 (1963); *Avent et al.* v. *North Carolina,* judgment vacated and remanded per curiam, 373 U.S. 375, 10 L.Ed.2d 420, 83 S.Ct. 1311 (1963); *Wright et al.* v. *Georgia,* 373 U.S. 284, 10 L.Ed.2d 349, 83 S.Ct. 1240 (1963).

99. *Kunz* v. *New York,* 340 U.S. 290, 95 L.Ed. 267, 280, 71 S.Ct. 312, 328 (1951); *Thomas* v. *Collins,* 323 U.S. 516, 89 L.Ed. 430, 65 S.Ct. 315 (1945), reh. den. 323 U.S. 819, 89 L.Ed. 431, 65 S.Ct. 557 (1945); *Danskin et al.* v. *San Diego Unified School District et al.,* 171 P.2d 885, 891 (Calif.1946).

100. 161 F.Supp. 549 (N.Y.1958).

101. See the following articles in which this question is raised: Alvin L. Goldman, "The University and the Liberty of Its Students—A Fiduciary

Theory," 54 *Kentucky Law Journal* 642 (1966); I. M. Heyman, "Some
Thoughts on University Disciplinary Proceedings," 54 *California Law
Review* 73 (March, 1966); Michael T. Johnson, "The Constitutional
Rights of College Students," 42 *Texas Law Review* 344 (February, 1964);
Arthur H. Sherry, "Governance of the University: Rules, Rights, and
Responsibilities," 54 *California Law Review* 23 (March, 1966).

102. 408 S.W.2d 935 (Texas 1966), reh. den. 1966.

103. See note 18 on the nature of mandamus.

104. 237 U.S. 589, 59 L.Ed. 1131, 35 S.Ct. 720 (1915).

105. See *Webb* v. *State University of New York*, 125 F.Supp. 910 (N.Y.1954).

106. *Sigma Chi Fraternity* v. *Regents of University of Colorado*, 258 F.Supp.
515 (Colo.1966).

107. 180 N.E.2d 889 (Ill.1962).

108. *Shinn* v. *People*, 16 Cal. Rptr. 165 (Calif.1961). Here the court observed
that "home education, regardless of its worth, is not the legal equivalent
of attendance in school in the absence of instruction by qualified private
tutors." See also *State ex rel. Shoreline School District No. 412* v. *Superior
Court for King County Juvenile Court*, 346 P.2d 999 (Wash.1959), reh.
den. 1960, where it was held that to qualify as a school, instruction must
adhere to the following three elements: (1) a qualified teacher, (2) a
pupil or pupils, and (3) a place of instruction. The court found that the
parents provided a place and a pupil but not a qualified teacher.

109. 263 P.2d 685 (Calif.1953).

110. 419 P.2d 896 (Kans.1966). See also *State* v. *Hershberger*, 144 N.E.2d 693
(Ohio 1955) holding that "By requiring the (parent) . . . to provide for
the proper education of his children his right to worship according to
the dictates of his conscience is in no way abridged and his right to
instruct his children in the tenets of his chosen faith is unquestioned."

111. 210 A.2d 208 (N.J.1965).

112. See *Railway Mail Association* v. *Corsi*, 326 U.S. 88, 89 L.Ed. 2072, 65
S.Ct. 1483 (1945). In this case the Court upheld New York's Civil Rights
Law which prohibited discrimination by labor organizations. In a concurring opinion Mr. Justice Frankfurter stated that "the insistence by
individuals on their private prejudices . . ., in relations like those now
before us, ought not to have a higher constitutional sanction than the
determination of a State to extend the area of nondiscrimination beyond
that which the Constitution itself exacts."

113. See Myron Lieberman, *op. cit.*, p. 17.

114. See *Mannis* v. *State of Arkansas ex rel. De Witt School District #1*, note
16. The court, with one dissent, held that the statute was a valid exercise
of the state's power in the interest of public health. In this connection,
see *Jacobson* v. *Massachusetts*, note 13.

115. See note 7.

116. 262 U.S. 390, 67 L.Ed. 1042, 43 S.Ct. 625 (1923).

117. 344 S.W.2d 636 (Mo.1961).

118. The court held that there was "mutuality of obligation between the

parties; on the part of the (academy) to provide the (student) with schooling for the school year; on the part of the (father) to pay the tuition agreed upon . . . ."

119. See *Wentworth Military Academy* v. *Marshall*, 283 S.W.2d 868 (Ark. 1955), where the academy reserved the right to dismiss without making specific charges "if any boy's presence is felt to be unwholesome or if he has a degrading influence on those around him, or has been guilty of conduct unbecoming a gentlemen, ..." The court held that the contract was mutual and enforceable because the academy could not dismiss the student without just cause.

120. See *Hoadley* v. *Allen*, 291 P. 601 (Calif.1930). See also *Hall* v. *Mt. Ida School for Girls*, 155 N.E. 418 (Mass.1927), where it was held to be a breach of contract for a girl who was admitted as a Miss to become a Mrs. It was held that, upon becoming a Mrs., the girl no longer fulfilled the terms of the contract, and recovery of the tuition by the school was allowed. However, see *Holton* v. *Cook*, 27 S.W.2d 1017 (Ark.1930), where the school was denied recovery because the student withdrew because of physical incapacity. The court held that where "there is nothing in the contract to the contrary, it will be implied that the total incapacity of either party excuses the performance."

121. *Miami Military Institute* v. *Leff*, 220 N.Y.S. 799 (1926). In this case the court stated: "I find the contract to be void as violating the constitutional rights of defendant's son in compelling him to attend and support a place of worship against his consent. * * * This to my mind, is so, unless the language of the Bill of Rights of the State Constitution of Ohio is composed of empty words, and the ideas and ideals of the American people as to freedom of conscience through all these years has been but a pleasant dream."

122. 344 F.2d 951 (Fla.1965). See also the conflicting opinions of federal district judges in *Guillory* v. *Administrators of Tulane University of Louisiana*, 203 F.Supp. 855 and 212 F.Supp. 674 (La.1962).

123. In *People ex rel. Tinkhoff et al.* v. *Northwestern University et al.*, 77 N.E.2d 345 (Ill.1947), reh. den. 1948, a student with the required qualifications brought a mandamus suit to compel the institution to admit him on the ground that it was a private corporation affected with a public interest. The court held, however, that the student had no legal right to be admitted to a non-public university, and that admission may be denied for any reason considered by the university to be adequate, and moreover, that no reason need be given for denying admission.

124. 338 P.2d 633 (Calif.1959).

125. *University of Miami et al.* v. *Militana*, 184 So.2d 701 (Fla.1966), reh. den. 1966. The court did conclude that there was no showing of arbitrariness or unreasonableness on the part of the college authorities. See also *Robinson* v. *University of Miami*, 100 So.2d 442 (Fla.1958) where a graduate student in education was withdrawn from a student-teacher program and later dismissed because of his fanatical views. He was un-

successful in his suit for specific performance. In this case, also, the court concluded that the institution acted in good faith and not arbitrarily or from malice.

126. 231 N.Y.S. 435 (1928). The student had agreed to the following university rule: "In order to safeguard those ideals of scholarship and the moral atmosphere which are in the very purpose of its founding and maintenance, the University reserves the right and the student concedes to the University the right to require the withdrawal of any student at any time for any reason deemed sufficient to it, and no reason for requiring such withdrawal need be given."

127. The express agreement is quoted above in note 126. The court observed that the institution's right to dismiss was not absolute but could only dismiss for reasons falling within two classes. Of course, it had "wide discretion in determining what situation does and what does not fall within the classes mentioned . . . ."

128. In *Baltimore University of Baltimore City* v. *Colton*, 57 A. 14 (Md.1904) it was held that mandamus was the proper remedy where the student had no other remedy at law. The court found that the institution had no formal rules regarding attendance and that the student had complied with all the informal policies. In *State ex rel. Nelson* v. *Lincoln Medical College et al.*, 116 N.W. 294 (Neb.1908) it was held that mandamus is the proper remedy where the student had completed her required course of study and had been recommended for graduation by her dean, but certain professors claimed she had failed a number of courses.

On the other hand, in *Booker et al.* v. *Grand Rapids Medical College*, 120 N.W. 589 (Mich.1909) Negro students who completed their first year in a non-public institution were denied admission to the second year because of their race. It was held that they had a right to be continued in attendance, but that "mandamus does not lie to compel a private corporation to perform its obligations resting on contract with an individual." Also in *State ex rel. Arbour* v. *Board of Managers of Presbyterian Hospital of New Orleans*, 59 So. 108 (La.1912), reh. den. 1912, a student nurse was dismissed at the end of her second year allegedly without reason. The court held that mandamus would not lie to enforce "obligations arising simply from contracts." It was held that the student would be entitled to a jury trial should she choose to ask for one.

129. 150 F.Supp. 626 (Mass.1957). Here the student protested vigorously the inadequacy of a scholarship award, but accepted it "under protest." The institution's catalog contained a provision reserving the right to dismiss a student "for appropriate reason."

See also *Barker* v. *Trustees of Bryn Mawr College et al.*, 122 A.220 (Pa.1923) where the college catalog provided that the college ". . . reserved the right to exclude at any time any student whose conduct or academic standing it regards as undesirable." A student was dismissed without notice or hearing. The court upheld the dismissal, saying that in view of the regulation, the college is not required to prefer charges and hold a trial before dismissing a student it regards as undesirable.

130. The concept of "business affected with a public interest" developed in connection with statutes regulating rates and fixing prices with respect to certain types of businesses. For a time the U.S. Supreme Court held that, unless a business was "affected with a public interest," a state statute fixing its rates, prices, or conditions of service was an unconstitutional deprivation of liberty and property without due process of law. Since 1934, when the Court decided *Nebbia* v. *People of State of New York*, 291 U.S. 502, 78 L.Ed. 940, 54 S.Ct. 505 (1934), state legislation regulating non-public activities and enterprises has been upheld if reasonable, whether or not the said activities were affected with a public interest. See generally *Constitution of the United States,* Revised and Annotated, 1963, pp. 1106–1108.

131. *Institute of the Metropolis* v. *University of the State of New York,* 289 N.Y.S. 660 (1936), affirmed 291 N.Y.S. 893 (1936). Also, see Thomas Blackwell, *College Law* (Washington: American Council on Education, 1961), pp. 25–27, and Merritt Chambers, *The Colleges and the Courts Since 1950* (Danville, Ill.: Interstate, 1964), pp. 167–176.

132. See for example: Alvin L. Goldman, "The University and the Liberty of Its Students—A Fiduciary Theory," 54 *Kentucky Law Journal* 642 (1966); "Symposium: Student Rights and Campus Rules," 54 *California Law Review* 1–178 (1966, including a Selected Bibliography on Aspects of Student Academic Freedom); Michael T. Johnson, "The Constitutional Rights of College Students," 44 *Texas Law Review* 344 (1964); Phillip Monypenny, "Toward a Standard for Student Academic Freedom," 28 *Law and Contemporary Problems* 625 (1963); and Comment, "Private Government on the Campus," 72 *Yale Law Journal* 1362 (1962).

133. Alvin L. Goldman, "The University and the Liberty of Its Students—A Fiduciary Theory," *loc. cit.*

134. For suggested legislative action, see "College Disciplinary Proceedings," 18 *Vanderbilt Law Review* 819 (1965). Among legislation which has been enacted in a few states are the "Fair Education Practices Acts" making it an unfair educational practice on the part of non-public educational institutions to exclude, limit, or otherwise discriminate against any persons seeking admission, because of race, religion, creed, color, or national origin. For example, see Massachusetts, *Annotated Laws,* Chapter 151C, Sections 1–5, and New York, *Education Law,* Section 313.

CHAPTER V

Tort Liability of Education Agencies and Personnel

A PERSON or agency involved in the education process may incur legal liability when his or its action or non-action is the legal cause of injury or damage to the person or property of another. For example, a teacher may incur legal liability because of the administration of corporal punishment to a pupil. A school board may incur legal liability because of failure to comply with a statute requiring liability insurance for its school buses. Some kinds of actions or non-actions that give rise to legal liability are classified in law as *torts*.

Some General Principles of the Law of Torts

A tort, as mentioned above, is a legal term used in reference to an action, or non-action, by a person or agency, which results in harm, injury, or damage to the person or property of another person or agency, and for which the law gives a remedy. From the beginning, courts have excluded from the area of tort those acts or failures to act that amount to breaches of contract, and also those acts or failures to act that amount to offenses against the state, i.e., crimes. Thus, the usual definition of a tort is "any private or civil wrong by act or omission, giving rise to a remedy which is not an action of contract."

The principles of the law of tort applied by American courts today are in part the result of centuries of development in which the courts of England disposed of thousands of cases, and in part the result of action by American legislatures. The basic concern in tort law is the development of principles for determining when and under what circumstances the economic loss resulting from harm to the person or property of P (the plaintiff) shall be shifted to D (the defendant) because of the acts or omissions of D (the defendant).

In the development of torts, there is evidence of the effort by courts and legislatures to strike a balance between the competing interest of the security of a person and his property on the one hand, and individual freedom of action on the other.

The principles of tort law developed to date cover a wide range of relationships and factual situations, and generally flow from three basic assumptions, resulting in three general categories of principles. The complex nature of a democratic industrial society requires for its orderly functioning that certain assumptions be made. With respect to tort liability it is assumed that:

1. A person will not, without privilege, intentionally interfere with certain interests of others in their person or property, and

2. A person, when acting or refraining from acting, will do so with *due* care as to the consequences which reasonably may be anticipated, and

3. A person who possesses or controls things likely to do harm if not restrained or controlled, will restrain or control those things.

Flowing from the first assumption are principles of tort law which, depending on the relations between the parties, fix liability for harm on a person who intentionally, and without privilege, interferes with another's interest in his person or property. Thus, if D communicates defamatory information about P, D may be liable in tort for the harm to P. However, if the relationship between D and P is that of chairman of a school board and school superintendent, D's communication may be privileged.

Flowing from the second assumption are principles of tort law which, depending on the relations between the parties, fix liability for harm if a person's action or non-action is below a recognized standard and interferes with another's interests in his person or his property. Thus, if D, to accommodate P at P's request, permits P to ride in D's car, and P is injured while so riding, D's liability for P's injury may depend on the standard of care imposed upon D, and this may depend on D's relation to P. If the relation between D and P is one of teacher and student, and D, while driving with ordinary but less than strict care, harms P, tort liability may be fixed on D.

Flowing from the third assumption are principles of tort law which, depending on the relations of the parties, fix liability for harm if a person possessing or controlling a thing likely to do harm fails to restrain or control the thing, and this failure results in interference with another's interest in his person or property. Thus, if D controls a building in which there exists an unprotected area likely to do harm, and P, an adult licensee, is harmed because of the unprotected area, D may not be liable in tort for P's harm. However, if P is a child and a trespasser, tort liability may be fixed on D if it is established that the unprotected area is an "attractive nuisance," i.e. a thing which attracts children's curiosity and invites them to play on, in, over, or with it.

In general, Anglo–American tort law imposes no liability unless it can be shown that there has been a harmful interference with an interest of someone in his person or property. If a harmful interference is shown, it is then necessary to establish at least two things: (1) that the person or agency charged with tortious conduct was under a *duty* to the person whose interest has been harmed *and* (2) that the failure properly to discharge this duty was the legal *cause* of the harm, i.e., that the person charged was legally at fault. The duty may arise from the relationship of the persons, or it may result from the possession or control of things or persons by the person charged. In the field of education this duty may arise from the relation of the educational institution to its professional and nonprofessional personnel, and/or pupils and students, and other persons as well. Also, it may result from the institution's possession of plant facilities and equipment.

Courts frequently employ the term "proximate cause" rather than "legal cause" in deciding negligence cases. When it is said that one of the things a plaintiff in a negligence suit must establish is that the defendant's failure to discharge properly his duty was the legal cause or proximate cause of the plaintiff's injury, the effort is being made to limit the defendant's liability. The defendant's negligent act may have been committed incident to the plaintiff's injury but the injury might have occurred in spite of the defendant's act. The defendant's negligent act may have been one of several events contributing to the plaintiff's injury. Because of these and other possibilities, something more must be shown than the fact that the defendant's negligent act was incident to the plaintiff's injury and may even have contributed to it. As Prosser points out, "(a)s a practical matter, legal responsibility must be limited to those causes which are so closely connected with the result and of such significance that the law is justified in imposing liability. Some boundary must be set to liability for the consequences of any act, upon the basis of some social idea of justice or policy."[1] It is important to keep these observations in mind when confronted with a court's statement that a particular defendant's negligent conduct was or was not the proximate cause of a particular plaintiff's injury.

As a general rule, tort liability is imposed upon the person whose action or non-action is the legal cause of the injury or damage complained of. Under the principles of tort law, however, tort liability may also be imposed upon the employer of the person found to be legally at fault. The legal principle that an employer is liable for the tortious action or non-action of his employee in connection with his employment is a principle of vicarious liability frequently called *respondeat superior*. State legislatures and courts are not in agreement as to whether this principle of *respondeat superior* should be applied so as to impose tort liability upon school boards and governing bodies of education institutions for the tortious conduct of teachers and other education employees.

Modern treatises on torts distinguish between (a) intentional torts, (b) negligent torts, and (c) torts where liability is imposed without regard to fault or intent.[2] Education cases, for the most part, fall into the first two categories.

DEFENSES TO TORT ACTIONS

The law recognizes two general types of defenses to tort actions. The first type includes the defenses of (1) no legal duty, and (2) no breach of legal duty. These defenses test whether the plaintiff has a cause of action, i.e. whether the essential components of an actionable tort are present. The second type of defense includes the defenses of (3) contributory negligence, (4) voluntary assumption of risk, (5) privilege, and (6) immunity. In general, defenses of this latter type concede that the essential components of an actionable tort exist but either operate to limit the amount of damage recoverable or bar completely any recovery by a particular plaintiff.

In the defense of *no legal duty,* the party charged with tortious conduct alleges that he was under no legal duty to the party whose person or property was damaged. There are well-established exceptions, but, in general, a landowner owes no affirmative legal duty to a trespasser, and a person owes no affirmative legal duty to a stranger.

In the defense of *no breach of legal duty,* the party charged concedes the existence of a legal duty but alleges that his conduct did not constitute a breach of that duty. The law recognizes that a higher degree of care must be exercised under some circumstances than is required under others. There is no breach of a legal duty if the party charged shows by competent evidence that he exercised that degree of care which the law requires. Part of the law of torts consists of rules establishing the degree of care required under particular circumstances.

In the defense of *contributory negligence,* the party charged concedes that he may not have exercised the requisite degree of care, but alleges that the party whose person or property was damaged failed to exercise the requisite degree of care for his own safety or the safety of his property.

In the defense of *voluntary assumption of risk,* the party charged alleges that the person or property of the complaining party was damaged because of a risk taken by the complaining party which he knew or ought to have known and voluntarily assumed. This is a familiar defense where spectators or participants in athletic contests are injured.

In the defense of *privilege,* the party charged alleges that the law recognizes in him a privilege to engage in the conduct which has caused the damage complained of. The law recognizes two types of privileges: one absolute, the other qualified. Certain officials are absolutely privileged to make otherwise defamatory statements about others. Whether a school board member who makes defamatory statements about the school superintendent is protected by an absolute or qualified privilege may depend on the law of the state in which the defamatory statements are made.

In the defense of *immunity,* the party charged alleges that the law renders him or it immune from tort liability for the conduct which has caused the damage complained of. Although employers may be liable for the tortious conduct of their employees under the doctrine of *respondeat superior,* under the law prevailing in many states, employers who are governmental agencies are protected or immunized from tort liability under the doctrine of governmental immunity. Moreover, in a few states, private employers engaged in nonprofit charitable activity are protected or immunized from tort liability under the charitable immunity doctrine.

The law of torts is complicated, sometimes illogical, and frequently very technical. The general statements made thus far are designed to give the reader only a broad perspective of the general field. The law at present recognizes a wide assortment of particular torts but the discussion that follows will be limited to an examination of some of the specific torts most frequently encountered in education cases, beginning with the intentional torts of defamation and battery.

Defamation

In general, actionable defamation is the unprivileged communication by the defendant to others of false statements that tend to degrade the plaintiff or hold him up to ridicule, disgrace, or hatred in the estimation of others. It is actionable *libel* if written, and actionable *slander* if spoken. In both kinds of defamation the plaintiff seeks compensation for the injury or damage to his reputation or good name. The statements complained of must not only be false, they must also be published, i.e., communicated to a person or persons other than the plaintiff before they are actionable.

Truth is a defense to an action for defamation but, even where it is shown that the statements complained of are false, the defense of privilege may be available to the defendant in certain situations. It may seem improper for the law to condone the publication of false and derogatory matter under any circumstances. However, much of law consists of balancing competing interests and, in defamation cases, the law recognizes the social interests involved in certain situations and gives them priority over the uncompensated damage to personal reputation. Thus, the law has always regarded it to be of major social importance that there be free and independent judicial and legislative proceedings. Accordingly, judges and legislators are encouraged to speak freely in the performance of their official duties without fear of defamation suits. To a lesser extent, the law also regards it as socially important to encourage other persons to speak freely in situations where the legitimate interests of such persons or third persons or the public may be advanced or protected thereby. It is for these and similar reasons that principles of the law of torts authorize persons under certain circumstances to interpose the defense of privilege when defamation actions are brought against them. In recognition of the fact that some interests entitled to be advanced or protected are of greater importance socially than others, the law recognizes two different types of privileges: the absolute privilege, and the qualified or conditional privilege. The availability of either type of privilege to education agencies and personnel is dependent in large part on state law and, therefore, varies from state to state.

THE ABSOLUTE PRIVILEGE

This privilege is a defense against tort liability for defamation without regard to the publisher's motives and whether or not he has reasonable grounds to believe that the statements made are true. In general, it is available to judicial, legislative, and major executive officers. The absolute privilege of judges with respect to statements made in judicial proceedings extends to jurors, parties to litigation, their counsel, and witnesses. The privilege is available to federal and state legislators with respect to statements made in the course of legislative proceedings but, in general, it does not extend to subordinate legislative bodies such as city councils. The privilege is also available to the major executive officers of the federal and state governments.

The decided cases reveal a conflict as to whether the absolute privilege is available to such education agencies as school boards or to education administrators such as superintendents. In *Smith* v. *Helbraun*,[3] a school superintendent brought a libel action against members of the school board because of alleged defamatory statements published in the board's minutes in relation to a board resolution relieving the superintendent of his official responsibilities. In reversing the trial court's ruling that the board members were protected only by a qualified privilege, the appellate court held that the members of a school board "are clothed with an absolute privilege for what is said or written by them in discharging their responsibilities." In contrast with *Smith* v. *Helbraun* is *Ranous* v. *Hughes*[4] where a teacher brought a libel action against the chairman of the school board because of alleged defamatory statements in a letter dismissing the teacher which was written by the chairman and sent to the school superintendent and the school principal. One of the grounds for the chairman's motion for summary judgment was that the dismissal letter was either absolutely or conditionally privileged. Obviously, if the letter was absolutely privileged, the motion should have been granted, but the trial court denied the motion. The appellate court held that school board members are not high-ranking executive government officials whose defamatory statements are absolutely privileged. Accordingly, the case was returned for trial to determine whether the chairman believed or had reasonable grounds to believe that the defamatory statements in the letter were true and whether the defamatory statements were necessary to a statement of the grounds for the teacher's dismissal.

THE QUALIFIED OR CONDITIONAL PRIVILEGE

This privilege is available to persons with respect to statements made to advance the legitimate interests of themselves, of third parties, or of the public, provided the statements are made reasonably and for a proper purpose. The availability of this defense depends, among other things, upon the nature and importance of the interest sought to be protected, the manner in which the statement is published, the person or persons to whom the statement is communicated, and the relevance of the statement to the interest sought to be protected or advanced. Unlike the absolute privilege, the availability of the qualified or conditional privilege depends on the motives of the publisher and also on whether the publisher has reasonable grounds to believe the statement is true.

There is no "rule of thumb" for determining when it is proper for a person to make a false statement and be protected from tort liability by the defense of qualified or conditional privilege. Officious intermeddling and tale-bearing are not protected, but a person does not have to be under a legal duty to make a statement in order to be protected. In general, it is sufficient if there is a moral duty, or generally accepted standards of decent conduct calling for a statement to advance or protect a legitimate interest.

Education personnel, along with persons generally, have a legitimate interest in their reputations. Accordingly, a person may be protected from a defamation suit if he makes a false statement in an appropriate manner if it appears that such statement is reasonably necessary to protect his own reputation against attack.

Education personnel may appropriately make statements for the purpose of protecting the interests of parents or students. Thus, in *Baskett et al.* v. *Crossfield et al.*,[5] it was held to be a college president's duty to write a letter to a student's parents advising them of morals charges against the student. In a libel action brought against the college president, the court found that the letter was written in good faith and without malice. Accordingly, the qualified privilege was available and the college president was held not liable for the statements contained in his letter.

Education personnel may exchange unverified information between themselves for the purpose of advancing or protecting their common interests. The publisher of false statements contained in such exchanges may be protected from tort liability by a qualified or conditional privilege. In *Forsythe* v. *Durham*[6] a high school principal heard a rumor concerning a student and communicated to the board that the rumor about the student was circulating among the students and teaching staff. In a slander action brought by the student against the principal, the trial court held in favor of the student. On appeal, however, it was held that it was the principal's duty to communicate the rumor to the board and that, in the absence of evidence of malice on the part of the principal, he was protected by a qualified privilege. It should be observed here that the *Restatements of Tort*'s position is that, if the interest which a person reasonably believes to be in great danger is of great value and if the harm which he reasonably believes is threatened thereto is a serious one, a person may be justified in communicating defamatory rumors and suspicions which are not supported by evidence sufficient to justify belief in the truth thereof.

As indicated above, the availability of the defense of qualified or conditional privilege depends, among other things, upon the status of the person or persons to whom the defamatory statements are communicated. The defense is not available if the recipients do not have the requisite interest in the matter to which the defamatory statements relate. Thus, in *Lipman* v. *Brisbane Elementary School District et al.,*[7] it was held that the qualified privilege was not available to individual members of a school board who, without board authorization, made defamatory statements to the press and the public about the school superintendent.

In the *Lipman* case the court also held that the school district was not liable because the actions of the individual board members were not authorized by the board. A different case might be presented if the board had authorized individual members of the board to work jointly with certain members of the public in the investigation of charges against the superintendent.[8]

Battery

Battery is the other intentional tort to be discussed here because it is frequently encountered in education cases. Reference is made to some of the cases in Chapter IV under *Discipline for Non-Scholastic Causes*. The brief discussion here is limited to the principles of tort law involved.

In brief, battery is the intentional and unpermitted contact with the plaintiff's person by acts of the defendant intended to result in such contacts. Actual harm is not necessary to the action but the plaintiff is assumed to consent to ordinary contacts allowed by social usage. One of the defenses to a tort action for battery is *discipline* which is somewhat analogous to the qualified or conditional defense of privilege in defamation actions.

The defense of discipline in tort actions for battery is based upon the fact that, under certain circumstances, the necessity for orderly discipline requires that persons charged with the control of others have authority to use force and restraint and to be protected so long as they act in good faith and in a reasonable manner. As the corporal punishment cases indicate, in determining whether a teacher has acted reasonably in administering corporal punishment, all of the relevant factors must be taken into consideration, including the nature of the offense, the age, sex and strength of the student, his past conduct, the nature of any instrument used, and the extent of the harm inflicted.

Negligence

The unintentional tort of negligence has been defined in various ways. A widely accepted definition is that given by the court in *Fouch* v. *Werner*:[9] "Negligence is either the omission of a person to do something which an ordinarily prudent person would have done under given circumstances or the doing of something which an ordinarily prudent person would not have done under such circumstances. It is not absolute or to be measured in all cases in accordance with some precise standard but always relates to some circumstance of time, place and person . . . ." Action or non-action is negligence when it creates an unreasonable risk of harm to some *general class of persons*. In order for a person injured by negligence to recover from the negligent person, it must be shown that the injured person was within the general class of persons to whom the negligent person owes a duty of care. The legal duty upon which negligence actions are based involves the duty of a person to use proper care in activities from which harm might reasonably be anticipated. Thus, the problems of negligence in the field of education can be considered in connection with the different relationships involved in the education process.

NEGLIGENCE IN RELATION TO ACADEMIC
AND ADMINISTRATIVE PERSONNEL

In the field of education, teaching personnel, supervisory personnel, and maintenance personnel have varying responsibilities and, accordingly, they have different duties, the improper discharge of which may constitute negligence and expose them to tort liability.[10]

Teaching Personnel. The duty of teaching personnel to exercise proper care in supervising students includes the duty to take appropriate steps to avoid dangers that reasonably could be antici-

pated. In *Morris* v. *Ortiz*[11] a student severely injured his hand
while moving a car top in an automobile mechanics class and it
was held that the teacher did not exercise proper care in supervising and instructing the students about moving the car top. The
court maintained that the instructor reasonably could have anticipated that injury might result from his pupils' unorganized
and unsupervised handling of a jaggedly cut metal car roof. On
the other hand, in *Wire* v. *Williams*[12] a majority of the court concluded that a physical education teacher could not reasonably
anticipate that the wooden handle attached to a six-foot rope
used for rope-jumping would be jerked from her hand and hit
and injure a student. It has also been held that, where a type of
physical education activity requires special training, the physical
education teacher should not permit or require untrained students
to participate in such activity. In *LaValley* v. *Stanford*[13] a teacher
was held liable in tort for injuries suffered by a student while
engaging in boxing, an activity for which the student had no
training.

The supervision of playground activities during recess periods
is customarily the duty of teachers. This duty includes the supervision of playground equipment. In *Eastman* v. *Williams*[14] a student was injured while playing on a merry-go-round on the school
playground during recess. The merry-go-round was defective and
the defect was known to the supervising teacher, but it was not
clear whether the student's injury was due to the defect or to the
student's conduct on the merry-go-round, which was allegedly contrary to school rules. The trial court directed a verdict for the
teacher but this action was reversed on appeal and the case was
remanded to the trial court. The appellate court was of the opinion that the teacher would be liable for actionable negligence if
it were shown "that the presence of the hole in the platform was
such that a prudent person in like circumstances . . . would have
thought that injury would be likely to result from an omission to
warn of such hole, or to prohibit the use of the merry-go-round."
This case demonstrates that the duty to supervise may require the
taking of affirmative action.

The absence of a teacher from the classroom may be evidence
of failure to exercise proper care or supervision. Of course, it
must appear that a teacher's breach of duty was the cause of the
injury complained of before the teacher can be held liable in tort.
In *Ohman et al.* v. *Board of Education of City of New York et al.*[15]

it appeared that a teacher was absent from the classroom for one hour and fifteen minutes storing supplies in a corridor room. During this period a rough-house developed in the classroom and a pencil thrown by one student to another struck a third student in the eye, causing a permanent injury. A majority of the court concluded that the tossed pencil, and not the teacher's absence, was the proximate cause of the injury. They held that, even if the teacher had been present in the room, the same accident might have occurred. Two dissenting judges were of the opinion that the teacher's absence was the proximate cause of the accident and injury. In *Chrisdofides* v. *Hellenic Eastern Orthodox Christian Church of New York*,[16] a rough-house took place in a classroom while the teacher was absent for a period of twenty-five minutes during which time one student stabbed another without provocation. The court held that the teacher's absence was the proximate cause of the stabbing. In this case, the student had been brandishing the knife for some minutes before the stabbing, and the court felt that, if the teacher had been present in the room, the knife would have been put away or confiscated and the injury thus prevented. Whether a particular breach of duty is the proximate or legal cause of an injury is often a mixed question of law and fact and courts have not developed or used any one test to be applied in all cases. It is sometimes said that all direct consequences of a breach of duty are proximate, regardless of whether or not they are foreseeable consequences. Whatever the test used, it is clear that courts do attempt to limit the legal responsibility for the consequences of negligent acts, so as not to make a negligent person liable in damages for *all* the consequences that might conceivably flow from his negligent conduct.

A somewhat unusual factual situation was presented in *Bogust* v. *Iverson*[17] where a student personnel officer, after several unsuccessful interviews with an emotionally disturbed student, advised against further interviews. A few days later the student committed suicide and her parents brought a negligence action against the personnel officer. The parents alleged, among other things, that the personnel officer was negligent in failing to alert the parents to their child's condition, and in failing to summon professional assistance. The court held, in effect, that, even if these allegations were proven true, it would be virtually impossible to prove that these failures were the proximate cause of the student's suicide.

Supervisory Personnel. Although supervisory personnel such as superintendents and principals do not always have the day-to-day contact with students that classroom teachers do, failure to exercise proper care in discharging their supervisory duties may expose them to tort liability. In *Eastman* v. *Williams*,[18] discussed above, a teacher-superintendent was also aware of the defective merry-go-round and had reported the defect to the maintenance department. The court intimated that the superintendent may have been obligated to prohibit the use of the merry-go-round until it was properly repaired. In the *Ohman* case,[19] also discussed above, a dissenting opinion stated that "the jury was . . . justified in finding that the principal was negligent in failing to adopt adequate regulations insuring proper supervision of classes in his school . . . ." In *Titus et al.* v. *Lindberg*[20] a nine-year-old pupil was seriously injured when he was struck by a paper clip as he arrived in the school yard ten minutes before school opened. It was alleged that a school board representative had advised pupils assigned to several different schools to gather in this particular school yard and wait for buses to take them to their assigned schools; that the paper clip had been shot from an elastic band by one of the waiting pupils; and that no provision was made to supervise the school yard during this period prior to the opening of the school although the principal of the school was aware of these arrangements and conditions. In an action for damages because of the injury, the court held, among other things, that the failure to take reasonable supervisory precautions could be said to be the proximate cause of the injury, and the principal therefore was liable.

Superintendents are often charged with certain statutory duties, but the nature of such duties determines whether they can be used as the basis for imposing tort liability against the superintendent. In general, it cannot be so used unless the statutory duty is mandatory as distinguished from discretionary. In *Bronaugh* v. *Murray et al.*[21] a statutory duty was imposed upon a superintendent to "see that the laws relating to the schools . . . and the regulations and policies of the district board of education are carried into effect." The board of education in turn was under a statutory duty to require operators of school buses to carry liability insurance. In violation of its statutory duty, the school board did not require a bus owner to carry liability insurance. The bus was involved in an accident in which a person was killed. In a tort action for damages, a judgment was rendered against the bus driver but he was bankrupt and unable to pay. Recovery was sought against the superintendent and the members of the board. In holding that the superintendent was not liable, the court observed that the statute does not "place any specific duty on the superintendent in regard to liability insurance . . . . It follows, therefore, that no individual liability falls on him." This holding is in accord with the general rule that, where a statute creates a duty but leaves its specific performance to judgment or discretion, the failure to perform that duty in a particular way does not constitute a proper basis for tort liability.[22] The liability of the school board in this case will be discussed later.

NEGLIGENCE IN RELATION TO GOVERNING BODIES OF EDUCATIONAL INSTITUTIONS

The common law rules with respect to the tort liability of governing bodies of educational institutions, both public and non-public, have been modified in many states by statute and/or court decisions. Statutes in some states restrict the application of the common law doctrine of governmental or sovereign immunity to public institutions and in a few states the doctrine has been repudiated by court decisions.

Where Immunity Is Recognized. The doctrine of sovereign or governmental immunity originated in the fiction that "the king can do no wrong" and has also been justified on the ground that money appropriated for governmental operations should not be dissipated by the payment of damages arising out of tort claims. While the doctrine has been severely criticized by some courts and law commentators, it is widely accepted as part of the American common law. The doctrine of charitable immunity is, in general, based upon the theory that the property of a charitable institution is a trust fund for certain purposes and these purposes should not be hampered by tort claims against such property. In some states, a non-public educational institution is immune from tort liability if it qualifies as a charitable institution.[23]

Where governmental immunity is recognized some courts have

held that this immunity does not extend to a nuisance created by a government agency. The conflict in the decisions over whether immunity from tort liability extends to liability for creating or maintaining a nuisance results in part from different applications of the term nuisance. Properly applied, and excluding the criminal area of public nuisance, the term nuisance, i.e., private nuisance, unlike the term negligence, is not a type of tort descriptive of a defendant's conduct. It refers to the unreasonable interference with a plaintiff's use and enjoyment of land because of the defendant's conduct. The defendant's conduct may be found to be trespass, an intentional tort, or it may be found to be negligence, an unintentional tort. For example, a school board may operate a parking lot for staff and students in such a manner as to cause dust and noise to interfere with the use and enjoyment of adjacent land. Depending on the circumstances, a court might find the school board's conduct to be an intentional trespass or unintentional negligence. In either event, the court might find the school board liable in tort for creating a nuisance. In determining whether the school board is immune from liability, it would seem that the crucial question should be whether the statute granting immunity is limited to negligence or extends to tort liability generally. However, courts do not usually concern themselves about the coverage of the immunity statute in terms of specific or general liability.

In *Ness* v. *Independent School District of Sioux City*[24] the plaintiff lived adjacent to a school playground on which students played baseball with the consent and under the supervision of the school district. Baseballs often came on to the plaintiff's property, damaging it, and students retrieving the baseballs also caused damage. Moreover, the baseball games created dust storms which allegedly interfered with the plaintiff's enjoyment of his property. The plaintiff alleged that the school district was maintaining a nuisance and the trial court issued an injunction. This action was upheld on appeal, the appellate court saying that " . . . immunity of a governmental agency for liability for negligence in the exercise of governmental functions does not exempt it from liability for a nuisance created and maintained by it." However, courts have generally been reluctant to classify governmental conduct as a nuisance. In *Husser* v. *School District of Pittsburgh*,[25] a public high school pupil was set upon and severely injured by a gang of juveniles as he left school at the end of the school day. The student brought a damage suit against the school district, alleging that the school district and its agents knew of the existence and recurrence of such gang attacks and that, in failing to take any measures to protect pupils entering and leaving school, the school district was maintaining a nuisance. The court held, however, that the school district was protected from tort liability by governmental immunity and that, while the failure of the school district to provide protection against gang attacks "may constitute negligence on the part of the school district," it did not constitute a nuisance in law. In *Bingham* v. *Board of Education of Ogden City*[26] the court, in effect, refused to recognize the maintenance of a nuisance as an exception to the doctrine of governmental immunity. In this case, a child fell into the burning embers of an unguarded incinerator maintained on the school grounds. In a suit for damages the court said, "Since the acts complained of were committed in the performance of a governmental function, the rule of immunity applies, even though the firing of the incinerator was performed in such a negligent manner as may be characterized as maintaining a nuisance."

It is held by some courts that governmental immunity is limited to governmental functions and that it does not apply to proprietary activities. Where this distinction is recognized, it is often a difficult distinction to make.[27] The operation of a summer camp open to the general public upon payment of an admission fee was held to be a proprietary activity of a school district in *Morris* v. *School District of the Township of Mount Lebanon*.[28] However, in *Shields* v. *School District of City of Pittsburgh*[29] it was held that the operation of a school playground by a school district during the summer vacation period was a governmental activity. Apparently there was no admission fee charged, but this may not be determinative. In *Boyer* v. *Iowa High School Athletic Association*[30] a spectator was injured while attending a high school basketball game for which he had paid an admission fee. In an action against the school district for damages the court held that governmental immunity protected the school district. "There is much authority that a school district exercises only governmental functions," the court observed.

The distinction made by some courts between governmental and proprietary functions appears to be an effort to limit the effective operation of the outmoded doctrine of governmental immunity. A comparison of the functions and activities which courts have held to be governmental with those which have been held to be proprietary gives rather convincing evidence that the distinction is more apparent than real.

Where a state statute provides that governmental immunity is retained only for certain specific acts, the court may have to determine whether an alleged injury was caused by the specific acts. In *Tardiff* v. *Shoreline School District*[31] a statute retained governmental immunity for injuries caused by athletic apparatus, equipment, appliances, etc. The question was whether a school district was immune from liability for an injury sustained by a pupil who fell from a rope cargo net used in the school gymnasium. The court held that, although the net was not manufactured for athletic purposes, it was athletic apparatus within the meaning of the statute. In an earlier case in the same state it was held that a baseball was not athletic apparatus![32]

Charitable immunity is available to protect non-public educational institutions in a few states only. In *Matute* v. *Carson Long Institute*[33] a student in a non-public academy brought suit to recover damages for injuries suffered in football practice. In denying recovery the court said that "there can be no question that the law of Pennsylvania grants immunity from tort liability to charitable institutions." However, later cases have abrogated the charitable immunity doctrine in Pennsylvania.[34]

Where Immunity Is Not Recognized. Where, because of statute or court decision, the doctrines of governmental and charitable immunity do not protect educational institutions from tort liability, such liability may result from the tortious conduct of the employees of the institution under the doctrine of *respondeat superior*. Under this doctrine, the innocent principal, employer, or master is liable for the torts of an agent, employee, or servant, committed while acting within the scope and during the course of his employment. In general, it is immaterial that the agent, employee, or servant acts in excess of his authority or contrary to instructions. Liability under the doctrine extends to an employee's intentional torts committed within the scope of his employment. Of course, an employee is always liable for his own torts whether or not his employer is liable. Under the doctrine of *respondeat superior*, the liability of the employer is based upon the tortious conduct of the employee, and the employer cannot be liable unless the employee is liable. In *Frank* v. *Orleans Parish School Board el al.*,[35] excessive disciplinary action by a teacher was the basis for a successful tort action against a teacher and the school board by whom the teacher was employed. The court held that the actions of the teacher in lifting, shaking, and dropping the boy were clearly in excess of that physical force necessary either to discipline the boy or protect himself. The school board and the teacher were therefore subject to liability for the injuries incurred as a result of the teacher's actions. In *Welch* v. *Dunsmuir Joint Union High School District*,[36] a football coach was found to have been negligent in caring for an injured player. In a damage suit, a judgment against the school district was sustained. It was held that the board's employee, directing and supervising the athletic event, failed to exercise even ordinary care. The employee having failed to exercise the requisite degree of care, the board became liable for the injuries sustained in part because of the employee's failure to exercise such care.

Members of governing bodies of public educational institutions are, as a general rule, classified as public officers and as such are immune from liability for tortious conduct in the performance of their duties that are discretionary or quasi-judicial in character, as distinguished from their ministerial duties. The reason for this immunity is said to be the desirability of freeing public servants from the fear of private suits when making decisions requiring their deliberation and judgment. Ministerial duties, those which a public officer is required to perform and where little or no judgment is required, cannot be affected by any fear of legal liability. Here again, a comparison of some of the duties which courts have held to be discretionary with those held to be ministerial permits one to question the soundness of the distinction.

In *Bronaugh* v. *Murray et al.*, discussed above, the school board was held to have breached its statutory duty to require school bus operators to carry liability insurance, and its members were held liable in a damage suit arising out of a death in an accident involving an uninsured bus. It was held that the statute imposed a "duty ministerial in nature," and where "no judgment or discretion on the part of the board is involved . . . board members who fail to act as directed by the statute can be liable individually." This decision implies that, where a statutory duty requires discretionary judgment on the part of the board, tort liability does not result from the board's failure to discharge this duty in a particular way. This was the holding in *Myer* v. *Carman*[37] where a statute required school boards to keep school buildings and grounds in safe condition at all times. In an action for damages for injuries sustained by a student who fell from an unguarded retaining wall on the school grounds, recovery against the board was denied. It was held that the statute in question vested the board with discretionary authority as to the manner of keeping the grounds safe.

Courts agree that there are circumstances which place a duty on school boards to provide for the supervision of students during non-school hours, and that a breach of this duty may be the proximate or legal cause of injuries to students. However, it is not easy to reconcile some of the decisions in which the issue is whether the presence of snow on the ground[38] or whether the sponsorship of a school club[39] gives rise to a duty to supervise during non-school hours. Nor is there an easily discernible distinction between cases holding that the breach of duty to supervise was the proximate or legal cause of a student's injury and cases holding that it was not.[40] Uncertainties such as these, sometimes occurring within a single state, present real educational problems. Of course, a showing that the governing body has recognized a potentially dangerous condition and has taken steps to protect against it may negate a charge of breach of duty and also provide a basis for the defense of voluntary assumption of risk on the part of the injured party. In *Cadieux* v. *Board of Education of City School District of City of Schenectady*,[41] a high school girl was injured while standing along the sidelines watching a football game. The school board had provided protected bleacher seats. In a suit for damages brought against the district, a summary judgment for the district was upheld on appeal. The appellate court held that " . . . a spectator at a sporting event assumes the obvious risk incident to the game, especially where he chooses to sit at an unsafe place despite the availability of protected seating."

The "Attractive Nuisance" Doctrine.[42] In determining the requisite care to be exercised by property owners or occupants with respect to various classes of persons, courts have distinguished between invitees, licensees, and trespassers. An invitee is one who comes on the premises at the express or implied invitation of the owner or occupant for the purpose of common interest or mutual benefit or in connection with the business of the owner or occupant. It is generally held that an owner or occupant owes an invitee a duty to exercise ordinary care to keep the premises in a reasonably safe condition. Thus, it was held in *Turner* v. *Caddo Parrish School Board*,[43] that a seventy-one-year-old woman attending a junior high school football game in which her grandson was playing was an invitee and not a mere licensee. Accordingly, the school board was liable in tort for injuries suffered by the woman while she was watching the game from the sidelines. The court observed that the school did not make any provision for seating the spectators and no effort was made to rope off or in any way indicate where spectators should stand. This was held to be actionable negligence.

A licensee is one who comes on the premises by consent or permission of the owner or occupant, but usually for purposes of his own, having no relation to the interests of the owner or occupant. The general view is that the owner or occupant owes no duty to a licensee to inspect and keep the premises safe but, if he knows of a dangerous condition and has reason to believe that the licensee would not discover it, he must either remedy the condition or warn the licensee. In *Gruhalla* v. *George Moeller Construction Co.*,[44] the pastor of a Catholic parish gave a Brownie troop permission to use a portion of the facilities of a newly opened Catholic school. A co-leader of the Brownie troop was injured when she stepped into a depression in an unlighted exit and brought suit for damages, alleging negligence. In deciding against her, the court held that she was not an invitee but a licensee and took the premises as she found them.

A trespasser comes on the premises without privilege or consent and it is generally held that the owner or occupant must merely refrain from intentional harms or wilful or wanton injury and that no duty is owed to keep the premises in safe condtion. The "attractive nuisance" doctrine is an exception to this general holding concerning trespassers. This doctrine imposes tort liability on owners and occupants under circumstances where the trespassers are small children. The *Restatement of Torts*[45] states that a landowner is liable for harm to young trespassing children caused by *a structure or other artificial condition,* if

" (a) the *place* where the condition is maintained is one upon which the possessor knows or should know that such children are likely to trespass, and

" (b) the *condition* is one of which the possessor knows or should know and which he realizes or should realize as involving an unreasonable risk of death or serious bodily harm to such children, and

" (c) the *children* because of their youth do not discover the condition or realize the risk involved in intermeddling in it or coming within the area made dangerous by it, and

" (d) the utility to the possesor of maintaining the condition is slight as compared to the risk to young children involved therein." This *Restatement,* with or without modification, has been adopted in many states. In *Saul* v. *Roman Catholic Church of Archdiocese of Santa Fe*[46] the Catholic school grounds were being prepared for the installation of a sprinkling system and several ditches and holes had been dug for this purpose. The excavations were unprotected. A ten-year-old child living in the area noticed the excavations one evening and began jumping from the sidewalk across a hole thirty inches deep. On the third jump across, he fell in and sustained a permanent leg injury. In a negligence action brought by the child's father it was alleged that the church was maintaining an "attractive nuisance." The court agreed. In its opinion, the harm to the child could and should have been reasonably foreseen from the maintenance of the condition complained of.

INSURANCE AGAINST TORT LIABILITY

It is reported that, as of 1965, seven states (Alaska, Arizona, California, Hawaii, Illinois, Minnesota, and Wisconsin) have abolished the governmental immunity of school districts.[47] In addition, this governmental immunity has been abolished in New York City and in the state of Washington, with certain exceptions.[48] Where governmental immunity has been abolished or is not recognized, and the school district purchases liability insurance, no special problems arise, although the terms of the insurance contract or policy may impose limitations.

In states other than those referred to above, where governmental immunity is recognized in whole or in part, school districts may be permitted or even required to purchase liability insurance. The effect of such purchases may be controlled by statutory provisions or may be determined by court decisions. In general, the purchase of liability insurance in these states is primarily to protect the school district against liability for its own acts which are not covered by governmental immunity, e.g. nuisance and propriɛtary acts. Whether and, if so, to what extent the purchase of liability insurance in these states constitutes a *waiver* of immunity from tort liability for torts otherwise covered by governmental immunity would seem to depend on the provisions of controlling statutes and current interpretations of those statutes. A controlling statute, as interpreted, may constitute a waiver of immunity at least to the extent of the face value of the insurance policy.

Under the general principles of insurance law, if an insurance carrier (usually called the insurer) is sued, it may set up any defenses available to the insured. However, statutes in some states provide that the insurance carrier cannot use governmental immunity as a defense.

In *Dillon* v. *York City School District*[49] a public high school pupil was injured when she slipped on an accumulation of ice and fell down a flight of stairs while going from one class to another. Suit was brought against the school district because of the negligence of its employees. The school district had purchased liability insurance. It was held that the school district was protected by governmental immunity and that this immunity was not waived by the purchase of liability insurance. The court observed that "The insurance policy protects the school district from possible liability incurred while engaged in proprietary functions." Governmental immunity was judicially abolished in Wisconsin in 1962 but the decision was given prospective effect only.[50] Prior to this decision, a high school pupil was injured while operating an unguarded power saw and suit was brought against the district which had purchased liability insurance. In denying recovery against the district, the court said that the insurance policy did not "require the carrier to forego the defense of governmental immunity (and) the mere presence of liability insurance does not constitute a waiver of the defense of governmental immunity."[51] In contrast, it was held in *Thomas* v. *Broadlands Community Consolidated School District No. 201*[52] that the purchase of liability insurance did constitute a waiver of governmental immunity to the extent of the policy. The court said, "The only justifiable reason for the immunity . . . is the sound and unobjectionable one that it is the public policy to protect public funds and public property, to prevent the diversion of tax moneys, in this case school funds, to the payment of damage claims. There is no justification or reason for absolute immunity if the public funds are protected," as they are where a policy of liability insurance is carried.

"Save Harmless" Statutes. Statutes in at least six states make it mandatory for school districts to "save harmless" their employees from claims arising out of the employees' negligence occurring in the course and within the scope of their employment. States with such statutes are California, Connecticut, Massachusetts, Minnesota, New Jersey, and New York. In these states, if a judgment is rendered against an employee of a school district in a tort action, the district is under a statutory obligation to pay the judgment or to reimburse the employee if he pays it. In general, school districts may purchase liability insurance to discharge this obligation.

In *Swainbank* v. *Coombs et al.*[53] the court held that Connecticut's "save harmless" statute did not impose a direct liability upon the school district for the tortious acts of its employees.

Education in the United States is a major undertaking, both in terms of the number of people directly participating in it and in terms of the state, local, and national expenditures involved. Under the Federal Constitution, the regulation of education is primarily the responsibility of the several states and this has resulted in wide variation in the regulation of the several relationships in the education process. The policy and practice in all states except Hawaii of subdividing the state into semi-autonomous local school districts results in a lack of uniformity in the disposition of legal problems in education even within a single state. This is true with respect to the imposition of tort liability as is illustrated by the court decisions discussed in this chapter. A question can be raised as to the educational soundness of the continued existence of these variations. There may be sound educational reasons why the development of many educational policies should be left to the several states, but are there any educationally sound reasons why local school boards should be left to determine whether the teachers they employ should be protected against negligence judgments by liability insurance purchased by the school district? This problem is further complicated by the conflict in the court decisions as to what constitutes proper supervision of students and whether the lack of proper supervision is the legal or proximate cause of a student's injury in any particular case. It is reported that at least forty-three cases involving student injuries were decided by the

nation's appellate courts during the two-year period, 1965 and
1966.[54] It was not possible to discover any statistics showing the
number of students injured each year in the classrooms throughout the nation. It is clear, however, that the principles of tort law
applicable in determining the liability of teachers and other education personnel for pupil injuries are the cause of considerable
uncertainty on the part of education personnel. Such uncertainty
can result in deficiencies in teaching and educational administration. It may be that the time has come to consider uniform state
laws that will treat the education enterprise in a manner similar
to the treatment accorded the industrial enterprise when workmen's compensation legislation was initiated.

Workmen's compensation laws developed because the principles of tort law were inadequate to deal equitably with industrial
injuries which were increasing substantially with the expansion of
industry. In a high percentage of industrial injury cases the losses
fell on injured employees because employers had available to them
the defenses of (a) contributory negligence, (b) voluntary assumption of risk, and (c) negligence of fellow-employees. The social un-
desirability of having employees bear the loss in industrial injury
cases prompted the enactment in practically all states of some type
of workmen's compensation laws. The underlying philosophy of
all these laws is that industrial accidents are the inevitable consequences of modern industry, and the losses to workers resulting
from such accidents should fall on industry rather than on the
workers. The uncertainties of litigation are replaced by statutory
benefits to injured parties for which the industrial employer is
primarily liable regardless of fault. Typically, such employers purchase liability insurance and benefits paid for losses due to injuries
become part of the cost of conducting the industrial enterprise.

It is suggested that proper research may reveal that the present
rules for determining liability for injuries arising out of activities
occurring in the education enterprise are inequitable and unsuited
to the conditions of modern education and that the losses from
such injuries should be regarded as part of the cost of modern
education, to be borne by the education enterprise rather than by
students and/or teachers.

Notes

1. William L. Prosser, *Law of Torts, 3rd Edition,* 1964.
2. See *Restatement, Second, Torts,* American Law Institute, 1965, and William L. Prosser, *op. cit.*
3. 238 N.Y.S.2d 212 (1963), 251 N.Y.S.2d 533 (1964). See also *Thompson v. Union Free School District No. 1 of Huntington,* 258 N.Y.S.2d 307 (1965) where the principal for business affairs of a school district communicated allegedly slanderous statements by telephone to a bus company about one of its bus drivers. The bus company had a contract with the school district to transport students. The court held that the school district had available to it the "protection of absolute privilege since it . . . performs executive and administrative duties relating to educational matters within its control and performs a function that is of import to the people within the district." And see *Lombardo et al.* v. *Stoke et al.,* 276 N.Y.S.2d 97, 222 N.E.2d 721 (N.Y.1966) where a public college president issued a statement as a defense against published charges that the college was discriminating against some of its employees. Two of the employees brought a libel action against the president alleging that his statement contained defamatory language. It was held that the president was acting on the direction of the college's governing body and that the governing body was "acting within the scope of (its) official powers (and) must be accorded the protection of absolute privilege."
4. 141 N.W.2d 251 (Wis.1966).
5. 228 S.W. 673 (Ky.1920), reh. den. 1921.
6. 200 N.E. 674 (N.Y.1936).
7. 359 P.2d 465 (Calif.1961), reh. den. 1961.
8. Compare *Hardy* v. *Vial et al.,* 311 P.2d 494 (Calif.1957), a case involving the tort of malicious prosecution.
9. 279 P.183 (Calif.1929).
10. Maintenance employees were held liable in tort for injuries to students in *Rose* v. *Board of Education of Abilene,* 337 P.2d 652 (Kans.1959) and in *Adams* v. *State Board of Education,* 103 S.E.2d 854 (N.C.1958).

    In *Esposito* v. *Emery,* 249 F.Supp. 308 (Pa.1965) a tort action for injury to a student was brought against the principal, assistant principal, director of administrative services, and the school janitor. The court held that, while agents and employees of the school district "may not be held vicariously liable for the torts of any other servant or agent," they are liable for their own personal tortious acts.
11. 415 P.2d 114 (Ariz.1966), reh. den. 1966.

12. 133 N.W.2d 840 (Minn.1965).

13. 70 N.Y.S.2d 460 (1947).

14. 207 A.2d 146 (Vt.1965).

15. 90 N.E.2d 474 (N.Y.1949).

16. 227 N.Y.S.2d 946 (1962). See also *Cirillo et al.* v. *City of Milwaukee et al.*, 150 N.W.2d 460 (Wis.1967) holding that a teacher may be held liable in tort for leaving his classroom for twenty-five minutes during which time there was a "rough-house" by students in which a student was injured. The court held that it cannot be held as a matter of law that the rough-house was the superseding cause of the injury.

17. 102 N.W.2d 228 (Wis.1960).

18. See note 14.

19. See note 15.

20. 228 A.2d 65 (N.J.1967).

21. 172 S.W.2d 591 (Ky.1943).

22. This immunity is sometimes referred to as an "absolute privilege" and is a defense against tort liability generally. The justification given is that certain persons performing public functions require freedom from the annoyance of litigation because it would hamper them in the performance of their activities. It extends to a wide range of public personnel and is to be distinguished from the absolute privilege to communicate defamatory information which is limited to a small category of high officials. In 5 *U.C.L.A. Law Review* 167, it is suggested that this immunity be abandoned and insurance coverage provided.

23. In general, charitable institutions are organized for religious, charitable, social, or educational purposes. They are nonprofit in that it is not contemplated that gains, profits, or dividends will be distributed to those who form the institution. See *Miller* v. *Concordia Teachers College of Seward, Nebraska*, 296 F.2d 100 (Neb.1961) where a student was shot by an intoxicated fellow student in a dormitory and tort action was brought against the non-public college, a charitable institution. Under Nebraska law such institutions are immune from tort liability, and the student was unsuccessful in his attempt to recover on contract.

24. 298 N.W. 855 (Iowa 1941). See also *Wayman* v. *Board of Education of Akron City School District*, 216 N.E.2d 637 (Ohio 1964) where it was held that a school board may be enjoined from operating a school parking lot in such a manner that it becomes a nuisance and inflicts damage upon neighboring property.

25. 228 A.2d 910 (Pa.1967).

26. 223 P.2d 432 (Utah 1950).

27. In distinguishing between governmental and proprietary functions, it is generally held that it is the nature of the activity that is determinative and not the location or department carrying on the activity. It is sometimes held that activities that compete with industry and labor are proprietary. On occasions it is said that pleasure activities are proprietary while health and education activities are governmental. In discussing the difficulty of applying the distinction, the court in *Plaza* v. *City of San*

Mateo et al., 266 P.2d 523 (Calif.1954), hearing den. 1954, concluded that "no rule of thumb has been evolved which can be applied with certainty . . . . each new activity claiming the courts' attention must be decided on its own peculiar facts." In this case, the court held that a city-operated golf course was a proprietary activity.

28. 144 A.2d 737 (Pa.1958). See also *Board of Education of Richmond County* v. *Fredericks,* 147 S.E.2d 789 (Ga.1966) holding that a school board may be held liable for injuries sustained by a paying spectator at a school athletic event where the injuries are the result of a defective condition in the seating facilities, which condition was known to the board. See also *Sawaya* v. *Tucson High School District No. 1 of Pima County,* 281 P.2d 105 (Ariz.1955) reh. den. 1955, where a court majority held that a school district leasing a stadium and charging admission to athletic events conducted therein is engaging in a proprietary activity and is not protected from tort liability by governmental immunity.

29. 184 A.2d 240 (Pa.1962).

30. 127 N.W.2d 606 (Iowa 1964).

31. 411 P.2d 889 (Wash.1966).

32. See *Barnecut* v. *Seattle School District No. 1,* 389 P.2d 904 (Wash. 1964).

33. 160 F.Supp. 827 (Pa.1958).

34. See *Heimbuch* v. *President and Directors of Georgetown College,* 251 F.Supp. 614 (D.C.1966).

35. 195 So.2d 451 (La.1967), reh. den. 1967.

36. 326 P.2d 633 (Calif.1958). See also *Miller* v. *Macalester College,* 115 N.W.2d 666 (Minn.1962) where a dramatics teacher in a non-public college assigned students to use a scaffold to take down ceiling spotlights after a dramatics production. The teacher gave only general directions on the use of the scaffold and, while it was being used by the students, it toppled over, seriously injuring a student. In a tort action, the college was held liable. The court held that the teacher was negligent in failing to instruct the students on the proper use of the scaffold and on the risks involved in its use.

37. 73 N.W.2d 514 (Wis.1955).

38. In *Cioffi* v. *Board of Education of City of New York,* 278 N.Y.S.2d 249 (1967) a school board was held liable in tort for injuries suffered by an eleven-year-old pupil who was struck by a piece of ice while pupils were throwing snow and ice on the school playground during unsupervised non-school hours. The court majority held that the school board was under a duty to provide adequate supervision because of the potentially dangerous conditions. But in *Lawes et al.* v. *Board of Education of City of New York et al.,* 213 N.E.2d 667 (N.Y.1965), in a situation similar to the one in *Cioffi,* it was held that snow on the ground does not constitute a special danger from snowball throwing requiring playground supervision during the lunch period. There were dissenting opinions in both cases.

39. In *Chappel* v. *Franklin Pierce School District No. 402,* 426 P.2d 471 (Wash.1967) it was held that a school district was liable in tort for in-

juries suffered by a student during off-campus initiation rites conducted by a school-approved and supervised student club, even though the school impliedly proscribed potentially harmful initiation stunts. It was held immaterial that the initiation rites might not possess any educational or cultural value. However, in *Coates v. Tacoma School District No. 10,* 347 P.2d 1093 (Wash.1960) it was held that a school district was not liable for injuries sustained by a student who was a member of a student club which had a school-appointed advisor but was not connected with any school activity. The student was injured following an unsupervised club initiation ceremony at a member's home several miles away from the school. The court held that (1) the doctrine of *respondeat superior* did not apply because the club advisor was not required to be a school district employee, and (2) the events resulting in the injury could not have been anticipated.

40. In *Chrisdofides v. Hellenic Eastern Orthodox Christian Church of New York,* note 16, where one student stabbed another one while the teacher was absent from the room for twenty-five minutes, it was held that the teacher's absence was the proximate cause of the stabbing because the student had been brandishing the knife several minutes before the stabbing and, had the teacher been present, the knife could have been confiscated before the stabbing. See also *Cirillo et al. v. City of Milwaukee et al.,* note 16. However, in *Ohman et al. v. Board of Education of City of New York et al.,* notes 15 and 19, where a teacher was absent from the room for over an hour during which period a pencil was thrown, causing injury to another student, it was held that the teacher's absence was not the proximate cause of the injury because, even if the teacher had been present, the accident might have occurred. See also *Kos et al. v. Catholic Bishop of Chicago et al.,* 45 N.E.2d 1006 (Ill.1942) holding that a non-public school is not liable for breach of contract to furnish "reasonably safe premises," where a student is struck in the eye by a scrubbing brush thrown by another student. The court held that the injury was caused by the deliberate and intervening act of another student.

41. 266 N.Y.S.2d 895 (1966).

42. It has been said that the word *nuisance* is used because of the supposed analogy to highway obstructions that may constitute a public nuisance. Its use is misleading because the concepts involved bear little relation to the concepts involved in the term *nuisance* in tort law as discussed on pages 141–43 in this chapter.

43. 179 So.2d 702 (La.1965).

44. 391 S.W.2d 585 (Mo.1965), reh.den. 1965.

45. The American Law Institute, an organization of distinguished American jurists, lawyers, and legal scholars, concluded that there was need to examine the decisional and stautory law in a number of areas including the field of torts, and attempt a statement of basic principles. This was done and one result was the Institute's *Restatement of the Law of Torts,* first published in four volumes in 1945. A second Restatement was published in 1964 and purports to represent developments since the 1945

publication. The *Restatements* are unofficial but they have been adopted with or without modification in many states and courts frequently cite them in support of their decisions.

46. 402 P.2d 48 (N.M.1965).

47. See Howard C. Leibee, *Tort Liability for Injuries to Pupils* (Ann Arbor, Mich.: Campus Publishers, 1965), p. 27.

48. Howard C. Leibee, *op. cit.*

49. 220 A.2d 896 (Pa.1966). See also *Branum* v. *State*, 145 N.W.2d 860 (Mich. 1966) holding that the purchase of liability insurance does not constitute a waiver of immunity, but that the statutory waiver of immunity with respect to government vehicles applies to governing bodies of constitutionally independent institutions of higher education.

50. See *Holytz et al.* v. *City of Milwaukee*, 115 N.W.2d 618 (Wis.1962).

51. *Niedfelt et al.* v. *Joint School District No. 1 of City of Viroqua*, 127 N.W.2d 800 (Wis.1964).

52. 109 N.E.2d 636 (Ill.1952), reh. den. 1953. In *Molitor* v. *Kaneland Community Unit School District No. 302*, 163 N.E.2d 89 (Ill.1959), governmental immunity was judicially abolished in Illinois.

53. 115 A.2d 468 (Conn.1955).

54. Research Division, National Education Association, *The Pupil's Day in Court: Review of 1965; The Teacher's Day in Court, Review of 1965; The Pupil's Day in Court, Review of 1966; The Teacher's Day in Court, Review of 1966* (Washington, D.C.: Research Division, National Education Association, 1966, 1967).

CHAPTER VI

Relations Between Church and Government in Education

THE early development of education in the United States was heavily influenced by the relationship between church and government in Colonial America. Free education was first established under the aegis of religious sects, and church-related schools, thus, had a profound impact on the early content and program of American education. Religion, however, not only permeated the educational process, but also played a major role in all aspects of government. One or another of the many religious sects was often given official governmental recognition, thus "establishing" that particular sect as the preferred religion. In part to eliminate such governmentally preferred religions and in part to reduce the sometimes bitter rivalries between different religious sects, the First Amendment to the Federal Constitution was adopted; it provides in part that "Congress shall make no law respecting an establishment of religion, or prohibiting the free exercise thereof." Many of the court decisions discussed in this chapter are concerned with the impact of this constitutional provision on the various relations involved in the education process.

As previously indicated, the regulation of education is a power reserved to the states by the Tenth Amendment of the Federal Constitution. State regulation of education is subject, however, to the limitations of the Federal Constitution on state action. One of these limitations is found in the Fourteenth Amendment which provides, ". . . nor shall any State deprive any person of life, liberty, or property, without due process of law; . . . ." As pointed out in Chapter IV, it is not a deprivation of "due process" for a state to require parents and guardians, under penalty of criminal prosecution, to enroll their children or wards in a qualified school. It will be recalled, however, that in *Pierce* v. *Society of Sisters*,[1] it was held that it is a deprivation of due process for a state to require all children to attend *public* schools. Thus, the rights of persons to operate non-public schools, and the rights of parents and guardians to send their children to such schools are rights protected against deprivation without due process of law. The U.S. Supreme Court has not spelled out with exactness all the personal rights protected by the due process clause against state deprivation, but in *Cantwell* v. *Connecticut*,[2] it was held that the concept of liberty embodied in the due process clause of the Fourteenth Amendment embraces the religious freedoms protected by the First Amendment. Under this interpretation, it is as though the First Amendment provides that neither the Congress *nor the states* shall make any law "respecting an establishment of religion, or prohibiting the free exercise thereof." In many of the court decisions discussed in this chapter, state laws challenged on the ground that they are laws respecting the establishment of religion or prohibiting the free exercise thereof.

It is to be noted that the First Amendment contains two different types of limitations on governmental action in the field of religion. Under the so-called *establishment clause,* the issue is whether the challenged governmental action is, in effect, a law respecting the establishment of religion. Under the so-called *free exercise clause,* the issue is whether the challenged governmental action is, in effect, a law prohibiting the free exercise of religion. The U.S. Supreme Court decisions in this area sometimes involve both limitations, but in general they provide guidelines both as to governmental action which is prohibited and governmental action which is permitted. Where it is held that a certain type of governmental action is permitted by the First Amendment, it may nevertheless be prohibited by state action (e.g. state legislation) which is undertaken in the exercise of the power reserved to the states by the Tenth Amendment.

In Chapter II it is pointed out that federal and state legislation and the official actions of federal and state agencies and officials are sources of law. The Congress and legislatures of the fifty states and government agencies and officials must make judgments that the laws they pass and the actions they take are constitutionally permissible. These judgments may stand until and unless the courts rule otherwise. Over the years a great deal of governmental action has been taken involving relations between religion and government in education. Much of this governmental action has been based upon legislative and administrative judgments and much of it has shown an attempt to apply the judicial guidelines which have been developed in a few U.S. Supreme Court decisions. These Court decisions up to January, 1968 have been concerned, for the most part, with public school laws relating to (1) compulsory flag salute or military training, (2) free textbooks or transportation, (3) released time programs, and (4) prayer recital and Bible reading. It seems appropriate, therefore, to examine the Court's decisions in these four areas with special reference to any guidelines they offer for legislative and administrative action with respect to education.

Compulsory Flag Salute and Military Training

Public school officials on occasions have required students to salute the flag and recite the "pledge of allegiance" as part of the public school program to promote respect for and interest in the Government. Such requirements have been challenged as laws violating the free exercise clause of the First Amendment.

In *West Virginia State Board of Education* v. *Barnette*,[3] a majority of the Court overruled a previous decision[4] and held that a school board resolution requiring students to participate in the pledge of allegiance and flag salute, under penalty of expulsion, violated the free exercise clause as well as other provisions of the First Amendment, and was therefore prohibited. The plaintiffs in this case were Jehovah's Witnesses who alleged that the requirements of the resolution were contrary to their religious beliefs. The Court majority and the dissenters differed as to the test to be applied when state action is challenged as a violation of First Amendment rights. For the majority, the test was whether the restrictions on First Amendment rights imposed by the challenged state action are necessary in order "to prevent grave and immediate danger to interests which the State may lawfully protect."[5] On the other hand, Mr. Justice Frankfurter, dissenting, expressed the view that the Supreme Court's "power does not vary according to the particular provision of the Bill of Rights which is invoked." In his opinion, the "Court's only and very narrow function is to

determine whether within the broad grant of authority vested in
legislatures they have exercised a judgment for which reasonable
justification can be offered." Frankfurter felt that the state action
in question met this test inasmuch as requiring the pledge of allegiance and flag salute was an appropriate means of promoting
good citizenship in school children.

In his dissent in the *Barnette* case, Frankfurter further expressed the view that the legal issue was not distinguishable from
the issue presented in *Hamilton* v. *Regents of the University of
California*[6] where a unanimous Court upheld a state law requiring
all male students enrolled in a state university to take a military
training course, as the law applied to a student who alleged that
such training was contrary to his religious beliefs. In this case the
student was under no legal compulsion to attend any institution of
higher education, whereas in the *Barnette* case the student was
subject to the compulsory attendance law. For the majority in the
Barnette case, this distinction was crucial. In the *Barnette* case and
in several other decisions, the Supreme Court has emphasized that
the free exercise clause prohibits governmental action which has
the effect of coercing persons to act contrary to their religious
beliefs.

Free Textbooks and Transportation

Many states use public funds to provide textbooks and/or transportation for students attending public elementary and secondary
schools. Some of these states include students attending church-
related schools as beneficiaries of their textbook and/or transportation subsidies. The use of public funds to provide textbooks
and/or transportation to students attending church-related schools
does benefit such schools. Because of this benefit to church-related
schools, such use of public funds has been challenged as governmental action "respecting an establishment of religion" in violation of the establishment clause of the First Amendment.

Court decisions involving government subsidies in education
make a distinction between aid given directly to students on the
one hand, and aid to the school or institution on the other. Where

governmental aid is given directly to students or their parents to assist students in acquiring an education, it may be said that the purpose of such aid is primarily for the benefit of the students and only incidentally for the benefit of the schools attended by such students. Under this view, governmental aid for students attending church-related schools is aid to such schools only incidentally. Is such incidental aid permitted by the First Amendment?

In a number of federal aid-to-education laws, Congress has given clear indication of its conclusion that government aid given directly to students does not violate the First Amendment where church-related schools incidentally benefit from such aid. The several "G.I. Bills" are familiar examples.[7] The U.S. Supreme Court's position on this question was obliquely given in *Cochran et al.* v. *Louisiana State Board of Education et al.*,[8] decided in 1930, and specifically set forth by the majority in the sharply divided opinion in *Everson* v. *Board of Education of the Township of Ewing et al.*,[9] decided in 1947.

In the *Cochran* case a state statute provided for the use of tax money to supply school books for the children of the state, including those enrolled in church-related schools. In a challenge to the statute, it was contended that supplying secular school books to children enrolled in private schools was using taxpayers' money for the private purpose of aiding private schools in violation of the Fourteenth Amendment. No reference was made to any possible conflict with the establishment clause of the First Amendment. The state court held that the tax money was being used for a public purpose and, therefore, there was no violation of the due process clause of the Fourteenth Amendment. In affirming the state court decision, the U.S. Supreme Court concluded that "The appropriations were made for the specific purpose of purchasing school books for the use of the school children of the state, free of cost to them. It was for their benefit and the resulting benefit to the state that the appropriations were made. . . . The schools . . . are not the beneficiaries. . . . What the statutes contemplate is that the same books that are furnished children attending public schools shall be furnished children attending private schools. . . . Among these books naturally, none is to be expected, adapted to religious instruction." If the Court saw any benefit at all to the schools it was not mentioned.

In the *Everson* case a state statute authorized public school districts to provide for the transportation of children to and from schools, including non-profit private schools. Pursuant to this statute, a township board of education authorized reimbursement to parents of money spent for the bus transportation of their children to and from schools, including Catholic schools. Suit was brought challenging the reimbursements to parents of Catholic school students, on the grounds that (1) the reimbursements used tax money for private purposes in violation of the Fourteenth Amendment, (this was the only contention made in the *Cochran* case) and (2) the reimbursements constituted governmental aid to Catholic schools in violation of the establishment clause of the First Amendment. In a six-to-three decision, the state's highest court upheld the statute and the school board action; the case was appealed to the U.S. Supreme Court. That Court, in a five-to-four decision, affirmed the decision of the state's highest court and held specifically that the establishment clause of the First Amendment had not been violated. Speaking for the majority, Mr. Justice Black described the meaning of the establishment clause in sweeping language which has been repeated in subsequent decisions.[10] In the majority opinion, the law authorizing the reimbursements to parents for money spent in transporting their children to Catholic schools was not a law aiding religion or supporting religious activities or institutions. On the contrary, it was held to be a law simply extending the state's public welfare benefits to all school children without regard to their religious belief. The majority likened the transportation services authorized by the law, to police, fire, and sewage disposal services. No reference is made in the majority opinion to any incidental benefits to religion.

The benefits to religion, however, are stressed by the dissenters. In his separate dissenting opinion, Mr. Justice Jackson expressed the view that it was immaterial whether the benefits of the law were primarily or only incidentally for the church school. In his opinion, "(t)he prohibition against establishment of religion cannot be circumvented by a subsidy, bonus or reimbursement of expense to individuals for receiving religious instruction and indoctrination." The dissenting opinion of Mr. Justice Rutledge, with whom Frankfurter, Jackson, and Burton joined, argues that the use of tax money in this case "does in fact give aid and encouragement to religious instruction" and that the "generating history" of the religious clauses of the First Amendment makes it clear that this type of aid is prohibited.

The *Cochran* and *Everson* cases together established the "child benefit doctrine" for testing whether certain types of governmental aid are permitted by the First Amendment. A substantial amount of federal and state aid-to-education legislation today is based upon this doctrine.

The logic of the *Cochran* decision, which held that the purchase of secular textbooks was for the benefit of students and the public and not for the benefit of the schools attended by the students, leads to the conclusion that tax funds used to purchase textbooks for church-related school students is also not a violation of the prohibitions of the First and Fourteenth Amendments against government aid or support to church-related schools. This has been the accepted view. However, whether the use of tax funds to purchase textbooks for church-related school students violates state constitutional or statutory provisions is a question of interpretation for the courts of the states faced with the question. A document issued in 1966 by the U.S. Department of Health, Education and Welfare[11] advises that in 1965 the use of tax funds for the purchase of textbooks for church-related school students was prohibited by judicial decisions or the opinions of the Attorneys General in eight states.[12]

The same H.E.W. document reports that in 1965 governmental transportation of students attending church-related schools was prohibited by judicial decisions or the opinions of the Attorneys General in eighteen states. The document also refers to a Mississippi statute providing that "Only those pupils of legal school age and in actual attendance in the public schools . . . shall be entitled to transportation within the meaning of the act." This statute is not open to different interpretations and there is no room for an application of the child benefit doctrine. However, state constitutional provisions of a more general nature, which prohibit the use of public funds to aid or support religion or religious institutions, may require interpretation as to whether or not they prohibit aid or support that is incidental under the child benefit doctrine.

In *Opinion of the Justices*,[13] the state's constitution provided that no public funds "shall be appropriated to or used by or in aid of any sectarian church or denominational school." This provision was interpreted as invalidating a state statute requiring school districts to provide free transportation for church-related school students where free transportation is provided for public school students. A state constitutional provision with similar language was involved in *Board of Education for Independent School District No. 52 et al. v. Antone,*[14] and the same interpretation was made. Concerning the legal effect of the U.S. Supreme Court's holding in the *Everson* case, the state court in the *Antone* case noted, "Notwithstanding the practical effect of the holding (in the *Everson* case), it essentially constitutes a ruling that the transportation of parochial pupils is not a Federal question, at least when tested by the First Amendment. As we view it, the decision does not change the effect of the State Constitution provisions."

Released Time Programs

In many communities various types of cooperative arrangements are made between local school boards and religious organizations under which public school students are released during the school day to participate on a voluntary basis in religious instruction. On occasions these arrangements have been challenged as violations of the establishment clause.

In *Illinois ex rel. McCullom v. Board of Education of School District No. 71, Champaign County, Illinois, et al.,*[15] an interdenominational religious organization arranged with a board of education to offer religious instruction to grades four through nine from thirty to forty-five minutes each week. These classes were conducted in the public school classrooms but admission to the classes was to be allowed only upon the express written request of parents, and then only to those classes designated by the parents. Students attending the religious classes were excused from secular classes during this period of religious instruction while students not attending such instruction continued their secular studies. Qualified religious teachers and teaching materials were furnished by the religious organization at no expense to the school board; the religious teachers, however, had to be approved by the public school superintendent. With one dissent, the U.S. Supreme Court held that this arrangement violated the establishment clause of the First Amendment because the facts "show the use of tax-supported property for religious instruction and the close cooperation between the school authorities and the religious council in promoting religious education." The Court majority rejected the contentions that the First Amendment forbids only governmental preference of one religion over another,[16] and that the First Amendment is not a prohibition against state action.[17] In his dissenting opinion, Mr. Justice Reed asserted that the Court had recognized many types of cooperation between religion and government as permissive under the First Amendment and expressed his concern that the majority did not indicate which part of the released time program violated the establishment clause. Later decisions indicate that the significant aspect of the released time program in this case was the use of public school buildings for conducting classes in religious instruction.

In *Zorach et al.* v. *Clauson et al.*,[18] decided four years after the *McCullom* decision, the U.S. Supreme Court in a six-to-three decision upheld a released time program. The essential difference between the released time program held unconstitutional in the *McCullom* case and the program approved in the *Zorach* case was that, under the *Zorach* program, students were released for sectarian observance, but the instruction was conducted at religious centers away from the public school premises. Mr. Justice Douglas, who voted with the majority in invalidating the program in the *McCullom* case, wrote the majority opinion in the *Zorach* case. He distinguished the program in the *McCullom* case in the following language: "In the *McCullom* case the classrooms were used for religious instruction and the force of the public school was used to promote that instruction. Here, as we have said, the public schools do no more than accommodate their schedules to a program of outside religious instruction. We follow the *McCullom* case, but we cannot expand it to cover the present released time program unless separation of Church and State means that public institutions can make no adjustments of their schedules to accommodate the religious needs of the people. We cannot read into the Bill of Rights such a philosophy of hostility to religion." This is a frank admission that the First Amendment does permit some governmental cooperation with and aid to religion. The question then becomes: What kind of cooperation and/or aid is permissible? The dissenters in *Zorach* saw no real distinction between the programs in that case and in the *McCullom* case. They saw, moreover, an element of coercion in the programs which would offend the free exercise clause.[19]

The ownership or control of the facilities in which religious education was carried on was the most important factor in the *McCullom* and *Zorach* cases. However, in *Moore* v. *Board of Education*,[20] although the facilities in which religious education was carried on were not owned or controlled by the public school authorities, a state court held that the public school's cooperation with the church was such that the released time program violated the requirements of the First Amendment. Factors other than ownership of the facilities were far more significant. The public school was situated on a plot of land owned by a Catholic Church and leased to the school board for ninety-nine years at a nominal charge. Church facilities were situated on the unleased portion of the same plot of land. Each school day the students were conducted by their teachers to the adjacent church building where, for one hour, they received religious instruction, often by the same teachers who gave them secular instruction. There would seem to be little doubt as to what the U.S. Supreme Court's reaction to such a program would be.

A state constitutional provision may be so construed as to prohibit the operation of the type of released time program held to be permitted in the *Zorach* case. In *Special District for Education and Training of Handicapped Children of St. Louis County* v. *Wheeler, et al.*,[21] the state constitution provided that the public school fund "shall be faithfully appropriated for establishing and maintaining free public schools and for no other purposes whatsoever." During the school year 1963–64, a public school district sent its speech teachers into parochial schools to provide speech therapy and, during the school year 1964–65, the school district offered speech therapy in public school buildings to parochial school children who were released from their parochial schools to attend these speech therapy classes. During the school year 1965–66, the school district again offered its speech therapy services to parochial school children in public school buildings but only after regular school hours. A state statute provided that all children shall "attend regularly some day school, public, private, parochial or parish." In an action for a declaratory judgment with respect to the 1963–64 and 1964–65 programs, the practices were held to be invalid. With respect to the 1963–64 program, it was held that

"The use of public school funds (in parochial school buildings) is not for the purpose of maintaining free public schools." With respect to the 1964–65 program the court took the seemingly narrow position that "By statute it is mandatory that each child 'attend regularly some day school.' This requirement is clear and unambiguous, and 'school' as written cannot be construed to mean 'schools.' "

Prayer Recital and Bible Reading

The U.S. Supreme Court decisions in *Engel et al.* v. *Vitale, Jr. et al.*,[22] and, to a lesser extent, *School District of Abington Township et al.* v. *Schempp et al.* and *Murray, III et al.* v. *Curlette et al.*,[23] touched off a national controversy over prayer recitation and Bible reading in the nation's public schools.

In the *Engel* case, the Court, with one dissent, held that requiring students in public schools to recite a state-composed denominationally neutral prayer is a violation of the establishment clause. The majority opinion recognized that many government-supported activities might be classified as aids to religion, such as reciting the Declaration of Independence or singing anthems, but concluded that "such patriotic and ceremonial occasions bear no true resemblance to the unquestioned religious exercise" of reciting the state-composed prayer. Mr. Justice Stewart, the single dissenter in the *Engel* decision, saw no valid distinction between reciting the state-composed prayer and the many other aids to religion which the majority thought were only patriotic and ceremonial exercises.

In the *Abington School District* and *Murray* cases, Mr. Justice Stewart was again the only dissenter. These cases involved statutes or regulations requiring recitation of the Lord's Prayer and Bible reading in public school classrooms. The majority opinion was delivered by Mr. Justice Clark; Justices Douglas, Brennan, and Goldberg delivered separate concurring opinions. The basic issue was whether state action requiring public schools to begin each school day with readings from the Bible and recitation of the Lord's Prayer violates the religious guarantees of the First Amendment, if individual students may be excused from participation

upon parental request. It was held that such exercises violate the
establishment clause of the First Amendment because they are
religious exercises supported by the state. In his dissenting opinion, Mr. Justice Stewart described the majority's description of
the limitations of the establishment clause as "insensitive" and
"mechanistic." In his view, the statutes and regulations in question
were sufficiently flexible to permit public schools to accommodate
Bible reading and prayers in a constitutional manner. He would
return the cases to the lower courts to take further evidence. He
contended that "The governmental neutrality which the First and
Fourteenth Amendments require . . . is the extension of even-
handed treatment to all who believe, doubt, or disbelieve—a refusal on the part of the State to weight the scales of private choice."

In the majority and separate concurring opinions in the *Engel,*
the *Abington School District,* and *Murray* cases, an attempt was
made to restate the meaning and scope of the establishment and
free exercise clauses of the First Amendment[24] and to provide tests
for determining whether government action in a given case is prohibited or permissible.[25] The effort to provide workable tests has
been only partially successful. In *Chamberlin et al. v. Dade County
Board of Public Instruction,*[26] a state statute authorized a number
of religious activities in the public schools, including the recitation
of prayers and Bible reading. The expressed legislative purpose
was to bring to the attention of public school children the importance of good moral training and good citizenship—a secular
purpose. The state's highest court upheld some of the authorized
practices, including prayer recitation and Bible reading. The U.S.
Supreme Court reversed this holding and remanded the case "for
further consideration in the light of *Murray* v. *Curlette* and *School
District of Abington Township* v. *Schempp* . . . ." On remand the
state court concluded that the expressed intent of the legislation
was secular, thus making the U.S. Supreme Court's decisions in-
applicable, and the state court reaffirmed its original judgment.
When the case again reached the U.S. Supreme Court, it was reversed "with respect to the issues of the constitutionality of prayer
and of devotional Bible reading pursuant to the Florida statute. . . ."

In the decisions banning prayer recitals and Bible reading in the
public schools, the U.S. Supreme Court found a conflict with the
establishment clause resulting from the official sponsorship and

supervision of religious activities by public school personnel. Under these circumstances it was held immaterial that participation by the students was optional and voluntary. The question whether spontaneous and voluntary religious activity in public schools without official sponsorship is permitted by the First Amendment was not considered in those cases. While the exact position of the U.S. Supreme Court is not yet known, its decision in *Cantwell* v. *Connecticut*[27] would seem to support the position that, under the free exercise clause of the First Amendment, students have the right to voluntary and personal prayer recital and Bible reading in the public schools subject only to reasonable limitations as to time, place, and manner. Two lower federal court decisions have direct relevance. In *Stein* v. *Oshinsky*,[28] the U.S. Court of Appeals, Second Circuit, held that student-initiated prayers are permissible, subject to the judgment of school authorities as to time and place. In *Reed* v. *Van Hoven*,[29] a federal district court held that public school students who wish to say prayers or read scriptures according to their choice in the morning before the school day begins and after the school day ends should be permitted to do so.

Unresolved Issues in Church–Government Relations in Education

There are legal issues involved in many areas of church-government relations in addition to the four areas discussed above. Until the U.S. Supreme Court gives further guidance, the decisions already analyzed provide the only guidelines for state courts, lower federal courts, legislatures, and other interested organizations and individuals. Some of these unresolved issues have been the subject of decisions rendered by state courts.

DUAL ENROLLMENTS

At least one state court has upheld dual enrollment or shared time programs. This type of program differs from the released time programs in that it contemplates that the same students will be enrolled in both public and non-public schools. Certain courses or subjects are taken in the public schools and other subjects or courses are taken in non-public schools. It has been said that "Shared time rests on the assumption that the child is primarily a creature of God, entrusted to his parents, nurtured by his church, and owing some obligation to his state for the performance of which he must be educated."[30] It is reported that dual enrollment or shared time arrangements exist "in at least 280 school systems in 35 states."[31] The U.S. Congress has indicated its belief that dual enrollments are constitutional by suggesting their use in carrying out the provisions of the Elementary and Secondary Education Act of 1965.[32] As late as November, 1967 the views of the U.S. Supreme Court were not known, but in *Morton et al.* v. *Board of Education of City of Chicago et al.*[33] a state court upheld a dual enrollment program with specific reference to the limitations of the First Amendment. The State School Code required all children between the ages of seven and sixteen to attend a public school "the entire time it is in session." Certain categories of children were excepted, including children attending private or parochial schools. School boards had statutory authority to "exercise all . . . powers . . . requisite or proper for the maintenance and the development of a public school system." The school board undertook an experimental dual enrollment plan whereby children in the residence zone for a certain public high school were permitted, upon the application of their parents, to take certain required courses at the public high school and the remainder at a nearby parochial high school. Suit was brought to enjoin the maintenance of this dual enrollment program on the ground, among others, that it violated the provisions of the First Amendment. The trial court dismissed the suit and this dismissal was upheld on appeal. The appellate court held that the school board, in accordance with the legislative enactment, had the power to "adopt and develop better methods of educating the children of this state, so long as the methods so adopted are otherwise consistent with the provisions of the School Code. . . ." The court observed that "Since the object of the compulsory attendance law is that all children be educated and not that they be educated in any particular manner or place, part-time enrollment in a public school and part-time enrollment in a non-public school is permitted . . . so long as the child receives a complete education."

There would seem to be educational advantages as well as dis-
advantages in a dual enrollment program. There is merit to the
contention that, in such programs, "The integration of diverse
religious groups in public school classes aids the democratization
which is one of the major purposes of the public school (and) the
contact between faculties and administrations of the two types of
schools tends to improve educational practice in both."[34] On the
other hand, it is said that "There are insuperable administrative
difficulties inherent in the shared-time plans. Among them are
scheduling, discipline, observation of holidays, accreditation, grad-
ing, and the maintenance of the proper relationship between two
school systems having diverse purposes (and) divisiveness is
strengthened rather than diminished by this plan."[35]

DIRECT APPROPRIATIONS

In *Horace Mann League of the United States of America, Inc.
et al.* v. *Board of Public Works of Maryland et al.*,[36] the state legislature had made direct appropriations of state funds to four
church-related colleges to be used for non-religious purposes.[37]
These appropriations were challenged on the grounds that they
were prohibited by the establishment clause. The state's highest
court divided four-to-three. In the majority opinion, where direct
appropriations to church-related institutions are challenged, the
dicta in the pre-*Abington School District* decisions reveal the judicial conclusion that tax-raised funds cannot be used to contribute
to the support of any sectarian institution.[38] In this light, the majority held that it is necessary to determine whether an institution
receiving direct contributions of public funds is sectarian as a
matter of law. It was held that every religious observance by an
institution does not make it sectarian as a matter of law. "(S)ectari-
anization depends upon a consideration of the observances themselves, and the mode, zeal, and frequency with which they are
made." If a consideration of these factors shows that the institution
is sectarian as a matter of law, then financing it by appropriations
of public funds violates the First Amendment, whether or not the
public funds are for the institution's secular activities. If, on the
other hand, a consideration of the factors shows that the institution
is not sectarian as a matter of law, then appropriations of public

funds to it do not violate the First Amendment. In applying these tests, the majority held that one of the colleges in question (Hood College) was not sectarian as a matter of law and the direct appropriations of public funds to it did not violate the First Amendment. This decision was appealed to the U.S. Supreme Court, which thereafter dismissed the appeal.[39]

The majority and the dissenters disagreed as to whether the *secular purpose and primary effect test* was applicable in determining the constitutionality of the direct appropriation of public funds to church-related schools. The dissenters contended that this test was applicable and that the direct appropriations to the four church-related colleges were for the secular purpose of supplying "added facilities which will help the secular educational activities of religious groups . . . ." The dissenters also held that there was no reasonable alternative, given the legislature's purpose of expanding and improving the facilities of higher education available in the state.

OTHER INCIDENTAL INVOLVEMENTS

In several of the U.S. Supreme Court decisions discussed above, members of the Court expressly recognized that, in addition to the specific governmental involvements before them for adjudication, there are numerous other existing governmental involvements in religious activity. In the *Everson* case, both the majority and dissenters recognized approvingly the government involvement where public funds are used to provide police and fire protection to members of religious sects and to property devoted to religious purposes. There are, however, sharp differences of views as to the relevance of these involvements to the specific involvement being challenged.

In his separate concurring opinion in the *Abington School District* case, Mr. Justice Brennan declared that ". . . not every involvement of religion in public life violates the Establishment Clause." He then stated his views concerning the following six categories of governmental involvements:

"A. The Conflict Between Establishment and Free Exercise." Included in this category are provisions for chaplains at military

and penal institutions, draft exemptions for ministers and divinity students, and excusal of children from public schools on their religious holidays. Mr. Justice Brennan implies that such involvements might be held constitutional in order to protect the free exercise rights of soldiers, prisoners, ministers, divinity students, and public school children.

"*B. Establishment and Exercises in Legislative Bodies.*" The reference here is to invocational prayers in federal and state legislatures and the appointment of legislative chaplains whose salaries are paid from public funds. The suggestion is that it was never intended that involvements of this type would be prohibited by the establishment clause.

"*C. Non-Devotional Use of the Bible in Public Schools.*" In this category, Mr. Justice Brennan includes the use of the Bible in connection with such secular subjects in the curriculum as literature and history. It is suggested that the appropriateness of the use of the Bible in the curricula of public schools should be "entrusted very largely" to public school officials who are more expert in these matters than members of the Supreme Court.

"*D. Uniform Tax Exemptions Incidentally Available to Religious Institutions.*" This is a self-explanatory category. Reference is made to the general practice of governments, federal and state, to extend tax exemption benefits to "educational, charitable and eleemosynary groups"; religious institutions are included "in spite of rather than because of their religious character." It is to be noted that this suggestion is similar to the reasoning of the majority in the *Everson* case supporting the conclusion that the use of public funds to defray the expense of transporting school children to and from school was in furtherance of a public welfare benefit.

It does not appear that the U.S. Supreme Court has ever measured tax exemptions to religious institutions against the requirements of the First Amendment. In *Murray* v. *Comptroller of the Treasury, State of Maryland, et al.*[40] it was said, "There are intimations or even expressions of opinions by individual Justices on the question here involved, but we agree with counsel that in no case has the Supreme Court given an opinion on or in specific terms discussed the constitutionality of tax exemptions of religious organizations." In this case the state court conceded that, "Indubitably, religious organizations benefit from the exemption. Economically, they are in the same position as though they paid taxes to the city and state and then received back the amounts paid in the form of direct grants." Nevertheless, the tax exemption was held not prohibited by the establishment clause, and one ground for this conclusion was that the religious organizations do perform secular general welfare functions as well as sectarian functions. Therefore, the state could reasonably determine that the tax exemption is primarily for the benefit of the secular functions even though sectarian functions are thereby benefited incidentally.

In *Lundberg* v. *Co. of Alameda et al.*,[41] it was again held that the tax exemption of property of a nonprofit church-related school does not conflict with the establishment clause of the First Amendment. The court held that ". . . The exemption was enacted to promote the general welfare thus encouraging the education of the young and not to favor religion, since it is not limited to schools maintained by religious groups but applies also to those operated by other charitable organizations. Under the circumstances, any benefit received by religious denominations is merely incidental to the achievement of a public purpose."

"E. Religious Considerations in Public Welfare Programs." It is not clear whether any involvements relating to education are intended to be included in this category, although the federal hot lunch program would seem to qualify. As with the involvements included in categories A and D, an inference can be drawn that Mr. Justice Brennan would consider the involvements included in category E to be constitutional in order to protect the free exercise rights of potential public welfare recipients. The Court's decision in *Sherbert* v. *Verner et al.*[42] supports such an inference.

"F. Activities Which, Though Religious in Origin, Have Ceased to Have Religious Meaning." Included in this category are patriotic exercises and activities used in public schools in which reference may be made to God but which no longer have a religious purpose or meaning. In *Engel et al.* v. *Vitale, Jr. et al.*,[43] it was said by way of dictum that the establishment clause did not prohibit the recitation in public schools of the Declaration of Independence although it contains references to the Diety.

Mr. Justice Brennan's six categories of governmental involvements and his conclusions as to the probable constitutionality of such involvements are dicta. It does not follow, however, that his conclusions in this regard should be ignored in the search for guidelines. Among the governmental involvements in religion that do not fit into any of Mr. Justice Brennan's categories are the formal recognition of religious holidays by public schools and the use of public funds to pay the tuition of students attending church-related schools or institutions of higher education. It has been observed that, in *Chamberlin* v. *Dade County Board of Public Instruction et al.,*[44] the trial court forbade the use of public schools for the religious observance of Christmas, Hanukkah, and Easter holidays, among other things, but the school board did not appeal this ruling.[45] Concerning tuition payments, reference has previously been made to the several "G.I. Bills" enacted by Congress.[46] It is to be noted that, under the 1944 G.I. Bill, authorization was given to pay the tuition directly to public and non-public educational institutions, whereas, under the 1952 and 1966 Bills, payments are made to the "eligible veteran." In at least one state court decision, discussed below, it has been held immaterial whether tuition payments are made to students or directly to the educational institution.

In *Swart* v. *South Burlington Town School District,*[47] the court held that payment by a public school district of tuition for students attending a parochial school was a "fusion of secular and sectarian education" and exceeded the limits of the Federal Constitution. In this case payments were made directly to the parochial school. In *Almond* v. *Day*[48] a state constitutional provision prohibited any appropriation of public funds to any school "not owned or exclusively controlled by the state." A state statute was enacted appropriating funds for the education of war orphans and a question was raised as to whether tuition could be paid from this appropriation for war orphans attending both public and non-public schools. It was held that, as to non-public school students, the appropriation was for the benefit of the non-public schools and the fact that "under the Act the funds may be paid to the parents or guardians of the children and not directly to the institutions does not alter their underlying purpose and effect."

Under the child benefit doctrine the payment of tuition would seem to be at least as beneficial to students as the payment for transportation or textbooks. On the other hand, where the tuition payments are made directly to the institution, it is difficult to argue that such payments are only incidentally beneficial to the institutions receiving such payments. Whether the payments are made directly or indirectly to the institutions, they normally become part of the institution's operating revenue.

In his dissenting opinion in the *Everson* case, with Frankfurter, Jackson, and Burton agreeing, Mr. Justice Rutledge disagreed with the majority conclusion that the transportation subsidized by public funds was not an essential part of the religious education of the parochial school students involved. He asserted that, where it is needed, transportation "is as essential to education as any other element," such as textbooks, school lunches, athletic equipment, etc. He implied that subsidizing these other elements with public funds is prohibited by the establishment clause. At another point in his dissent, Rutledge asserted that "(n)o rational line can be drawn between payment for transportation and payment for" tuitions, teachers' salaries, buildings, equipment and other materials.

In 1965 the Michigan legislature enacted a law requiring public school boards to extend nine types of auxiliary services to all non-public school students if they are extended to public school students. A challenge to this legislation is pending in the Michigan courts.[49] In *Flast et al.* v. *Gardner et al.*, it is alleged that, pursuant to the authority of the Elementary and Secondary Education Act of 1965 enacted by the Federal Congress, federal funds are being used to furnish instruction and instructional materials for use in religious and sectarian schools. A challenge to this use of federal funds is now pending before the U.S. Supreme Court.[50]

In appraising governmental regulation of the relations between government and religion in education, two basic limitations imposed by the Federal Constitution are sometimes difficult to harmonize. On the one hand, the First and Fourteenth Amendments require the Federal and state governments to recognize the right of religious groups to operate educational institutions. Moreover, with respect to their compulsory school attendance laws, states must recognize church-related schools with appropriate programs as legal substitutes for public schools. On the other hand, the First Amendment prohibits the Federal and state governments from providing direct aid and support to church-related schools. Recognized, as they must be, as integral parts of the total educational system of the nation, sectarian educational institutions are preferred over public schools by many Americans for a variety of reasons.

While the secular education which is fused with sectarian education in church-related schools may or may not be the same as the secular education provided in public schools, it is the legal equivalent of the education considered essential to the successful functioning of the American democratic society. The First Amendment, as interpreted, does not prohibit the inclusion of the study of religion in public school curricula. Mr. Justice Clark, speaking for the Court majority in the *Abington School District* case, attempted to make clear the distinction between teaching religion for the purpose of indoctrination, which is prohibited in the public schools, and teaching about religion as a cultural phenomenon, which is permitted and even advocated in the *Abington School District* decision. The American Association of School Administrators has expressed the view that "Whatever else the Supreme Court decisions may or may not have done, they have stimulated the public schools to a search for appropriate means to deal effectively with religion as one of the great influences in man's history." However, there is considerable difference of opinion as to how successful the public schools have been in this regard.

The cost of education has been increasing steadily, both for educational institutions and for the students attending them. Governments are primarily responsible for financing public education. Those who have the duty to prepare budget estimates for financing public education normally take into consideration the estimated number of students who will elect to enroll in non-public, including church-related, schools. In this process it may be possible to reduce budget estimates solely because church-related schools supply some of the education that government has obligated itself to provide. To the extent that such reductions take place, governments may consider themselves obligated, morally or politically, to provide some support for church-related educational institutions. Legally, valid support is limited by the First Amendment as it is judicially interpreted. The child benefit doctrine offers some opportunity for valid government aid (incidental or indirect) to church-related schools, but the fact that this doctrine was devised by a bare majority of a sharply divided U.S. Supreme Court raises doubts as to its continuing vitality and makes extensions of the doctrine legally hazardous.

The holding of the state court majority in the *Horace Mann* case, that direct government appropriations to church-related schools that are not legally sectarian are permitted by the First Amendment, suggests some steps which church-related schools can take to qualify for government support. Even assuming the U.S. Supreme Court eventually adopts or approves the *Horace Mann* test, however, the question remains as to whether the secularization of church-related schools is educationally beneficial. There may be important educational values in the programs of legally sectarian church-related schools that should be preserved. Should this prove to be the case, then one solution to the financial problems of sectarian institutions would be to reduce the programs of such schools to the point where they can be supported entirely by private contributions. There are no easy answers but there may be alternatives, and educators, because of their special competence, have a professional obligation to assist in the formulation and development of procedures and programs in this area that are both educationally and legally sound.

Notes

1. Chapter II, pp. 18–19.
2. 310 U.S. 296, 84 L.Ed. 1213, 60 S.Ct. 900 (1940).
3. 319 U.S. 624, 87 L.Ed. 1628, 63 S.Ct. 1178 (1943). See also *Holden et al. v. Board of Education of City of Elizabeth*, 216 A.2d 387 (N.J.1966), where the court upheld pupils who refused to salute the flag on the grounds of "conscientious scruples" growing out of the pupils' adherence to a religion claimed by some to have political and racial overtones. The court said, "The First Amendment . . . guarantees to plaintiffs the right to claim that their objection to standing is based upon religious belief, and that the sincerity or reasonableness of this claim may not be examined by this or any other Court."
4. *Minersville School District* v. *Gobitis*, 310 U.S. 586, 84 L.Ed. 1375, 60 S.Ct. 1010 (1940).
5. The "clear and present danger doctrine" as a test for determining the constitutionality of governmental action restricting First Amendment liberties was first enunciated in 1919 by Mr. Justice Holmes speaking for a unanimous Court in *Schenck* v. *United States*, 249 U.S. 47, 63 L.Ed. 470, 39 S.Ct. 247 (1919). However, in recent decisions, its application has been uneven. See Osmond K. Fraenkel, *The Supreme Court and Civil Liberties* (New York: Oceanic Publications, Inc., 1963), pp. 39–41, and Paul G. Kauper, *Civil Liberties and the Constitution* (Ann Arbor: University of Michigan Press, Ann Arbor Paperbacks, 1966), pp. 110, 122.
6. 293 U.S. 245, 79 L.Ed. 343, 55 S.Ct. 197 (1934).
7. Under the "Serviceman's Readjustment Act of 1944" federal funds were paid to the educational institution, public or non-public, which covered "the customary cost of tuition, and such laboratory, library, health, infirmary and other similar fees as are customarily charged . . . and books, supplies, equipment and other necessary expenses . . . ."

   Under the "Veterans' Readjustment Assistance Act of 1952" federal funds were paid to each eligible veteran who was pursuing a program of education or training in any public or non-public school or educational institution.

   Under the "Veterans' Readjustment Benefits Act of 1966" federal funds are paid to each eligible veteran as an educational assistance allowance for subsistence, tuition, fees, supplies, books, equipment, and other educational costs. The veteran may enroll in a public or non-public school or educational institution.
8. 281 U.S. 370, 74 L.Ed. 913, 50 S.Ct. 335 (1930).

9. 330 U.S. 1, 91 L.Ed. 711, 67 S.Ct. 504 (1947), reh. den. 330 U.S. 855, 91 L.Ed. 1297, 67 S.Ct. 962 (1947). See also *Fox* v. *Board of Township of West Milford,* 226 A.2d 471 (N.J.1967) and *Rhoades* v. *School District of Abington Township,* 226 A.2d 53 (Pa.1967). App. dism. 389 U.S. 11, 19 L.Ed.2d 7, 88 S.Ct. 61 (1967).

10. The description reads: "The 'establishment of religion' clause of the First Amendment means at least this: Neither a state nor the Federal Government can set up a church. Neither can pass laws which aid one religion, aid all religions, or prefer one religion over another. Neither can force nor influence a person to go to or to remain away from church against his will or force him to profess a belief or disbelief in any religion. No person can be punished for entertaining or professing religious beliefs or disbeliefs, for church attendance or non-attendance. No tax in any amount, large or small, can be levied to support any religious activities or institutions, whatever they may be called, or whatever form they may adopt to teach or practice religion. Neither a state nor the Federal Government can, openly or secretly, participate in the affairs of any religious organizations or groups and vice versa. In the words of Jefferson, the clause against establishment of religion by law was intended to erect 'a wall of separation between church and State.' "

11. *State Laws Related to Transportation and Textbooks for Parochial School Students and Constitutional Protection of Religious Freedom,* U.S. Department of Health, Education and Welfare, Office of Legislation, Superintendent of Documents Catalog No. FS 5.220:20087. This document contains a brief description of the laws of the fifty states and Puerto Rico relating to transportation and textbooks for students attending church-related schools.

12. In *Board of Education of Central School District No. 1, Towns of East Greenbush et al.* v. *Allen,* 273 N.Y.S.2d 239 (1966), the state constitution provided that "Neither the state nor any subdivision thereof shall use . . . any public money . . . in aid or maintenance . . . of any school or institution of learning wholly or in part under the control or direction of any religious denomination . . . ." It was held that this provision was violated by a state statute authorizing the use of public funds to purchase textbooks for the use of parochial school students. The court also held that the statute violated the First Amendment as interpreted by the U.S. Supreme Court in the *Engel* (see note 22) and *Abington School District* (see note 23) cases. No mention was made of the *Cochran* decision.

   In *Dickman* v. *School District No. 62C, Oregon City of Clackamas County,* 366 P.2d 533 (Ore.1961) the state constitution prohibited the use of public moneys "for the benefit of any religious or theological institution." It was held that this provision was violated when a school board furnished free textbooks to pupils enrolled in parochial schools. The court held that the *Everson* (see note 9) case was distinguishable but that "even if it were not our conclusion would be the same."

13. 216 A.2d 668 (Del.1966).

14. 384 P.2d 911 (Okla.1963). See also *McVey et al.* v. *Hawkins et al.,* 258

S.W.2d 927 (Mo.1953); *Snyder v. Town of Newtown et al.,* 161 A.2d 770 (Conn.1960); *Matthews* v. *Quinton,* 362 P.2d 932 (Alaska 1961); *State ex rel. Reynolds* v. *Nussbaum,* 115 N.W.2d 761 (Wis.1962); *Visser et ux.* v. *Nooksack Valley School District No. 506, Whatcom County et al.,* 207 P.2d 198 (Wash.1949), reh. den. 1949. See also *Squires et al.* v. *Inhabitants of City of Augusta,* 153 A.2d 80 (Me.1959), where it was held that a city which operated under a charter empowering it to enact laws "not inconsistent with the Constitution and laws of this state," lacked the necessary power to use public funds for the transportation of parochial school pupils, in view of the absence of similar or enabling state legislation or constitutional provision.

15. 333 U.S. 203, 92 L.Ed. 649, 68 S.Ct. 461 (1948).

16. This "no preference doctrine" was supported by early commentators. See *Constitution of the United States,* Revised and Annotated, 1963, p. 846.

17. The contention that the restrictions of the First Amendment relating to religion were not intended to apply to state action still has its advocates. For a well-documented statement in support of this contention, see William F. O'Brien, "The States and 'No Establishment,'" *Washburn Law Journal,* Spring, 1965.

18. 343 U.S. 306, 96 L.Ed. 954, 72 S.Ct. 679 (1952).

19. Mr. Justice Black contended, ". . . Here the sole question is whether New York can use its compulsory education laws to help religious sects get attendants presumably too unenthusiastic to go unless moved to do so by the pressure of this state machinery. That this is the plan, purpose, design and consequence of the New York program cannot be denied. The State thus makes religious sects beneficiaries of its power to compel children to attend secular schools. Any use of such coercive power by the state to help or to hinder some religious sects or to prefer all religious sects over non-believers or vice versa is just what I think the First Amendment forbids."

Mr. Justice Frankfurter said, "The pith of the case is that formalized religious instruction is substituted for other school activity which those who do not participate in the released time program are compelled to attend. The school system is very much in operation during this kind of released time. If its doors are closed, they are closed upon those students who do not attend the religious instruction, in order to keep them within the school. That is the very thing which raises the constitutional issue. It is not met by disregarding it. Failure to discuss this issue does not take it out of the case."

Mr. Justice Jackson stated, "This released time program is founded upon a use of the State's power of coercion, which, for me determines its unconstitutionality. Stripped to its essentials, the plan has two stages: first, that the State compel each student to yield a large part of his time for public secular education; and second, that some of it be 'released' to him on condition that he devote it to sectarian religious purposes."

20. 212 N.E.2d 833 (Ohio 1965). The court also held that segregation on religious grounds was not illegal.

21. 408 S.W.2d 60 (Mo.1966), reh. den. 1966.

22. 370 U.S. 421, 8 L.Ed.2d 601, 82 S.Ct. 1261 (1962).
23. 374 U.S. 203, 10 L.Ed.2d 844, 83 S.Ct. 1560 (1963).
24. For example, speaking for the majority in the *Engel* case, Mr. Justice Black stated, ". . . Although these two clauses may in certain instances overlap, they forbid two quite different kinds of governmental encroachment upon religious freedom. The Establishment Clause, unlike the Free Exercise Clause, does not depend upon any showing of direct governmental compulsion and is violated by the enactment of laws which establish an official religion whether those laws operate directly to coerce nonobserving individuals or not . . . ."

Speaking for the majority in the *Abington School District* and *Murray* cases, Mr. Justice Clark asserted that the establishment clause prohibits "a fusion of governmental and religious functions or a concert or dependency of one upon the other to the end that official support of the State or Federal Government would be placed behind the tenets of one or of all orthodoxies . . . ." The free exercise clause guarantees ". . . right of every person to freely choose his own course . . . free of any compulsion from the state . . . and (withdraws) all legislative power respecting religious belief or the expression thereof . . . ." In his concurring opinion, Mr. Justice Douglas stated that the "Establishment Clause is not limited to precluding the State itself from conducting religious exercises. It also forbids the State to employ its facilities or funds in a way that gives any church, or all churches, greater strength in our society than it would have by relying on its members alone . . . . Financing a church either in its strictly religious activities or in its other activities is equally unconstitutional, as I understand the Establishment Clause. Budgets for one activity may be technically separable from budgets for others. But the institution is an inseparable whole, a living organism, which is strengthened in any department by contributions from other than its own members."

25. Speaking for the majority in the *Abington School District* case, Mr. Justice Clark stated, "The test may be stated as follows: What are the purpose and primary effect of the enactment? If either is the advancement or inhibition of religion then the enactment exceeds the scope of the legislative power as circumscribed by the Constitution. That is to say that, to withstand the strictures of the Establishment Clause, there must be a secular legislative purpose and a primary effect that neither advances nor inhibits religion." In his separate concurring opinion, Mr. Justice Brennan stated, ". . . the Constitution enjoins those involvements of religious and secular institutions which (a) serve the essentially religious activities of religious institutions; (b) employ the organs of government for essentially religious purposes; or (c) use essentially religious means to serve governmental ends where secular means would suffice."

26. Mem. 374 U.S. 487, 10 L.Ed.2d 1043, 83 S.Ct. 1864 (1963). 377 U.S. 402, 12 L.Ed.2d 407, 84 S.Ct. 1272 (1964).
27. Mem. 309 U.S. 626, 84 L.Ed. 987, 60 S.Ct. 589 (1940). 310 U.S. 296, 84 L.Ed. 1213, 60 S.Ct. 900 (1940).
28. 224 F.Supp. 757 (N.Y.1963), 348 F.2d 999 (N.Y.1965). See also *Opinion of*

the Justices, 228 A.2d 161 (N.H.1967), where the court upheld legislation which would require the opening of every class day in the public schools with a period of silence for meditation.

29. 237 F.Supp. 48 (Mich.1965).
30. See Harry L. Sterns, "Shared Time," *Theory Into Practice*, IV, No. 1 (Ohio State University, February, 1965), p. 16.
31. See Sam Duker, *The Public Schools and Religion—The Legal Context* (New York: Harper & Row, 1966), pp. 221–224.
32. Section 205 (a)(2) of the Act requires the local education agency to include "special educational services and arrangements (such as dual enrollment, educational radio and television, and mobile educational services and equipment) in which educationally deprived children who are enrolled in non-public schools can participate."
33. 216 N.E.2d 305 (Ill.1966).
34. See Sam Duker, *op. cit.*, p. 222.
35. *Ibid.*, p. 223.
36. 220 A.2d 51 (Md.1966).
37. Four separate statutes provided matching grants totaling two and a half million dollars for the construction of such buildings as a dormitory and classroom building, a science wing and dining hall, and science buildings.
38. In *Everson* the Court said, "No tax in any amount, large or small, can be levied to support any religious activities or institutions, whatever they may be called, or whatever form they may adopt to teach or practice religion."
   In *Zorach* the Court said, "Government may not finance religious groups . . . ."
   In *Engel* it was observed that "when . . . financial support of government is placed behind a particular religious belief," the First Amendment is violated.
39. See *Ohio ex rel. Eaton* v. *Price, Chief of Police*, 360 U.S. 246, 3 L.Ed.2d 1200, 79 S.Ct. 978 (1959), where Mr. Justice Brennan, in explaining the Court's notation of probable jurisdiction, stated, "Votes to affirm summarily, and to dismiss for want of a substantial federal question, it hardly needs comment, are votes on the merits of the case . . . ."
40. 216 A.2d 897 (Md.1966).
41. 298 P.2d 1 (Calif.1956), reh. den. 1956.
42. 374 U.S. 398, 10 L.Ed.2d 965, 83 S.Ct. 1790 (1963).
43. See note 22.
44. 143 So.2d 21 (Fla.1962), reh. den. 1962.
45. See Sam Duker, *op. cit.*, p. 178.
46. See note 7.
47. 167 A.2d 514 (Vt.1961).
48. 89 S.E.2d 851 (Va.1955).
49. *O'Hare et al.* v. *Detroit Board of Education et al.*
50. 389 U.S. 985, 19 L.Ed.2d 212, 88 S.Ct. 218 (1967). See note 40, Chapter VII.

CHAPTER VII

Federal Education Legislation

As indicated in the Introduction, federal legislation is one of the sources of education law. Although no express power over education is delegated to Congress by the Federal Constitution, the Congress has, in the exercise of its express and implied powers, enacted legislation that has had a profound effect upon American education.

During the Constitutional Convention, there was discussion about establishing a national university. Some years later, in his 1796 message to Congress, President Washington recommended the establishment of such a university, stating that, "Amongst the motives to such an Institution, the assimilation of the principles, opinions, and manners of our Country men, but [sic] the common education of a portion of our Youth from every quarter, well deserves attention. The more homogeneous our Citizens can be made in these particulars, the greater will be our prospect of permanent Union; and a primary object of such a National Institution should be, the education of our Youth in the science of Government."[1] Although Congress did not adopt this recommendation, there is little if any evidence of congressional doubt over the Federal Government's power to legislate in the field of education. The Congress, functioning under the Articles of Confederation, approved grants of federal land in 1787 to aid a system of common schools in the Northwest Territory. It has been estimated that more than two hundred and fifty pieces of federal education legislation have been enacted by Congress and signed into law by the President since the present Constitution was adopted in 1788.[2]

The magnitude and varied nature of the education programs in which the Federal Government is involved is revealed in the comprehensive report submitted to the House of Representatives Committee on Education and Labor by Congresswoman Edith

Green in June, 1963.[3] This report states, "All told, 42 departments, agencies, and bureaus of the Government are involved in education to some degree. The major programs in education are being conducted by nine agencies, departments, and subdivisions." Significantly, this report also states that "Never in the history of providing Federal Aid to higher education has Congress drawn a line between public and private colleges and universities. . . . Traditionally, aid to higher education has been provided by the Government to public and private institutions without regard to corporate status or religious affiliation. . . . Private elementary and secondary schools participate in the Federal Surplus Property Act program and the national school lunch program. . . . Their teachers also participate in institutes supported by" federal agencies.[4] Among other things, the report refers specifically to the use of federal funds for (a) educational facilities and equipment, (b) support of students, (c) support of teachers, (d) curriculum strengthening, and (e) research in colleges and universities. Also reported is the fact that "the Government's educational activities cost $2.2 billion a year, based on figures, for the most part, for the fiscal year 1962," and "Of this total figure, approximately half, or $1.1 billion provided direct support to the educational system of the United States."

This manifest interest in, and reliance upon education, at the national level has, in general, been in the form of contributions of federal property and funds for specified educational purposes. Excluding the educational activities in areas where the primary responsibilities of the national government are clear,[5] congressional policy, in contrast to congressional power, has, in general, reflected national needs at different periods in the country's history. In addition, however, major issues have helped to shape congressional policy concerning federal aid to that education which traditionally has been the direct responsibility of the several states.

One issue affecting congressional policy in recent years relates to the conflicting views as to congressional responsibility where the beneficiaries of federal subsidies practice racial segregation. In dealing with this issue, Congress included provisions in the Civil Rights Act of 1964 that, in effect, prevent the allocation of federal funds to racially segregated school systems or educational institutions. The U.S. Department of Health, Education and Welfare has issued guidelines to effect these provisions. The legal effect of these guidelines is not entirely clear and judicial reactions to them have been referred to in Appendix I.

At least two other issues have involved questions of federal policy and of federal power as well. The problem of federal control of education has involved the question of federal power to make conditional grants that result in federal control, to some degree, of the intrastate educational activity supported or aided by such grants. This question of federal power has been resolved in favor of the power to make such grants. On the other hand, in the church-state issue the question of congressional *power* to authorize grants that in some degree benefit religion or religious educational institutions has not been resolved.

On the policy question of federal control of education, there has always been controversy over the regulatory effect of conditional grants under which Congress dictates the manner in which federal grants can be used. This policy question is no doubt responsible for the fact that federal education grants have tended to be selective or categorical rather than general. During the past decade, however, there has been a marked expansion in the scope of such legislation. Congress has, at the same time, sought to allay the fear of federal control by including express disclaimers in its enactments.[6]

The issue of federal control of education has also involved the question of the Tenth Amendment[7] limitations on congressional power to make conditional grants. In the early days this Amendment was thought to prohibit the expenditure of federal funds for the education of the people of the several states.[8] As late as 1936 the U.S. Supreme Court, in *United States* v. *Butler et al.,*[9] used language implying that conditional grants to states of federal property or funds in aid of intrastate education might violate the Tenth Amendment. In *Steward Machine Co.* v. *Davis,*[10] however, the Supreme Court seems to have removed any doubt about congressional power to make grants conditioned on compliance with federal regulations. The *Butler* case involved a federal tax on the processing of certain agricultural products, the proceeds of the tax being used to pay farmers who complied with the production regulations set out in federal regulations. This legislation was challenged as an attempt by Congress to interfere with the regulation of intrastate agricultural production reserved to the states under the Tenth Amendment. A majority of the Court held the legislation unconstitutional. The legislation was described as a congressional attempt to use federal funds to "purchase compliance" with the federal regulation of matters reserved to the states. The dissenting Justices maintained that the tax moneys were being used to provide for the general welfare and that the legislation was "necessary and proper." In the *Davis* case federal legislation was upheld which, in effect, could be said to be an attempt by Congress to "purchase compliance" with federal regulations relating to intrastate unemployment. The *Davis* case involved a federal tax on employers, the proceeds of which were to be used to pay unemployment benefits. Under the legislation, an employer in a state which had enacted federally approved unemployment legislation received a credit against his federal tax for taxes paid to the state. The Court held that relief of unemployment was a proper object of federal expenditure under the general welfare clause and the challenged legislation was a legitimate attempt to solve the unemployment problem by the cooperation of the Federal and state governments. Strengthening educational systems and institutions would seem to be as appropriate an object of federal expenditure as relief of unemployment.

Any doubt as to whether Congress may make conditional grants without violating the Tenth Amendment was removed by the Supreme Court decision in *Oklahoma* v. *U.S. Civil Service Commission*[11] involving a federal statute providing grants-in-aid to states for highway construction. The statute provided that the amount to be granted to a state would be diminished if the state refused to remove a state official who engaged in partisan political activity contrary to the requirements of the federal Hatch Act. This statute was challenged as a violation of the Tenth Amendment. In upholding the statute, the Court stated, "While the United States is not concerned and has no power to regulate local political activities as such of state officials, it does have power to fix the terms upon which its money allotments to the state shall be disbursed." The *Davis* and *Oklahoma* cases provide most of the answers to questions that might be raised in any challenge to federal education legislation on the ground that such legislation violates the provisions of the Tenth Amendment. For the most part, constitutional support for such legislation is found in the direct grant to Congress of the power to "provide for the common defense and the general welfare of the United States."[12] Additional support is found in the "necessary and proper clause" of Article I, Section 18 of the Federal Constitution.[13]

The church-state issue involves not only the question of the extent to which Congress *should* involve the Federal Government in relations with church-related educational institutions, but also the question of congressional *power* to authorize grants that may benefit religion or religious institutions to some degree, because of the limitations of the establishment and free exercise clauses of the First Amendment.[14] The June, 1963 report by Congresswoman Green reveals that church-related educational schools and institutions, their teachers and students, have benefited from federal education grants. The following summary analyses of some of the provisions of five recent congressional Acts relating to education indicate the possibilities for federal involvements in religion.[15] Senate Report No. 85, 90th Congress, 1st Session,[16] states that these and other Acts "include, by application, church-related institutions among their beneficiaries. The extent of this inclusion is not, according to Department officials, accurately definable. In some cases the acts have not been in operation long enough to make a determination but the legislative history portends broad utilization of such institutions in these new Federal education programs."

The National Defense Education Act, as amended [17]

Title I contains language from which the conclusion can be drawn that Congress, in enacting this legislation, was exercising its power to provide for the common defense by insuring "trained manpower of sufficient quality and quantity to meet the national defense needs of the United States." Concerning congressional policy, this Title reaffirms the principle "that the States and local communities have and must retain control over and primary responsibility for public education."

Title II—*Loans to Students in Institutions of Higher Education.* Under this Title federal funds are made available for capital contributions to low-interest, long-term student loan funds. Partial forgiveness of loans is authorized for student borrowers who become teachers. In H.E.W.'s *Annual Report* for 1966, it is stated that "about a million students have borrowed approximately $834 million from such funds since they were established at participating colleges and universities."

Title IV—*National Defense Fellowships.* The 1958 Act authorized the use of federal funds to provide for fifteen hundred fellowships per year. 1964 amendments increased the number to seventy-five hundred for 1967 and the same for 1968. H.E.W. documents report that the fellowships granted for 1966–67 "bring to 17,500 the grand total of awards made over the 8-year program. Total Federal support for these fellowships amounts to about $188,335,-150."

Title VI—*Language Development.* Grants of federal funds to establish and operate foreign-language centers are authorized under this Title. Federal funds for foreign-language fellowships are also authorized. H.E.W. documents report that in the 1965–66 school year there were ninety-eight centers on sixty-one campuses which taught modern foreign languages and studies related to the areas in which the languages are used. It has been reported that approximately twenty-six hundred fellows have studied modern foreign languages on grants awarded under this Title.

Title VII—*Research and Experimentation in More Effective Utilization of Television, Radio, Motion Pictures, and Related Media for Educational Purposes.* The H.E.W. *Annual Report* for 1966 states that projects approved under this Title during the year included forty-one research and experimentation projects and forty information dissemination projects. The total financial commitment in fiscal 1966 reportedly amounted to three hundred and nineteen million dollars.

Title VIII—*Area Vocational Education Programs.* It is reported that federal funds under this Title which amends the Vocational Education Act made it possible for more than two hundred thousand youths and adults to enroll in area vocational schools for the 1963–64 school year.

Title XI—*Institutes.* Federal funds are available under this Title for stipends to enable teachers in a variety of subjects and teachers of educationally disadvantaged children to participate in short-term or regular session institutes. H.E.W. reports indicate that, in fiscal 1966, twenty-two long-term and five hundred and thirty-two short-term institutes were approved. Federal funds made available for institutes during this period amounted to $34,987,000.

The Elementary and Secondary Education Act of 1965, as amended.[18]

This Act has as its stated purpose, "to strengthen and improve educational quality and educational opportunities in the Nation's elementary and secondary schools." As originally enacted the Act contained five titles. During the 89th Congress Title VI was added.

Title I—*Financial Assistance to Local Educational Agencies for the Education of Children of Low-Income Families.* This Title authorizes grants of federal funds "to provide financial assistance . . . to local educational agencies serving areas with concentrations of children from low-income families to expand and improve their educational programs by various means (including pre-school programs) which contribute particularly to meeting the special educational needs of educationally deprived children." In order to qualify for federal funds a local school board is required to give proper assurance that such funds will be used for programs for educationally deprived children attending non-public as well as public elementary and secondary schools. The Senate Committee on Labor reported in November, 1967[19] on the Elementary Act of 1967. Referring to the progress that had been made under this Title, the report states that an estimated "8.3 million children were reached . . . (and that) . . . a total of $987.6 million was spent on programs designed to meet the special needs of the educationally deprived."

Title II—*School Library Resources, Textbooks, and Other Instructional Materials.* This Title authorizes the grant of federal funds to state educational agencies for the acquisition of school library resources. The federal funds must be allocated pursuant to a state plan that must assure that the library resources acquired with federal funds can be used by pupils and teachers in both public and non-public schools. Such library resources, however, cannot be used for religious instruction or worship. The report on the 1967 Act referred to above states that because of federal funds provided under this Title, "3,637 new public school libraries were established. 49 million students and 1.9 million teachers in public and nonpublic elementary and secondary schools now have access to books and materials acquired with Federal assistance."

Title III—*Supplementary Educational Centers and Services.* Grants of federal funds to local educational agencies are authorized under this Title for programs of supplementary educational services, "but only if there is satisfactory assurance that in the planning of that program there has been, and in the establishing and carrying out of that program there will be, participation of persons broadly representative of the cultural and educational resources of the area to be served." Provision must be made for the participation of children enrolled in non-public schools. The report on the 1967 Act states, "The Commissioner . . . has approved for support 2,235 proposals costing $208 million . . . . Title III programs have served nearly 10 million public and nonpublic elementary and secondary school pupils, 93,000 preschool children, 250,000 out-of-school youth, 255,000 classroom teachers, and 131,000 parents and other adults."

Title IV—*Educational Research and Training.* This Title amends the Cooperative Research Act of 1954.[20] It authorizes grants of federal funds "to universities and colleges and other public or private agencies, institutions, and organizations and to individuals, for research, surveys, and demonstrations in the field of education . . . and for the dissemination of information derived from educational research . . . ." It is expressly provided that "no grant shall be made . . . for training in sectarian instruction or, for work done in an institution whose program is specifically for the education of students to prepare them to become ministers of religion or to enter upon some other religious vocation or to prepare them to teach theological subjects." The 1966 *Annual Report* of H.E.W. states that "grants totalling $7.2 million were awarded in fiscal year of 1966 to 92 institutions in support of 178 training programs in educational research" under this Title.

Title VI—*Education of Handicapped Children.* Added during the 89th Congress, this Title authorizes grants of federal funds for personnel recruitment, training, programs and research, pursuant to state plans which, among other things, give assurance that handicapped children who are enrolled in private elementary and secondary schools will participate in such programs.

The Higher Education Act of 1965, as amended [21]

The stated purpose of this Act is "to strengthen the educational resources of our colleges and universities and to provide financial assistance for students in post-secondary and higher education."

Title I—*Community Service and Continuing Education Programs.* Under this Title federal funds are authorized to assist in financing the development and execution of state plans under which institutions of higher education, both public and non-public, cooperate with communities in solving such problems as youth opportunities, health, housing, and employment in urban and suburban areas. H.E.W.'s *Annual Report* indicates that during fiscal 1966, five hundred and fifty projects were funded involving approximately three hundred and ten institutions of higher education.

Title II—*College Library Assistance and Library Training and Research.* Basic, special, and supplemental grants of federal funds for library resources are authorized under this Title, which expressly provides that no grant may be made for library resources for use "for sectarian instruction or religious worship, or primarily in connection with any part of the program of a school or department of divinity." H.E.W. reports indicate that during the fiscal year 1966, grants were made to 1,830 institutions. Grants under this Title are also available for programs to train librarians and during the fiscal year 1966 grants for this purpose were made to twenty-four institutions for one hundred and thirty-nine graduate fellowships in library and information science. These fellowships carried stipends of two thousand dollars per fellow.

Title III—*Strengthening Developing Institutions.* Federal funds are available under this Title to assist in the establishment and execution of cooperative agreements between developing institutions and other institutions, organizations, and business entities. Provision is also made for grants for national teaching fellowships to encourage individuals to teach in developing institutions. The term "developing institution" is defined as "a public or nonprofit educational institution" provided it is not an institution whose program "is specifically for the education of students to prepare them to become ministers of religion or to enter upon some other religious vocation or to prepare them to teach theological subjects." The H.E.W. *Annual Report* for 1966 indicates that during the first year of operation, grants were made for eighty-four cooperative agreements involving one hundred and fifteen developing institutions, sixty-six cooperating institutions, and nine business entities. Two hundred and sixty-three national teaching fellowships were included in the cooperative agreements.

Title IV—*Student Assistance*. Under this Title federal funds are provided for educational opportunity grants to needy undergraduate students selected by their institutions. Federal funds are also provided for federally subsidized student loans and to finance programs to identify talented youths of exceptional financial need and encourage them to complete their education. H.E.W. reports indicate that during fiscal 1966 grants were made to 1,419 institutions for approximately one hundred and thirty-four thousand students. Work-study programs accommodated an estimated one hundred and ninety thousand students and forty-two contracts for talent search programs were approved.

Title V—*Education Professions Development*. Federal funds are available under this Title to increase the number of qualified teachers, especially in the elementary and secondary schools. Funds are also provided for the establishment of a National Teacher Corps of experienced teachers and teacher-interns. It is expressly provided that payments under this Title "for religious worship or instruction or training for a religious vocation or to teach theological subjects" are not authorized. The H.E.W. *Annual Report* for 1966 states that during that year awards were made to forty-two institutions to assist in the operation of teacher training programs and sixteen hundred persons were selected for the National Teacher Corps.

A 1967 amendment to this Title authorizes federal grants to states to support local community efforts to attract and train persons in the community to serve as teachers and teacher-aides to meet critical teacher shortages. Concerning training programs carried on under this amendment, it is expressly provided that states must give assurance "that no person will be denied admission to training programs. . . . because he is preparing to teach or serve as a teacher aide in a private school."

The Higher Education Facilities Act of 1963, as amended [22]

This Act includes a congressional finding that the "security and welfare of the United States" requires the immediate increase in higher education facilities. The Act's stated purpose is to assist public and nonprofit institutions of higher education in acquiring certain facilities.

Title I—*Grants for Construction of Undergraduate Academic Facilities.* Under this Title federal funds are available for the construction of academic facilities for public community colleges, public technical institutes, and institutions of higher education other than public community colleges and technical institutes.

Title II—*Grants for the Construction of Graduate Academic Facilities.* This Title makes federal funds available for the "construction of academic facilities for graduate schools and cooperative graduate centers."

Title III—*Loans for Construction of Academic Facilities.* Federal funds are available under this Title to "make loans to institutions of higher education or higher education building agencies for the construction of academic facilities."

Title IV—*General Provisions.* This Title provides, among other things, that, "The term 'academic facilities' shall not include . . . any facility used or to be used for sectarian instruction or as a place for religious worship, or any facility which . . . is used or to be used primarily in connection with any part of the program of a school or department of divinity. . . ." It is also provided that a higher education building agency may be a public or other nonprofit institution.

The 1966 H.E.W. *Report* states that in the fiscal year 1966 one thousand and sixty-three grants were made under Title I, ninety-five under Title II, and one hundred and forty-four loans were made under Title III. It has been reported elsewhere that among the largest grants in the fiscal year 1967 were Title I grants ranging from 2 to 3.7 million dollars for gymnasiums, libraries, and other academic buildings. There were Title II grants ranging from 1.3 million to 2.6 million dollars for a law school, science buildings, and other academic buildings, and Title III loans ranging from 3.5 to 4.3 million dollars for community college campuses, libraries, biological science buildings, and a building for general instruction and research.

The Economic Opportunity Act of 1964, as amended [23]

This Act's stated purpose is "to mobilize the human and financial resources of the Nation to combat poverty in the United States." The Act includes a congressional finding that "The United States can achieve its full economic and social potential as a nation only if every individual has the opportunity to contribute to the full extent of his capabilities and to participate in the workings of our society."

Title I—*Work Training and Work–Study Programs.* Under this Title federal funds are available for the establishment and operation of (a) Job Corps, (b) Work Training programs, (c) Work–Study programs, and (d) Special Impact programs. Public or nonprofit private institutions and agencies may qualify as sponsors of work and training programs, and receive federal funds to assist in the operation of work-study programs. It is expressly provided, however, that such programs may not involve "the construction, operation, or maintenance of so much of any facility used or to be used for sectarian instruction or as a place for religious worship; . . . ."

Title II—*Urban and Rural Community Action Programs.* Under this Title federal funds are available to public or nonprofit private agencies to conduct such programs as "Project Headstart," "Follow Through," and "Upward Bound." It is expressly provided that "No financial assistance shall be extended under this title to provide general aid to elementary and secondary education in any school or school system; but this shall not prohibit the provision of special, remedial, and other noncurricular assistance." It is reported that the number of children participating in Headstart programs rose from 561,356 in 1965 to 572,171 in 1966 and that in 1966 Upward Bound programs involved 224 institutions and 20,148 students. It is reported elsewhere that approximately six percent of the community action programs are operated or coordinated by church-affiliated organizations.

It is clear from this summary review of pertinent provisions of some recent pieces of federal education legislation that Congress has involved the Federal Government in religion to some degree. It is not clear, however, which, if any, of these involvements are prohibited by the First Amendment. A brief discussion of this unresolved issue is, therefore, appropriate.

First Amendment Limitations

In the Supreme Court decisions discussed in Chapter VI, where the issue was whether particular state laws violated the First Amendment, members of the Court have been sharply divided. They have agreed, however, that the First Amendment does not prohibit every government involvement with religion or religious activity. In the dicta of several decisions it is asserted that the direct appropriation of public funds to religious institutions violates the First Amendment. The few Supreme Court decisions concerning the limitations of the First Amendment on congressional legislative power give little clue as to how the Court will react to the Federal Government's involvement with religion in the federal education legislation of the type just discussed.

The use of federal funds by religious organizations was upheld by the Supreme Court in two early decisions but in neither decision were any guidelines developed for future legislation. In *Quick Bear* v. *Leupp et al.*,[24] the Court held that the First Amendment did not prohibit the payment of Indian Treaty and Trust Funds to the Bureau of Catholic Missions for the operation of a school for Indian children. The federal legislation appropriating the money for the Treaty and Trust Funds specifically provided that no appropriation from the funds would be made "for education in any sectarian school." The Commissioner of Indian Affairs, apparently at the request of a number of Indians, entered into a contract with the Bureau of Catholic Indian Missions under which the Bureau would be paid from the Treaty and Trust Funds for operating a school on the Sioux Indian Reservation. The legality of this contract was challenged on the ground that it required the expenditure of public funds for the support of a sectarian school. In upholding the contract the Court determined that the money in the Treaty and Trust Funds was not public funds but belonged to the Sioux Indians to be used by them to educate their children in schools of their choice. The Court suggested that invalidation of the contract might violate the rights of the Indians protected by the free exercise clause of the First Amendment. In the other early decision of *Bradfield* v. *Roberts*,[25] the Court upheld the appropriation of federal funds for the construction of a hospital operated by a religious organization. It was held that the operation of the hospital was an wholly secular activity.

Recent federal education legislation, especially the legislation enacted during the past decade, evinces a congressional policy decision to extend federal support to an increasingly wide range of educational activity. From the language employed by Congress in this legislation it is not unreasonable to conclude that, in the judgment of Congress, it is permissible under the First Amendment to appropriate federal funds to provide (a) secular educational aid and services to students enrolled in church-related schools, (b) for secular research by students enrolled in and teachers employed by church-related institutions, and (c) educational facilities and equipment for church-related institutions to be used exclusively for secular purposes. No one doubts that the Supreme Court possesses the constitutional power to review congressional education legislation and to determine whether any provisions thereof are prohibited by the First Amendment. Whether the Court should, as a matter of judicial policy, review such legislation is a question involving, among other things, the relations between the Court and the Congress, a matter not present in the state legislation decisions discussed in Chapter VI.

In numerous decisions it has been observed that the exercise of the Supreme Court's power to declare Acts of Congress unconstitutional is a grave and solemn duty and at all times a matter of much delicacy.[26] In declining to review decisions involving the constitutionality of congressional legislation the Court's disclaimer may be on the constitutional ground that no "case or controversy" exists.[27] With few exceptions Supreme Court review is a discretionary matter with the Court and in exercising this discretion the Court may impose judicial self-restraint and decline to review even though the constitutional power to do so exists. Thus, the Court has said that it will avoid deciding constitutional issues except where strictly necessary, because, among other things, serious consideration is due the judgment of Congress in the exercise of its constitutional powers.[28] On other occasions it has been said that the Supreme Court reserves its review power for issues of national concern.[29] Subject to these limitations and restraints, however, the Supreme Court has reviewed many Acts of Congress and has often held them to be unconstitutional.[30]

One of the grounds advanced by the Court in declining to review a taxpayer's suit challenging the constitutionality of federal-spending legislation is that a federal taxpayer, as such, does not have a sufficient interest in the Federal Treasury to justify judicial intervention in his behalf by the courts. The problem of *standing to sue* is a hurdle that must be cleared before the Court will consider the issue of whether any provisions of the recent federal education legislation are prohibited by the First Amendment. A brief analysis of this problem follows.

The Standing to Sue Hurdle

As already stated, the jurisdiction of the federal courts is limited by Article III, Section 2 of the Federal Constitution to *cases or controversies.* This is familiar law, but whether a particular issue and the manner in which it is presented to the Court constitutes a case or controversy is, in the final analysis, a matter for the Supreme Court of the United States to determine.

In *Smith et al.* v. *Adams*[31] it was held, in substance, that cases and controversies mean claims of litigants brought before the courts for determination by such proceedings as are established by law or custom for the protection or enforcement of rights, or the prevention, redress, or punishment of wrongs. The term implies the existence of present or possible adverse parties. Subsequent decisions have stressed the importance of adverse parties with real interests and an actual controversy.

Where the Supreme Court determines that the issue and the manner in which it is presented lack the essential components of

a case or controversy, the Court determines, in effect, that the
Federal Constitution prohibits a review or adjudication of the
issue. As indicated above, however, apart from the no case or controversy limitation, the Court may, in its discretion, apply its own
judicial self-restraint to further limit its review of constitutional
issues. Where the Supreme Court declines to review an issue on
the ground that the petitioner has no substantial interest, and
therefore no standing to sue, it is not always clear whether the
Court's action is based on the constitutional limitation of Article
III or on its self-imposed restraint. The precise basis for the
Court's action may be crucial, however, to the success of current
efforts to enact congressional legislation authorizing judicial review of several pieces of recent federal education legislation.

In the frequently cited case of *Frothingham* v. *Mellon et al.*,[32]
a federal taxpayer challenged the constitutionality of the expenditure of federal funds under the Federal Maternity Act on the
ground that the expenditures amounted to a taking of her property and using it for an unconstitutional purpose in violation of
the due process clause of the Fifth Amendment. Without passing
on the question as to whether using federal funds to further the
purposes of the Maternity Act was constitutional, the Court held
that the plaintiff's economic interest, as a federal taxpayer, was
not sufficiently substantial to give her standing to challenge the
constitutionality of the Maternity Act. The Court said that as a
federal taxpayer, the plaintiff's "interest in the moneys of the
Treasury—partly realized from taxation and partly from other
sources—is shared with millions of others, is comparatively minute
and indeterminable; and the effect upon future taxation, of any
payment out of the funds, so remote, fluctuating and uncertain,
that no basis is afforded for an appeal to the preventive powers of
a court of equity." It is not clear whether the Court's action was
based upon the limitation of Article III, or upon its discretionary
power of judicial self-restraint.

Many members of Congress and persons with varying interests
have concluded that it is in the national interest to have a judicial
review to determine the constitutionality of various provisions
of recent federal education legislation, and that the standing to
sue hurdle should be removed. During the 89th Congress the Senate Committee on the Judiciary held hearings and solicited views
from constitutional law authorities on the question whether the

standing to sue hurdle erected by the *Frothingham* decision is a constitutional limitation. Based on the hearings and opinions received, the Committee concluded that the *Frothingham* decision is not based on a constitutional limitation. Accordingly, the Committee recommended the passage of Senate Bill 2907 which provides for a judicial review of nine different pieces of federal education legislation.[33] Final action on this Bill was not taken by the 89th Congress but the Bill was reintroduced in the 90th Congress as Senate Bill 3.[34] This Bill purports to give standing to sue to three classes of plaintiffs: (1) any public or other nonprofit agency or institution which is or may be prejudiced by loans or grants under any of the listed Acts, (2) corporate or individual taxpayers, and (3) all citizens. As of March, 1968 no final action had been taken on the Bill by the 90th Congress. In the meantime, however, the Supreme Court has indicated that it may provide answers to some of the problems to which the Senate Bill is addressed.

On October 17, 1967 the Supreme Court noted probable jurisdiction in *Flast et al.* v. *Gardner et al.*,[35] a case challenging the constitutionality of certain provisions of the Elementary and Secondary Education Act of 1965 on the ground that the religious freedom provisions of the First Amendment are being violated. The plaintiffs are federal taxpayers, one is the mother of children enrolled in the New York City public schools. The gist of the complaint is that pursuant to congressional authorizations in Titles I and II of the Elementary and Secondary Education Act federal funds are being used to finance instruction and guidance services, and furnish textbooks, library resources and other materials to sectarian schools in violation of the First Amendment. With respect to the standing to sue issue the plaintiffs, through their counsel, contend that the *Frothingham* decision is not based upon a constitutional limitation and, moreover, that the doctrine of judicial self-restraint is not applicable to complaints based upon the First Amendment. A federal district court of three judges, with one dissent, dismissed the complaint on the ground that under the *Frothingham* decision the plaintiffs have no standing to sue.[36] As noted above, when the plaintiffs petitioned the Supreme Court for review, probable jurisdiction was noted. It appears, therefore, that the Court will, at least, rule on the question whether the plaintiffs have standing to sue.

There appears to be no easy answer to the question of who

should have standing to challenge federal expenditures on the
ground that the religious freedom provisions of the First Amendment are being violated. If the *Frothingham* decision is based on
judicial self-restraint, it is understandable that the Supreme Court
may wish to require plaintiffs to show a substantial economic injury in order to have standing to challenge federal expenditures
on due process grounds. Every federal taxpayer has an economic
interest in all federal expenditures from the general treasury.
Every federal taxpayer, and every citizen for that matter, presumably wants Congress to authorize expenditures of federal
funds only to the extent permitted by the Constitution. It does
not follow, however, that being a federal taxpayer or a citizen
should give one standing to challenge every federal expenditure
on due process grounds. On the other hand, the Court has repeatedly held that rights protected by the establishment and free
exercise clauses of the First Amendment are personal rights of an
high order belonging to every citizen. It is generally held that
these First Amendment rights may not be infringed by congressional majorities or even by the majority vote of the people short
of a constitutional amendment. To say that a citizen must have a
substantial economic interest that is being injured before he has
standing to challenge federal expenditures on religious freedom
grounds, is to ignore or minimize the nature of every citizen's
interest in the religious freedoms protected by the First Amendment. Even if the *Frothingham* decision should not be applied to
challenges of federal expenditures on First Amendment grounds,
the Supreme Court may, nevertheless, wish to impose some requirements that will enable it to keep the case load of the federal
courts within manageable limits.

In *Doremus* v. *Board of Education of Borough of Hawthorne*,[37]
the Supreme Court held that plaintiff taxpayers lacked standing to
challenge a state statute that provided for the reading of the Bible
in public schools because they showed no "direct and particular
interest." In his dissent in the three-judge court decision in the
Flast case District Judge Frankel suggested that the plaintiffs in the
Doremus case "made no allegation that any added tax moneys were
being expended for Bible reading" and that this pleading de-
ficiency was fatal.[38] It has also been suggested that the parents in
the *Doremus* case had no substantial interest in the education at
issue in that case because they had no children enrolled in the

school at the time of the hearing.[39] It may be that the Court will hold that in order to have standing to challenge federal education expenditures on religious freedom grounds under the First Amendment, a plaintiff must show a direct interest in the education at issue, as by having children enrolled in a school that is a beneficiary of federal loans or grants. In the *Flast* case now before the Supreme Court one of the plaintiffs is the mother of children enrolled in the public schools, and thus the Court will be in a position to indicate whether such an interest is required in order to have standing to sue.[40] The Court need not be too concerned, however, about its delicate relations with Congress because many Congressmen have gone on record as being anxious to have a judicial review of recent federal education legislation—a review that hopefully will provide Congress with some sorely needed guidelines.

Notes

1. Eighth Annual Address to Congress, December 7, 1796.
2. For a list of enactments by the 88th Congress, 1963–64, see *Enactments by the 88th Congress Concerning Education and Training, 1963–1964* (Washington: U.S. Government Printing Office, 1964). In the first of an eight-unit series titled *Federal Legislation on American Education (Grades K–12)* (Chicago: Science Research Associates, Inc., 1965), reference is made to sixty major items of federal legislation related to education enacted by Congress between 1777 and 1965.
3. The report, titled *The Federal Government and Education,* was printed as House Document No. 159, 88th Congress, 1st Session, by House Concurrent Resolution 203.
4. *Ibid.,* pp. 140–141.
5. Areas of primary national responsibility are, for example, the service academies, education in the District of Columbia, in the territorial possessions, and the education of American Indians.
6. For example, Section 102 of the National Defense Education Act of 1958, as amended, provides: "Nothing contained in this Act shall be construed to authorize any department, agency, officer, or employee of the United States to exercise any discretion, supervision, or control over the curriculum, program of instruction, administration, or personnel of any educational institution or school system."
7. The Tenth Amendment provides: "The powers not delegated to the United States by the Constitution, nor prohibited by it to the States, are reserved to the States respectively, or to the people."
8. In vetoing the Morrill Bill of 1859, President Buchanan asserted, "I presume the general proposition is undeniable that Congress does not possess the power to appropriate money in the Treasury, raised by taxes on the people of the United States, for the purpose of educating the people of the respective States."
9. 297 U.S. 1, 80 L.Ed. 477, 56 S.Ct. 312 (1936).
10. 301 U.S. 548, 81 L.Ed. 1279, 57 S.Ct. 883 (1937). See also *Helvering* v. *Davis,* 301 U.S. 619, 81 L.Ed. 1307, 57 S.Ct. 904 (1937).
11. 330 U.S. 127, 91 L.Ed. 794, 67 S.Ct. 544 (1947).
12. See Article I, Section 8 of the Federal Constitution.
13. This clause grants to Congress the power, "To make all laws which are necessary and proper for carrying into execution the foregoing powers, and all other powers vested by this Constitution in the Government of the United States, or in any department or officer thereof."

14. These clauses have been discussed in Chapter VI.

15. In compiling the information regarding the five statutes, the following publications were referred to: The *Annual Report* of the Department of Health, Education and Welfare for 1966; *The Quiet Revolution,* Second Annual Report of the Office of Economic Opportunity, 1966; various issues of *American Education,* a periodical published by the Department of Health, Education and Welfare; *Senate Report No. 726,* 90th Congress, 1st Session; and *Federal Legislation on American Education,* Science Research Associates, Inc., 1965–66.

16. See note 34.

17. Public Law 85-864, 72 Stat. 1580. This Act has been amended fourteen times up to and including the 1967 amendment by P.L. 90-247, 81 Stat. 783.

18. Public Law 89-10, 79 Stat. 27. This Act has been amended twice up to and including the 1967 amendment by P.L. 90-247, 81 Stat. 783.

19. Senate Report No. 726, 90th Congress, 1st Session.

20. Public Law 83-531, 62 Stat. 533.

21. Public Law 89-329, 79 Stat. 1219. This Act has been amended six times up to and including the 1967 amendment by P.L. 90-257, 81 Stat. 783.

22. Public Law 88–204, 77 Stat. 363. This Act has been amended four times up to and including the 1966 amendment by P.L. 89–769.

23. (Anti-Poverty Act) Public Law 88-452, 78 Stat. 508. This Act has been amended seven times up to and including the 1967 amendment by P.L. 90-222, 81 Stat. 672.

24. 210 U.S. 50, 52 L.Ed. 954, 28 S.Ct. 690 (1908).

25. 175 U.S. 291, 44 L.Ed. 168, 20 S.Ct. 121 (1899).

26. See 16 Am. Jur. 2d 293, Section 107 and cases cited.

27. Article III of the Federal Constitution limits the jurisdiction of the federal courts to cases or controversies.

28. See statement of Mr. Justice Rutledge in *Rescue Army et al.* v. *Municipal Court of Los Angeles,* 331 U.S. 549, 91 L.Ed. 1666, 67 S.Ct. 1409 (1947).

29. For a general discussion of the doctrine of judicial self-restraint, see *Constitution of the United States,* Revised and Annotated, 1963, pp. 629–634.

30. *Ibid.,* pp. 1387–1401 for a list of seventy-four congressional acts held unconstitutional between 1803 and 1964.

31. 130 U.S. 447, 32 L.Ed. 895, 9 S.Ct. 466 (1889).

32. 262 U.S. 447, 67 L.Ed. 1078, 43 S.Ct. 597 (1923).

33. See Senate Report No. 1403, 89th Congress, 2nd Session. Section 1 of the Bill refers specifically to: the Higher Education Facilities Act of 1963, Title VII of the Public Health Services Act, the National Defense Education Act of 1958, the Mental Retardation Facilities and Community Mental Health Centers Construction Act of 1963, Title II of the Act of September 30, 1950, the Elementary and Secondary Education Act of 1965, the Cooperative Research Act, the Higher Education Act of 1965, and the Economic Opportunity Act of 1964.

34. For an analysis of Senate Bill 3, see Senate Report No. 85, 90th Congress, 1st Session.

35. 389 U.S. 895, 19 L.Ed.2d 212, 88 S.Ct. 218 (1967).

36. *Flast et al.* v. *Gardner et al.,* 267 F.Supp. 351 (N.Y.1967).

37. 342 U.S. 429, 96 L.Ed. 475, 72 S.Ct. 394 (1952).

38. 267 F.Supp.

39. *Flast et al.* v. *Gardner et al.,* Plaintiffs' Memorandum of Law on Motion to Dismiss, p. 8, submitted to the district court of three judges.

40. On June 10, 1968, the U.S. Supreme Court, with one dissent, held in *Flast* v. *Cohen* that the plaintiffs, as federal taxpayers, had standing to sue. *Frothingham* v. *Mellon* is distinguished and the narrow holding of the Court is that a Federal taxpayer has standing to challenge a specific congressional expenditure on the ground that it is prohibited by the Establishment Clause of the First Amendment.

Before and After Brown *v.* Board of Education of Topeka, Kansas

S ome of the legal and educational problems spawned by the *Brown* decisions of 1954 and 1955[1] stem from the U.S. Supreme Court's early interpretations of the Civil War Amendments to the Federal Constitution[2] and the educational policies and practices adopted in accordance with those early interpretations.

As early as 1883 the Supreme Court held that the right to equal protection of the laws guaranteed by the Fourteenth Amendment protects persons against racial discrimination by *state action* but does not protect against discrimination by non-public or private action.[3] This interpretation is still honored although the list of activities embraced by the term *state action* has been enlarged substantially in recent years. It is still consistent with judicial interpretation of the Federal Constitution for non-public or private education to be administered on a racially discriminatory basis.

In 1896 the U.S. Supreme Court held that state action requiring the separation of the races is not inconsistent with the equal protection clause of the Fourteenth Amendment, if equal treatment and opportunity are provided for members of the races so separated.[4] The statute which the Court upheld required segregation of the races in railway transportation, but significantly the Court relied in part on the early Massachusetts case of *Roberts* v. *City of Boston*[5] in which racial segregation in public education was upheld. In 1927 the U.S. Supreme Court found no constitutional objection to the classification of an Oriental girl with Negroes in assigning her to a public school.[6] This separate but equal doctrine prevailed in public education until 1954—approximately fifty-eight years. During this period, dual systems of public education were established in seventeen states and the District of Columbia, and were optional in four other states.[7] Some educators questioned the educational soundness of separate but equal education, but, for the most part, members of the education profession accepted the situation. The dominant legal issue during this period was whether the public education provided separately for Negro students was equal as a matter of law. The pressure for equality under the separate but equal systems did remove some of the most obvious inequalities through the expensive and piece-meal process of litigation. Some idea of the magnitude of the disparity between the public education offered to Negro students as compared to that offered to white students can be gathered from an official report in 1954 that "the estimated cost of 'equalizing' Negro schools is in excess of two billion dollars."[8]

During the fifty-eight-year reign of the separate but equal doctrine in public education, many proponents of the doctrine stoutly contended that substantial equality existed. It is now widely accepted that, as a general rule, Negro students in racially segregated public schools received, and still receive, education substantially inferior to the education available in public schools in which all or a high percentage of white students are enrolled. The separate and unequal or inferior treatment of Negroes in public education was supported by racial segregation and discrimination in such other important areas as employment, housing, and transportation.

Between 1938 and 1950, the U.S. Supreme Court was called upon to examine more closely the equality aspects of the separate but equal doctrine. As applied to state-supported education, the Supreme Court in *Missouri ex rel. Gaines v. Canada, Registrar of the University of Missouri et al.,*[9] *Sweatt v. Painter et al.,*[10] and *McLaurin v. Oklahoma State Regents for Higher Education,*[11] evolved tests for determining whether racial segregation in public higher education meets the requirements of the equal protection clause of the Fourteenth Amendment. In the *Gaines* case a state could not satisfy the equality requirement by subsidizing the legal education of Negro students outside the state. In the *Sweatt* and *McLaurin* cases the equality requirement could not be satisfied by the enforced isolation of Negro professional and graduate students from their white counterparts. Finally, in 1954 in *Brown v. Board of Education of Topeka, Kansas,*[12] the Supreme Court held that state action requiring the separation of students by race in public elementary and secondary education does not satisfy the equality requirement because it "generates a feeling of inferiority" in minority group students "as to their status in the community." A unanimous Court concluded that "in the field of public education the doctrine of 'separate but equal' has no place. Separate educational facilities are inherently unequal."

In 1955 the Supreme Court implemented its 1954 decision. In summary:

(1) Federal district courts "will require" local school agencies and officials to "make a prompt and reasonable start toward full compliance with" the 1954 ruling.

(2) Once a prompt and reasonable start is made, federal district courts may grant additional time "to carry out the ruling in an effective manner."

(3) "The burden rests upon" local school agencies and officials "to establish that such time is necessary in the public interest and is consistent with good faith compliance at the earliest practicable date."

(4) ". . . the vitality of (the) constitutional principles" established in the 1954 ruling "cannot be allowed to yield simply because of disagreement with them."

(5) Federal district courts are directed to "take such proceedings and enter such orders and decrees as are necessary" to accomplish desegregation "with all deliberate speed . . . ."

In the seventeen states and the District of Columbia where racial segregation in public education was required by state constitutional or statutory provision, the reaction ranged all the way from prompt and effective compliance to massive and effective resistance.[13]

In *Cooper* v. *Aaron et al.*[14] the Supreme Court declared that community hostility to desegregation is not a relevant factor in determining whether there has been "a prompt and reasonable start" in any particular case or whether particular desegregation plans will accomplish compliance "with all deliberate speed."

In *Evans et al.* v. *Buchanan et al.*[15] the Third Circuit Court of Appeals affirmed that it is appropriate for a state board of education to formulate desegregation plans for all segregated school districts in the state.

In *Brewer* v. *Hoxie School District No. 46 of Lawrence County, Arkansas*[16] the Eighth Circuit Court of Appeals affirmed a lower court order enjoining protest organizations from interfering with a school board's voluntary desegregation plans.

In *Griffin* v. *County School Board of Prince Edward County*[17]

the Supreme Court held that a state may not constitutionally authorize one county in the state to close all its public schools and
support non-public schools in attempting to avoid desegregation,
while free public education is made available in the rest of the
state.

Desegregation plans. Since 1955 a variety of desegregation plans
have been before federal district courts for judicial appraisal.
Between 1955 and 1958, eight states enacted *pupil placement laws*
under which administrative agencies were delegated authority to
place or assign students to particular schools on the basis of a sometimes lengthy list of specified factors not directly related to race
but often directly related to the fact, once vehemently denied, that
under the separate but equal doctrine Negro schools were inferior.[18] In *Shuttlesworth* v. *Birmingham Board of Education of
Jefferson County, Alabama,*[19] a federal district court held a pupil
placement law to be constitutional on its face, and on this narrow
ground the Supreme Court affirmed this holding.[20]

Although *grade-a-year* plans beginning at the first grade have in
the past received judicial approval,[21] more recent decisions indicate that such plans no longer fulfill the requirements of desegregation with "deliberate speed."[22] Another plan that has evoked
conflict in judicial reaction is the *free choice of school* plan limited
by the availability of classroom space. Under this plan, a Negro
student, to a limited extent, is free to choose between a segregated
Negro school and an integrated or mixed school. It has been held
that "a free, private choice of segregation does not violate the
Constitution."[23] In other cases school boards have not succeeded
in getting court approval of freedom of choice plans.[24]

Other plans have been formulated, but it is to be noted that,
in each of the three plans referred to above, the continued existence of dual school systems is contemplated. There is a serious
question as to whether such plans can be said to constitute compliance with the Supreme Court's rulings of 1954 and 1955.

Geographical zoning of attendance areas plans have been approved where there was no evidence that area boundary lines have
been "gerrymandered" to accomplish segregated schooling.[25]
However, it has also been held that it must be proved that the attendance areas were drawn for a legitimate educational purpose.[26]
Where a geographical zoning plan included transfer rules based
on race, the Supreme Court held it unconstitutional.[27] It has been

reported that as of 1963 the "two types of plans which have been consistently approved as desegragation plans (are) (1) geographical-zoning-of-attendance-areas plans, and (2) free-choice-of-schools plans."[28]

Congressional concern over the slow pace of desegregation in public education as supervised by federal district courts is reflected in two specific provisions included in the Civil Rights Act of 1964.[29] Title IV of the Act authorizes the Attorney General to initiate compliance actions in the courts,[30] and Title VI authorizes the Department of Health, Education and Welfare to withhold federal funds[31] from school districts found not to be in compliance with the Supreme Court's rulings in *Brown* v. *Board of Education of Topeka, Kansas*. In carrying out its responsibilities under Title VI, H.E.W. has issued "Guidelines for measuring compliance."[32] Among other things, the Guidelines prohibit "the continued maintenance of a dual structure of separate schools for students of different races." The establishment of non-racial attendance zones and free choice of schools plans are appropriate desegregation plans under the Guidelines under certain conditions. Plans based upon geographical attendance zones may constitute compliance if a "single system of non-racial attendance zones is established" and each student is "assigned to the school serving his zone of residence." Only certain types of transfers are allowed under the Guidelines.[33] Plans based upon free choice of schools may also constitute compliance if each student "is required to exercise a free choice of schools once annually," and no choice may be denied "for any reason other than overcrowding." The Guidelines recognize that "a free choice plan tends to place the burden of desegregation on Negro or other minority group students and their parents" and, therefore, provide "that the single most substantial indication as to whether a free choice plan is actually working to eliminate the dual school structure is the extent to which Negro and other minority group students have in fact transferred from segregated schools."[34]

Significantly, the Guidelines recognize the relevance of the integration of teaching staffs in any effective desegregation plan. It is expressly provided that "the racial composition of the professional staff of a school system must be considered in determining whether students are subjected to discrimination in educational programs."[35]

It has been noted that the two desegregation plans most consistently approved by the lower federal courts have been based upon geographical attendance zoning and free choice of schools. The H.E.W. Guidelines also recognize these two types of plans but only under certain conditions, one of the conditions being the dismantling of dual school systems based on race and the establishment of a unitary non-racial system. Thus, the test of desegregation plans applied by the lower federal courts may be different from that found in the H.E.W. Guidelines.

The issue as to whether, and if so to what extent, federal courts should consider H.E.W. Guidelines in determining the validity of desegregation plans has been adjudicated in several lower federal court cases.[36] *United States* v. *Jefferson County Board of Education et al.*[37] is a three-judge federal court decision involving appeals from district court decisions in Alabama and Louisiana. The court held, with one dissent, that while the H.E.W. Guidelines are not binding on the courts they should be given *great weight,* and that to do so is not an abdication of the judicial function. The court majority held that the Guidelines are "within the scope of the congressional and executive policies embodied in the Civil Rights Act of 1964." A profoundly significant conclusion of the court majority was that, where there has been a *de jure* system of segregated education the dual system must be dismantled in order to comply with the rulings in *Brown.*[38] On behalf of the local school boards, it was contended that the Guidelines are contrary to the constitutional intent expressed in the Civil Rights Act of 1964. The court majority responded that this contention is based upon the dictum in *Briggs* v. *Elliott*[39] which the court held as inconsistent with the second *Brown* decision and the "later development of decisional and statutory law in the area of civil rights."

Another of the issues in the *Jefferson County* case was whether a "freedom of choice" plan of desegration is an acceptable method of compliance with the rulings in *Brown.* The majority were of the view that, while the "method has serious shortcomings," it is acceptable if certain conditions are met which "make it more than a mere word of promise to the ear."[40] It is obvious that the "freedom of choice" acceptable to the court is not one where the choice is between a segregated school on the one hand and a desegregated school on the other. The dissenting opinion took the position that the dictum in *Briggs* is good law, i.e., that the Constitution does not require integration, it merely forbids discrimination. In the view of the dissenter, the freedom of choice can be between a segregated school and a desegregated school.

In *Clark et al.* v. *Board of Education of Little Rock School District et al.*,[41] the two principal issues were whether the H.E.W. Guidelines should be viewed by the courts as providing minimum standards for desegregation as held in the *Jefferson County* case, and whether a "freedom of choice" plan of desegregation must provide mandatory annual choice of schools. The court held that to view the H.E.W. Guidelines as providing minimum standards would be to abdicate judicial responsibility to an administrative agency, and that no mandatory annual freedom of choice is necessary in the absence of a showing that constitutional rights have been violated by a non-mandatory annual freedom of choice plan. The *Jefferson County* case was distinguished on the grounds that it involved a different circuit with different problems and with a system based on dual attendance zones.

In the first of its *Brown* decisions, the U.S. Supreme Court adopted a lower court finding that "segregation of white and colored children in public schools has a detrimental effect upon the colored children. The impact is greater when it has the sanction of law." However, its rulings were limited to that segregation sanctioned by law. That is, the *Brown* decisions were limited to the racial segregation in public education that is required or expressly permitted by law. Subsequent decisions hold that racial segregation by school agencies or officials is within the prohibitions of *Brown,* even though no state laws require or permit such segregation.[42]

De facto segregation in public education. Even where racial segregation in public education is not required or expressly permitted by law, and even where it does not result from purposefully discriminatory action on the part of school agencies or officials, it may still exist because of the application of the neighborhood school policy in a geographical area heavily populated by racial minorities because of racially segregated housing patterns. This phenomenon is often referred to as *de facto* school segregation, and is so referred to here.[43] The U.S. Supreme Court has not yet determined whether *de facto* segregation is unconstitutional, and there is a conflict in the court decisions. In *Bell et al.* v. *School*

City of Gary, Indiana[44] it was held that a school board has no affirmative obligation "to change innocently arrived at school attendance districts by the mere fact that shifts in population either increase or decrease the percentage of either Negro or white pupils."[45] As of June, 1967 the most recent federal court decision holding that *de facto* school segregation is unconstitutional is *Hobson* v. *Hansen*,[46] involving the public schools in the District of Columbia. A number of federal district courts and at least one state court have reached the same conclusion.[47] In one way or another, these courts say that minority group children have a constitutional right to integrated public education and that, while the neighborhood school policy is not *per se* unconstitutional, it must give way to constitutional considerations.

Although the weight of judicial opinion is at present against the view that public school agencies and officials are required by the Federal Constitution to take affirmative action to eliminate *de facto* school segregation, the legal authority to take such action voluntarily is affirmed as a general rule. It has been contended that official action to remedy *racial imbalance,* which is the term most often employed, is to act on the basis of race contrary to the requirements of the Federal Constitution. In a majority of the court decisions, these contentions have been overruled.[48]

It is reported that six states have acted officially to deal with the the problem of *de facto* segregation or racial imbalance in their public school systems.[49] Until and unless the legality of these official actions is adjudicated by the courts one can only speculate about their validity and, where it is alleged that such actions violate provisions of the Federal Constitution, the U.S. Supreme Court must give the final answer. In 1967 the courts of two different states rendered decisions concerning the legality of racial imbalance statutes enacted by the legislatures of their respective states. In *School Committee of Boston* v. *Board of Education et al.,*[50] the Massachusetts Racial Imbalance Act of 1965[51] was challenged on the ground that it constituted a denial of equal protection. The Act was upheld because the court found that no pupil had in fact been excluded from a public school on account of his race. In contrast, the Illinois court in *Tometz et al.* v. *Board of Education, Waukegan City School District No. 61*[52] held, with one dissent, that the Armstrong Act, enacted by the Illinois legislature in 1965 to deal with racial imbalance, violated provisions of both the Federal and Illinois Constitutions. The court majority construed the Armstrong Act as official action requiring school districts to consider race as a factor in the revision of school district boundaries and, for that reason, a violation of the equal protection clause of the Fourteenth Amendment of the Federal Constitution as interpreted by the U.S. Supreme Court in the *Brown* decisions of 1954 and 1955. As previously indicated, other courts have reached the opposite conclusion, and only the U.S. Supreme Court can resolve this disagreement. The majority decision in the *Tometz* case, that the Armstrong Act violates provisions of the Illinois Constitution, is of special importance to education policy makers in Illinois. It is unfortunate that the majority were not more explicit in stating their reasons for this conclusion.[53]

There is general agreement that the problems of *de jure* and *de facto* segregation in education are among the most crucial in contemporary American education. Effective solutions may well depend upon what members of the education profession, especially classroom teachers, are prepared to do. It has been suggested that educators should "consciously, deliberately, and systematically undertake the testing and/or demonstration of the scientific validity, pedagogical soundness and democratic feasibility of racial desegregation in American society."[54] There is evidence of serious concern over this problem at the national organizational level. The Educational Policies Commission of the National Education Association and the American Association of School Administrators recently examined certain of the issues in some detail and has published some governing principles.[55] Among the Commission's conclusions is the following: *"Segregation on grounds of race is bad.* In education, it denies children, white or Negro, a chance to obtain a broader perspective on the society. It complicates the overcoming of racial stereotypes. In middle class schools, it breeds a sense of innate superiority which is unjustified and unhealthy. It causes Negroes to feel that they are being discriminated against and produces the inherently unequal circumstances of which the Supreme Court spoke in 1954. Conversely, contacts among children of varied backgrounds are essential to education. Pupils learn much from each other. Laws or customs which enforce segregation cannot prevent contact between cultures; they merely prevent those types of contact which would do the most good. They do not insulate cultures; they only prolong incompatibility." The Commission warns that "the simple mixing of races in a school does not of itself solve all problems of integration," and observes that minority group students may suffer because they are unable to compete academically with their contemporaries from the majority group who are the products of the more affluent segment of society. It may be true that students from lower income groups and segregated racial minorities will not be able to perform academically as well as their middle class contemporaries. There is evidence, however, that minority group students perform better when mixed with middle class students than they do in segregated classrooms, and that middle class students do just as well in integrated classrooms as they do in homogeneous, segregated classrooms.[56] This evidence refutes the arguments of those who are in favor of "ability grouping" to achieve quality education. Members of the education profession have a responsibility to develop methods for teaching classes composed of students from different subcultures without resorting to ability groupings or "track systems." In *Hobson* v. *Hansen*[57] the court enjoined the continuation of a track system under which students were separated into tracks according to their academic development because such a system was found to violate the constitutional rights of minority group students. This case presents the possibility that creeping legalism may overtake the makers of educational policy in searching for quality education in our pluralistic society.

Notes

1. 347 U.S. 483, 98 L.Ed. 873, 74 S.Ct. 686 (1954) and 349 U.S. 294, 99 L.Ed. 1083, 75 S.Ct. 753 (1955).
2. The Thirteenth, Fourteenth, and Fifteenth Amendments.
3. The *Civil Rights Cases*, 109 U.S. 3, 27 L.Ed. 835, 3 S.Ct. 18 (1883).
4. *Plessy* v. *Ferguson*, 163 U.S. 537, 41 L.Ed. 256, 16 S.Ct. 1138 (1896).
5. 55 Mass. (5 Cushing) 198 (Mass.1850).
6. *Gong Lum* v. *Rice*, 275 U.S. 78, 72 L.Ed. 172, 48 S.Ct. 91 (1927).
7. The Report of the United States Commission on Civil Rights (Washington, D.C.: U.S. Government Printing Office, 1959) stated that "immediately prior to the Supreme Court decision in the *School Segregation Cases*," Alabama, Arkansas, Delaware, Florida, Georgia, Kentucky, Louisiana, Maryland, Mississippi, Missouri, North Carolina, Oklahoma, South Carolina, Tennessee, Texas, Virginia, West Virginia, and the District of Columbia were requiring segregation by constitutional or statutory provision, and Arizona, Kansas, New Mexico, and Wyoming were permitting segregation in varying degrees or under specified conditions.
8. Jack Greenberg, *Race Relations and American Law* (New York: Columbia University Press, 1959), p. 209, Quoting from Brief of the United States on the Further Argument of the Questions of Relief in Brown v. Board of Education, p. 17.
9. 305 U.S. 337, 89 L.Ed. 208, 59 S.Ct. 232 (1938), reh. den. 305 U.S. 676, 83 L.Ed. 437, 59 S.Ct. 356 (1939).
10. 339 U.S. 629, 94 L.Ed. 1114, 70 S.Ct. 848 (1950).
11. 339 U.S. 637, 94 L.Ed. 1149, 70 S.Ct. 851 (1950).
12. See note 1.
13. See Greenberg, *Race Relations and American Law, op. cit.,* pp. 215–274, and Reed Sarratt, *The Ordeal of Desegregation* (New York: Harper and Row, 1966); Report of the United States Commission on Civil Rights, 1959, *op. cit.,* Part Three, pp. 173–244.
14. 358 U.S. 1, 3 L.Ed.2d 5, 78 S.Ct. 1401 (1958).
15. 256 F.2d 688 (Del.1958), reh. den. 1958, cert. den. 358 U.S. 836, 3 L.Ed.2d 72, 79 S.Ct. 58 (1958).
16. 238 F.2d 91 (Ark.1956).
17. 377 U.S. 218, 12 L.Ed.2d 256, 84 S.Ct. 1226 (1964).
18. For a list of seventeen such factors, see Report of the United States Commission on Civil Rights, 1959, *op. cit.,* p. 241.
19. 162 F.Supp. 372 (Ala.1958). See also *Carson et al.* v. *Warlick*, 238 F.2d 724 (N.C.1956), cert. den. 353 U.S. 910, 1 L.Ed.2d 664, 77 S.Ct. 665 (1957), holding North Carolina's law constitutional on its face.

20. 358 U.S. 101, 3 L.Ed.2d 145, 79 S.Ct. 221 (1958).

21. *Kelley et al. v. Board of Education of City of Nashville, Davidson County, Tennessee et al.,* 270 F.2d 209 (Tenn.1959).

22. See *Gaines et al. v. Dougherty County Board of Education et al.,* 334 F.2d 983 (Ga.1964), reh. den. 1964, where the court required that a grade-a-year plan of desegregation commence simultaneously at both the first and twelfth grades; the court, in addition, placed the burden of proof on the local school board "to show cause why further acceleration of the complete desegregation should not be required." Also, *Evans et al. v. Ennis,* 281 F.2d 385 (Del.1960), reh. den. 1960, where the court disapproved a grade-a-year plan for the reason that it did "not follow the intent and substance of the rulings of the Supreme Court in *Brown . . . .*"

23. See Report on Education, United States Commission on Civil Rights, 1961, p. 17, citing among other cases *Briggs et al. v. Elliott et al.,* 132 F.Supp. 776 (S.C.1955).

24. In *Houston Independent School District et al. v. Ross et al.,* 282 F.2d 95 (Texas 1960), the court branded the plan as a "palpable sham and subterfuge designed only to accomplish further evasion and delay." See also *Boson et al. v. Rippy et al.,* 285 F.2d 43 (Texas 1960), reh. den. 1961.

25. *Bush et al. v. Orleans Parish School Board et al.,* 230 F.Supp. 509 (La. 1963).

26. *Davis v. Board of Education of Charleston Consolidated School District No. 7 of Mississippi County, Missouri,* 216 F.Supp. 295 (Mo.1963).

27. See *Goss et al. v. Board of Education of City of Knoxville, Tennessee et al.,* 373 U.S. 683, 10 L.Ed.2d 632, 83 S.Ct. 1405 (1963).

28. 1963 Staff Report, Public Education, submitted to the United States Commission on Civil Rights, p. 52.

29. Public Law 88-352, 78 Stat. 241.

30. Section 407 of Title IV authorizes the Attorney General under certain circumstances to institute a civil action in the name of the United States against a school board if he believes such action is meritorious.

31. Sections 601–605 of Title VI prohibit discrimination in federally assisted programs and authorize federal agencies to effect such prohibitions by issuing regulations, and withholding federal financial assistance to effectuate compliance with such regulations. An H.E.W. regulation (45 C.F.R., par. 80.4(a), 1964) directs the Commissioner of Education to approve applications for financial aid to public schools *only if* such school or school system agrees to comply with a court order or submits a desegregation plan satisfactory to the Commissioner.

32. See Revised Statement of Policies for School Desegregation Plans under Title VI of the Civil Rights Act of 1964, December 1966, as amended for the school year 1967–68, U.S. Department of Health, Education and Welfare, Office of Education.

33. See Subparts B and C of the Statement of Policies (Guidelines).

34. See Subparts B and D of the Statement of Policies (Guidelines).

35. See Subpart B, paragraph 181.13 of the Statement of Policies (Guidelines).

36. See *Clark et al. v. Board of Education of Little Rock School District et al.,*

374 F.2d 569 (8th Cir.1967); *United States of America et al.* v. *Jefferson County Board of Education et al.,* 372 F.2d 836 (5th Cir.1966), and *Singleton* v. *Jackson Municipal Separate School District,* 348 F.2d 729 (5th Cir.1965).

37. See note 36.

38. In the view of the majority, the *Brown* ruling "requires conversion of the dual zones into a single system. Faculties, facilities, and activities as well as student bodies must be integrated."

39. 132 F.Supp. 776 (S.C.1955) wherein the court stated, "Nothing in the Constitution or in the decision of the Supreme Court takes away from the people freedom to choose the schools they attend. The Constitution, in other words, does not require integration. It merely forbids discrimination. It does not forbid such segregation as occurs as the result of voluntary action. It merely forbids the use of governmental power to enforce segregation."

40. The conditions stipulated by the majority were that: (1) by 1967–68 all grades should be desegregated, (2) mandatory free choice should be made annually, (3) adequate notice should be given, (4) students in segregated grades and students with special needs should have the right to transfer, (5) services, facilities, activities, and programs must be fully integrated, (6) schools within the system must be substantially equal, (7) compliance reports should be submitted to the court annually, and (8) faculty and staff must be desegregated.

41. See note 36.

42. See *Clemons et al.* v. *Board of Education of Hillsboro, Ohio,* 228 F.2d 853 (Ohio 1956), cert. den. 350 U.S. 1006, 100 L.Ed. 868, 76 S.Ct. 651 (1956) where, notwithstanding state laws against school segregation, attendance zones were gerrymandered, and the court held that the ruling of the *Brown* case was violated. See also *Taylor* v. *Board of Education of City School District of City of New Rochelle,* 191 F.Supp. 181 (N.Y.1961), where gerrymandering was held to be in conflict with the *Brown* decision.

43. In the Report of the United States Commission on Civil Rights—1967, *Racial Isolation in the Public Schools,* Vol. I (Washington, D.C.: U.S. Government Printing Office), the term used is *adventitious school segregation.* See also p. 223, note 25, of the same publication for a collection of materials on the subject in various legal periodicals.

44. 324 F.2d 209 (Ind.1963), cert. den. 377 U.S. 924, 12 L.Ed.2d 216, 84 S.Ct. 1223 (1964).

45. The same conclusion was reached in *Avery et al.* v. *Wichita Falls Independent School District et al.,* 241 F.2d 230 (Texas 1957), cert. den. 353 U.S. 938, 1 L.Ed.2d 761, 77 S.Ct. 816 (1957). See also *Deal et al.* v. *Cincinnati Board of Education et al.,* 369 F.2d 55 (Ohio 1966); *Swann et al.* v. *Charlotte–Mecklenburg Board of Education,* 369 F.2d 29 (N.C. 1966), and compare *Springfield School Committee et al.* v. *Barksdale et al.,* 348 F.2d 261 (Mass.1965).

46. 269 F.Supp. 402 (D.C. 1967).

47. See *Barksdale et al.* v. *Springfield School Committee et al.,* 237 F.Supp.

543 (Mass.1965), reversed in part in 348 F.2d 261; *Blocker* v. *Board of Education of Manhasset, New York,* 226 F.Supp. 208 (N.Y.1964); *Jackson* v. *Pasadena City School District,* 382 P.2d 878 (Calif.1963), reh. den. 1963; and *Branche et al.* v. *Board of Education of Town of Hempstead, School District No. 1, et al.,* 204 F.Supp. 150 (N.Y.1962).

48. See *Katalinic* v. *City of Syracuse,* 254 N.Y.S.2d 960 (1964) where the court said, "even if the Court were convinced that the sole purpose in closing the Junior High School . . . and in transferring the students to (the other) . . . school was for the correction of a situation of racial imbalance, which it is not, the Court still would be of the opinion that at this time, it has no power to hold that said action would be arbitrary and capricious or a Constitutional Violation." See also *Balaban et al.* v. *Rubin et al.,* 250 N.Y.S.2d 281, cert. den. 379 U.S. 881, 13 L.Ed.2d 87, 85 S.Ct. 148 (1964). In *Fuller* v. *Volk,* 230 F.Supp. 25 (N.J.1964) the court held that "a local board of education is not constitutionally prohibited from taking race into account in drawing or redrawing school attendance lines for the purpose of reducing or eliminating de facto segregation in its public schools."

49. See Report of the United States Commission on Civil Rights—1967, *Racial Isolation in the Public Schools, op. cit.,* p. 229, where it is stated that "California, Massachusetts, New York, New Jersey, Wisconsin, and Connecticut have taken the position, in executive or judicial statements, that racial isolation in the schools has a damaging effect on the educational opportunities of Negro pupils."

50. 227 N.E. 2d 729 (Mass. 1967), app. dism. 36 L.W. 3279.

51. Massachusetts General Laws, Chapter 15.

52. Docket No. 40292, Agenda 23, March 1967.

53. The majority rely upon Section 22 of Article IV of the Illinois Constitution and the 1874 case of *Chase* v. *Stephenson,* 71 Ill.383. However, the dissent appears to be on firm ground in holding that neither the constitutional provision nor the decision are relevant to the issue in the *Tometz* case.

54. Charles U. Smith, "Race Relations and the New Agenda for Higher Education," *Phi Delta Kappan,* May, 1965.

55. See the report of this Commission, *American Education and the Search for Equal Opportunity* (Washington, D.C.: National Education Association, 1965).

56. See Report of the U.S. Commission on Civil Rights—1967, *Racial Isolation in the Public Schools, op. cit.,* pp. 128–140, 160–161. See also Cole S. Brembeck, *Social Foundations of Education* (New York: John Wiley and Sons, Inc., 1966), pp. 496–497.

57. See note 46.

APPENDIX II

Collective Negotiations in Public Education

THE status of teachers in the formal organization and administration of public elementary and secondary educational systems has changed substantially during the past decade. The most significant changes have been wrought by teachers' increased reliance on their organizations, through which teachers engage in collective negotiations with their employers, the school boards. There is some evidence of a growing interest in collective negotiations on the part of teachers in institutions of higher education. The term, collective negotiations, as used here, refers to the processes and procedures *established by law* under which employees, through representatives selected by them, participate in decision-making with respect to issues and subjects which, under the traditional authority structure, would be decided by employers or their designates.

Employee-employer relationships in education embrace a variety of subjects and issues which may be divided loosely into two categories. One category, relating primarily to teacher welfare issues, includes such subjects as teacher qualifications, hours of work, rates of pay, promotions, retirements, and dismissals. The other category, relating primarily to issues of educational policy, includes such subjects as curriculum, textbooks, class size, extracurricular activities, teaching assignments, and teaching aids.[1] In public elementary and secondary education, decisions with respect to some of these issues and subjects are made by the states, through their legislatures, in the exercise of the state's plenary power over education. As has been shown, decision-making power is often delegated by state legislatures. In the absence of express delegation of decision-making power, the traditional authority structure in elementary and secondary education allocates administrative and supervisory authority to governing bodies and their administra-

tors. Teachers, to be sure, may be and have been consulted as a
matter of policy, but they participate in decision-making only to
the extent that they are invited to do so. In higher education, on
the other hand, the traditional authority structure typically provides for considerable involvement in decision-making by teachers
and/or committees of teachers.

Various types of teachers' organizations have existed at local,
state, and national levels for many years. The National Education
Association, first established in 1857, is a national organization
with state and local affiliates. The American Federation of
Teachers, first formed in 1916, is an affiliate of the AFL–CIO and
has local organizations throughout the nation. Through these and
other organizations teachers have voiced their objections to the
traditional authority structure in education. The Teacher Tenure
and Civil Service laws which have been enacted in many states are
examples of legislative response to the expressed concerns of
teachers' organizations. However, regulations affecting the status
of teachers and their organizations vary widely from state to state.
As late as 1930, a state court upheld a school board regulation
prohibiting the employment of teachers who were members of a
federation of teachers.[2] Laws in a few states still purport to prohibit public employees, including public school teachers, from
forming or joining labor organizations,[3] but it would appear that
the right to organize or to join organizations is a right to freedom
of association protected from unreasonable restrictions by the First
and Fourteenth Amendments of the Federal Constitution.[4]

There are differences of opinion as to whether it is reasonable
to restrict the rights of public employees to organize, simply because they are public rather than private employees. Opinions also
differ as to whether teachers, as professional persons, should engage in collective negotiations. Such differences of opinion have
contributed to the fact that, although collective negotiations in
private industry and business became acceptable and operative in
the 1930's, they did not begin to gain general acceptance in public
employment until the 1960's. In some respects recent developments in public education have followed the pattern established
earlier for private business and industry. It is appropriate, therefore, to note the basic features in collective bargaining as it has
developed in private employment.

Prior to 1914, federal courts held that organizations of employees were subject to the provisions of the Sherman Anti-Trust Act[5] prohibiting conspiracies in restraint of trade, but in that year Congress enacted the Clayton Act[6] which had the effect of giving employees the right to organize for the purpose of bargaining collectively with their employers without violating the Sherman Act. While the Clayton Act protected the right of employees to organize, it was not until the enactment of the National Labor Relations Act in 1935[7] that Congress created for employees the statutory right to organize and to bargain collectively with their employers *through representatives of their own choosing*. This Act also placed a statutory obligation on employers subject to the Act to recognize the representative selected by employees as the exclusive representative of all the employees in the appropriate unit, and to bargain in good faith with such representative with respect to employees' wages, hours, and other conditions of employment. The Act specifically provides for the establishment of the National Labor Relations Board as an independent administrative agency to effect the purposes of the Act. In 1947 Congress enacted the Labor–Management Relations Act[8] which made some important changes in the 1935 Act, but the basic features referred to above were not changed.

The 1935 and 1947 Acts, hereafter referred to as federal labor legislation, do not apply to public employee-employer relations and are further limited to employee-employer relations in the private sector only where such relations affect interstate commerce. An important question is whether and, if so, to what extent, the basic features of the federal labor legislation serve as guidelines in the development of collective negotiations in public employment, and more specifically in employment in public education. In this regard, it should be noted that the federal labor legislation imposes a statutory obligation on employers to bargain collectively with representatives of their employees concerning matters traditionally dealt with unilaterally by employers. In addition, the processes considered essential in collective bargaining are identified and administrative procedures established for using these processes to reach a formal agreement or collective bargaining contract.

The following features of the federal legislation are selected to determine the impact of such legislation on the development of collective negotiations in employment in public education:

(1) establishing the right of employees to negotiate or bargain collectively with their employers through representatives of their own choosing; (2) imposing on employers the legal obligation to negotiate or bargain with their employees' representatives; (3) establishing procedures for determining the categories of employees to be represented, i.e., unit determinations;[9] (4) establishing procedures for determining the employees' representatives, i.e., representation determinations;[10] (5) establishing the issues or subjects which may be bargained about or negotiated, i.e., the scope of bargaining or negotiation; and (6) establishing or designating an agency to administer the legislation.

With respect to public employees, it may be recalled that, as early as 1912, Congress recognized the right of federal employees to organize for the purpose of improving their working conditions. No specific provision was made for the official recognition of such organizations, but the heads of many federal agencies voluntarily developed collective negotiation relationships with representatives of federal employee organizations. Few of the basic features of the federal legislation relating to the private sector were present. In 1955 the Committee on Labor Relations of the American Bar Association made the following statement in its report:

> A government which imposes upon private employers certain obligations in dealing with their employees may not in good faith refuse to deal with its own public servants on a reasonably similar basis, modified of course to meet the exigencies of public service.

Finally, in 1962 President Kennedy issued Executive Order 10988 on Employee–Management Cooperation in the Federal Service. This Order and supplemental documents issued thereafter provided for the participation of federal employees in the formulation and implementation of personnel policies affecting them. It is generally agreed that this Order greatly reduced the public resistance to collective negotiations in public employment. The basic features of the Order and supporting documents are: (1) federal employees are granted the right to form or join employee organizations; (2) federal agencies are required to accord informal, formal, or exclusive recognition to employee organizations; (3) where exclusive recognition is accorded, the agency and the representative organization are required to "meet at reasonable times and confer with respect to personnel policy and practices and matters affecting working conditions, so far as may be appropriate subject to law and policy requirements"; and (4) certain management rights are specifically excluded from the scope of conferences.[11]

What has been the development of employee organization and collective bargaining in public education? In *Norwalk Teachers' Association* v. *Board of Education of City of Norwalk*,[12] decided in 1951, a state court held that, in the absence of enabling legislation, (1) public school teachers may organize, (2) a school board may, but is not legally obligated, to negotiate with such teachers' organization, (3) a school board may agree to arbitrate certain issues but may not by general arbitration agreement surrender the legal responsibilities and broad discretion delegated to it by the legislature, (4) a school board may not agree to a closed shop, and (5) public school teachers may not strike to enforce their demands. It does not seem unreasonable to assume that courts in many other states might reach the same or similar conclusions in the absence of enabling legislation.

In recent years there has been a sharp increase in the number of states in which collective negotiation legislation has been enacted either relating to public employment generally or to public school employment in particular. The eleven state statutes enacted by early 1968 include seven which relate specifically to public school employment and four which relate to public employment in general, the latter, of course, including public school employment.[13] The statutes vary considerably in the extent to which they include the basic features of the federal legislation. In all of the statutes, the right of individual teachers to confer with their school boards is recognized. In all statutes the right of teachers to organize and to select organizations to represent them is also recognized. However, the right of teachers to bargain, negotiate, or meet and confer with school boards through organizations or representatives of their own choice is limited in several statutes. Only seven of the eleven state statutes contain provisions specifically obligating school boards to bargain, negotiate, or meet and confer with teachers' representatives.[14] There may be an implied obligation on school boards in three of the four remaining state statutes but the fourth state statute specifically provides that there is no statutory obligation on school boards to meet and confer with organizations representing teachers.[15]

The position taken in this discussion is that an essential requisite of a collective negotiation statute in public education is the imposition of a statutory obligation on school boards to negotiate with teachers' representatives. This position is taken because of the belief that, so long as a school board has the option to negotiate or not to negotiate, there is no substantial change in the traditional authority structure in public education. This is not to assert or deny that there is a need to change substantially the traditional authority structure. Rather, it is to suggest that statutes requiring the use of statutory processes and procedures only if a school board chooses to negotiate are different from statutes obligating school boards to negotiate and also to use certain processes and procedures. Both types of statutes are examined because both constitute education laws.

The statutory right of teachers to bargain, negotiate, or meet and confer with school boards through representatives of their own choosing. There are two related issues here: one involves the determination of the groups or units of public school personnel eligible to choose the teachers' representatives, i.e., unit determinations; and the other involves the determination of the teachers' representative. Unit determinations are designed to limit the selection of their representative to those employees with common interests. A question often raised in this regard is whether employees who supervise have interests in common with the employees whom they supervise. As concerns representation determinations, some statutes reveal a legislative intention to limit the kinds of organizations which may be chosen by teachers or other public employees to represent them.

Under the California statute, the unit entitled to choose its representatives includes all public school employees, "excepting those persons elected by popular vote or appointed by the Governor of this state." The representative chosen may be "any organization which includes employees of a public school employer and which has as one of its primary purposes representing such employees in their relations with that public school employer." The statute provides, however, that, if there is more than one employee organization representing certified employees, each such organization shall be entitled to a proportionate representation on a *negotiating council.* Thus, the California legislature has adopted proportionate representation instead of exclusive representation where teachers are represented by more than one organization.[16] Public school teachers in California, therefore, have representation of their own choosing only to a limited extent.

Under the Connecticut statute, certified professional employees may elect to have three different kinds of units for the purpose of choosing representatives. If a majority of *all* such employees below the rank of superintendent so vote, there can be one unit. However, teachers may vote for a separate unit, as may administrative and supervisory personnel. The unit or units decided by majority vote have the statutory right to choose as their representatives "any organization or organizations of certified professional employees" and such organization becomes the exclusive representative of all certified professional employees in the appropriate unit.

Under the Minnesota statute, teachers, defined as certificated persons excepting superintendents, have the right to form or join teacher organizations, defined as "any organization or labor union or part of such organization which includes only teachers of a public school as members." There is no provision in the statute expressly granting teachers the right to choose teacher organizations as representatives. However, the statute does obligate school boards to recognize teachers' organizations as representatives of teachers who are members of such organizations. It is further provided that "(w)hen more than one teacher organization has as members teachers employed in the district, the board shall grant recognition to a committee of five teachers selected by these organizations on a proportionate basis determined by membership. The committee shall be known as the teachers' council and consist only of teachers employed by the district." Minnesota, like California, has adopted proportionate representation rather than exclusive representation. Unlike the teachers in California, however, Minnesota teachers are limited in their choice of representatives to organizations including teachers only. The right of teachers to choose their representatives is thus even more limited in Minnesota than it is in California.

The Nebraska statute provides that "(c)ertificated public school employees shall have the right to form, join, and participate in the activities of organizations of their own choosing for the purpose of representation. . . ." There is also a provision that "(o)rganizations of certified public school employees shall have the right to represent their members. . . ." It is expressly provided that school boards are not obligated to do so, but if by majority vote a school board elects to meet or confer with the representatives of an organization of certified employees, and more than one such organization requests recognition, the school board "may recognize as representative the organization which has for the last two preceding years enrolled a majority of the certificated school employees. . . ." It would appear that teachers may only be represented by *organizations of certificated school employees,* but the statute does not define these organizations. Unless the organizations which teachers choose to join are considered to be organizations of certified school employees, it is clear that teachers in Nebraska do not have the right to meet or confer with school boards through representatives of their choice.

The Oregon statute grants to certified school personnel the right to be represented by a committee of such personnel elected by majority vote of such personnel below the rank of superintendent. The committee so elected has the right to confer, consult, and discuss in good faith with the school board. It is clear from a reading of the statute, however, that teachers in Oregon do not have the right to confer, etc. with school boards through representatives of their own choice.

Under the Rhode Island statute, certified teachers are expressly granted the "right to bargain collectively with their respective school committees and be represented by an association or labor organization. . . ." The statute also provides that "(t)he organization selected by majority vote (of certificated teachers) shall be certified as the exclusive bargaining agent of the teachers."

The Washington statute is addressed to the rights of employee organizations rather than to the rights of teachers represented by the organizations. An employee organization is defined as "any organization which includes as members certificated employees of a school district and which has as one of its purposes the representation of the employees in their employment relations with the school district." A certificated employee is defined as "any employee holding a regular teaching certificate of the state who is employed by any school district with the exception of the chief administrative officer of each local district." The statute expressly grants representation rights to the employee organization which shall "have won a majority in an election to represent the certificated employees within its school district, ..." Presumably only certified employees are eligible to vote for the representative but the statute is silent on this point.

In addition to the seven states with statutes relating specifically to public school personnel there are four states with statutes relating to public employment in general, which includes public school employment; they are Massachusetts, Michigan, New York, and Wisconsin.

The Massachusetts statute defines a public employee as "any employee of a municipal employer, whether or not in the classified service of the municipal employer, except elected officials, board and commission members, and the executive officers of any municipal employer." Thus, public school employees are included. Employee organization is defined as "any lawful association, organization, federation or council having as a primary purpose the improvement of wages, hours and other conditions of employment." The statute grants to employees, as defined, the right "to present proposals . . . through representatives of their own choosing." It is provided that an employee organization, as defined, "recognized by a municipal employer or designated as the representative of a majority of the employees in an appropriate unit, shall be the exclusive bargaining agent for all employees of such unit. . . ." The state labor relations commission is required to decide in each case "whether the appropriate unit . . . shall be the municipal employer unit or any other unit thereof." However, a professional employee is defined in great detail and it is expressly provided that "no unit shall include both professional and nonprofessional employees unless a majority of such professional employees vote for inclusion in such unit." With respect to public school employees the statute refers to "a superintendency union formed in accordance with general or specific law" but superintendents are not specifically excluded from units including teachers.[17]

Under the Michigan statute, public employees, including public school employees, are granted the right to "negotiate or bargain collectively with their public employers through representatives of their own free choice." No specific reference is made to public school employees, but the statute requires the state's labor mediation board to "decide in each case . . . the appropriate unit for the purposes of collective bargaining as provided" in another statute which declares that employees "holding executive or supervisory positions" are excluded from units of employees.[18] The collective negotiation statute specifically provides that "(r)epresentatives designated or selected . . . by the majority of the public employees in a unit appropriate for such purposes, shall be the exclusive representatives of all the public employees in such unit. . . ."

The New York statute defines a public employee as "any person holding a position by appointment or employment in the service of a public employer" with exceptions not relevant here. Thus, public school employees are included. Employee organization is defined in considerable detail as "an organization of any kind having as its primary purpose the improvement of terms and conditions of employment of public employees" with specific exceptions, such as organizations with membership policies that discriminate because of race, color, creed, or national origin. The statute grants public employees, as defined, the right to join "any employee organization of their own choosing," and also the "right to be represented by employee organizations to negotiate collectively with their public employers. . . ." Every government, as defined in the statute, through its legislative body is empowered to establish procedures for unit and representation determinations. Pending the establishment of such procedures, the public employment relations board, created by the statute, is required to make unit and representation determinations. Community of interest is one of the standards to be used in making unit determinations. In making representation determinations the choice of the public employees in the unit is to be ascertained, by election if necessary. The employee organization, as defined, which is chosen by the public employees in the unit must affirm that it does not assert the right to strike, or to assist or to participate in such strike, before it can be certified as the bargaining representative.

Under the Wisconsin statute, municipal employees, including employees of school districts, are granted the right to "affiliate with labor organizations of their own choosing and the right to be represented by labor organizations of their own choice in conferences and negotiations with their municipal employers . . . ." The state employment relations board is empowered to make unit and representation determinations.[19]

The statutory obligation imposed on school boards to bargain, negotiate, meet, confer and/or discuss specified issues or items with teachers' representatives. Statutes in seven states—California, Connecticut, Massachusetts, Michigan, Minnesota, New York, and

Rhode Island—impose specific obligations on school boards in their relations with teachers' representatives. The nature of these obligations vary from statute to statute and their meaning and effect are matters of statutory interpretation ultimately for the courts. Where an independent agency is established or designated to administer the statute, that agency typically will have the initial interpreting responsibility. The statutes of five of the seven states —Connecticut, Massachusetts, Michigan, New York, and Rhode Island—impose on school boards a statutory obligation to *bargain or negotiate in good faith* with teacher representatives. This specific obligation is similar to the obligation imposed on both employers and employee representatives by the federal labor legislation. Under federal labor legislation, although there is no obligation to reach an agreement, the obligation to bargain in good faith has been interpreted to mean that the parties to the bargaining must make a bona fide effort to reach an agreement. The National Labor Relations Board and the federal courts have rendered decisions involving the issue whether there has been a refusal to bargain in good faith. These decisions are of persuasive authority in the interpretation of the five state statutes in which obligatory language similar to that used in the federal legislation has been adopted.

The statutes in California and Minnesota obligate school boards to meet and confer with teachers' representatives rather than to bargain or negotiate in good faith. In neither state have the words "meet and confer" been judicially construed.

The statutes in Oregon and Washington contain no provisions expressly obligating school boards to bargain, negotiate, or meet and confer with teachers' representatives. However, the Washington statute provides in effect that the teachers' representatives "shall have the right . . . to meet, confer and negotiate" with school boards, and the Oregon statute provides in effect that committees of teachers elected by teachers "shall have the right to confer, consult and discuss in good faith" with school boards. It is certainly arguable that, in establishing these rights for teachers' representatives, the legislatures have created an implied obligation on school boards.

The Nebraska statute also establishes the right of teachers to "participate in the activities of organizations of their own choosing for the purpose of representation on all matters of employment relations." However, this statute expressly provides that "no board

of education . . . shall be required to meet or confer with representatives of an organization of certificated school employees unless
a majority of the members of such board determines to recognize
such organization." Therefore, in Nebraska, the statutory right of
teachers to be represented by organizations of their choice does
not result in any implied obligation on school boards to meet and
confer with such representatives.

The Wisconsin statute contains no provisions expressly obligating municipal employers, including school boards, to bargain,
negotiate, or meet and confer with teachers' representatives.
Whether this obligation can be implied from the statutory rights
granted to public school employees does not appear to have been
judicially determined.

Scope of negotiations. The eleven statutes examined here vary
in the kinds of issues or items which are proper subjects of bargaining, negotiation, meetings, and conferences or discussions between teachers' representatives and school boards. The statutes of
eight states, in general, limit the scope of negotiations to teacher
welfare or economic issues. The statutes of Connecticut, Massachusetts, Michigan, Minnesota, New York, Oregon, Rhode Island,
and Wisconsin define the scope of negotiation by the economic
phrase, "wages, hours and conditions of employment," or some
variation of this phrase.[20] It is to be noted that this phrase is similar
to the one used in the federal legislation, and is found, in addition,
in all four statutes which relate to public employment generally.
A liberal construction of the "conditions of employment," when
applied to public school teachers, might include some educational
policy issues.[21]

The California statute requires school boards to meet and confer with representatives of employee organizations or a negotiating
council upon request "with regard to all matters relating to employment conditions and employer-employee relations, and in addition . . . all matters relating to the definition of educational
objectives, the determination of the content of courses and curricula, the selection of textbooks, and other aspects of the instructional program to the extent such matters are within the discretion
of the public school employer or governing board under the law."

Under the Nebraska statute, as previously pointed out, school
boards have no statutory obligation to meet or confer with repre-

sentatives of teachers' organizations unless there is a majority vote of the board to do so. If there is such a vote, the representative of the employee organization which has been recognized by the board is required to give the board a written request to meet and confer, specifying "the areas to be discussed by the parties." While the board has a statutory right to accept or reject requests, there is no statutory limitation on the kinds of issues or items a school board may agree to meet or confer about, and it is expressly provided that "such meetings shall be good faith negotiations in regard to the matters set forth in the request to meet and confer and the acceptance thereof."

The Washington statute authorizes the school board and representatives of an employee organization to consider jointly "proposed school policies relating to, but not limited to, curriculum, textbook selection, in-service training, student teaching programs, personnel hiring and assignment practices, leaves of absence, salary schedules and noninstructional duties."

Impasse procedures. Most collective negotiation statutes require the school board and the teachers' representative to make a bona fide effort to reach an agreement on the issues within the scope of negotiations. Typically, however, the statutes make it clear that neither party is under any statutory obligation to agree to a proposal or to make a concession. Thus, bona fide negotiations may result in a persistent disagreement or impasse. The procedures for resolving impasses include fact finding, conciliation, mediation, and either advisory or binding arbitration.

Fact finding may be initiated in a number of ways. Typically, it is conducted by an outside party or panel and results in a report with recommendations for resolving any impasse. There is general agreement that the effectiveness of fact finding is enhanced by the express or implied authority to publish the findings.

In conciliation and mediation, an outside party confers with the negotiating parties in an effort to assist them in resolving any impasse. A mediator may be empowered to make recommendations, but the recommendations are in no way binding.

In arbitration, the negotiating parties submit an impasse to an outside party who makes a decision in the form of award. An arbitrator's award may be advisory or binding. Where a statute requires the submission of impasses to either advisory or binding arbitration, the process is known as compulsory arbitration. Without a statutory mandate, however, negotiating parties may agree to submit an unresolved issue to arbitration; this is known as voluntary arbitration. The legal capacity of a public school board to enter into a voluntary binding arbitration agreement is open to question.[22] There would seem to be no legal question, however, where a statute authorizes binding arbitration.

The California statute requires school boards to "adopt reasonable rules and regulations for the administration of employer-employee relations" under the statute. However, it contains no specific provisions relating to impasses.

Under the Connecticut statute, election disputes relating to unit and representation determinations "shall be submitted to a board of arbitrators for a binding decision with respect thereto." Disagreements as to terms and conditions of employment "shall be submitted to the secretary of the state board of education for mediation." He is authorized to make advisory recommendations. If mediation fails, either party may submit unresolved issues "to an impartial board of three arbitrators" for an advisory decision. If either party refuses to arbitrate, "an action to compel arbitration may be instituted . . . ."

The Massachusetts statute provides that, if there are unresolved disputes arising out of negotiations, "either party or the parties jointly may petition the state board of conciliation and arbitration to initiate fact finding." This state board is also required to be available for conciliation and arbitration. The use of other arbitration tribunals is authorized.

The Michigan statute does not contain any provisions referring specifically to impasses. The state labor mediation board, however, is required to mediate grievances when petitioned to do so.

Under the Minnesota statute, matters not agreed upon are referred to an adjustment panel for settlement. The panel is authorized to hold hearings and make findings. The statute is silent concerning the effect of these findings.

The Nebraska statute provides that "(i)f the parties cannot agree . . . the dispute shall be submitted to a fact-finding board . . ." which is required to "hear and review the matters relating to the dispute and . . . render a report of its opinion which shall recommend a basis for settlement of the dispute." It is expressly provided that "in no case shall (the recommendations) be binding on the school district."

The New York statute creates a public employment relations board. Among the many responsibilities of this board are the resolution of unit and representation disputes and the establishment of "panels of qualified persons broadly representative of the public to be available to serve as mediators or members of fact-finding boards." The board is specifically required, upon request, to appoint mediators and "if the impasse continues" to appoint fact-finding boards, which, under certain circumstances, shall make public their findings and recommendations. If, after publication, the parties do not accept the recommendations of the fact-finding board, "and the impasse continues," the public employment relations board is expressly authorized "to take whatever steps it deems appropriate to resolve the dispute . . . ."

The Oregon statute provides that, "(w)henever it appears . . . that a persistent disagreement . . . exists," either of the parties may request the appointment of consultants who may determine a reasonable basis for settlement and recommend it to the negotiating parties.

Under the Rhode Island statute "(a)ll unresolved issues shall be brought to arbitration."

Under the Washington statute, any unresolved issues may be referred to "a committee composed of educators and school directors appointed by the state superintendent of public instruction." This committee is required to make advisory recommendations.

Under the Wisconsin statute, the state employment relations board is authorized to initiate fact finding if the negotiating parties are "deadlocked." The employment relations board is also authorized to "function as a mediator in disputes between municipal employees and their employers upon the request of both parties."

Strikes by public school teachers. Only five of the eleven state statutes examined here contain specific provisions against strikes by public school teachers or by public employees including public school teachers. However, none of the other six statutes authorize such strikes, and judicial opinion that such strikes are against public policy is almost uniform. The New York statute contains the most detailed provisions against strikes by public employees, including public school teachers.[23]

The following chart summarizes the contents of this discussion.

Notes

1. There have been and are honest differences of opinion as to whether certain subjects fall into one category or the other.
2. See *Seattle High School Chapter No. 200, American Federation of Teachers et al.* v. *Sharples et al.,* 293 P.994 (Wash.1930).
3. A North Carolina statute prohibits public employees in general from joining labor organizations. A Texas statute prohibits public officials from recognizing labor organizations as representatives of public employees. A South Carolina attorney general's opinion upholds an ordinance prohibiting municipal employees from joining labor organizations.
4. See *NAACP* v. *Alabama,* 357 U.S. 449, 2 L.Ed.2d 1488, 78 S.Ct. 1163 (1958).
5. 26 Stat. 209 (1890); 15 U.S.C. 1–7.
6. 38 Stat. 730 (1914).
7. 49 Stat. 449 (1935); 29 U.S.C. 151.
8. 61 Stat. 136 (1947); 7 U.S.C. 6289. Among other things, this Act makes it an unfair labor practice for the employee representative as well as the employer to refuse to bargain in good faith.
9. Unit determination procedures limit the employees who are eligible to participate in the selection of an employee representative. Typically, the purpose of the unit determination is to establish a unit of employees with common interests.
10. Representation determination procedures are primarily to provide for the selection of the representative of the employees. Such procedures are important where more than one qualified organization seeks representation rights.
11. Section 7 (2) of the Order provides: "Management officials of the agency retain the right, in accordance with applicable laws and regulations, (a) to direct employees of the agency, (b) to hire, promote, transfer, assign, and retain employees in positions within the agency, and to suspend, demote, discharge, or take other disciplinary action against employees, (c) to relieve employees from duties because of lack of work or for other legitimate reasons, (d) to maintain the efficiency of the Government operations entrusted to them, (e) to determine the methods, means, and personnel by which such operations are to be conducted, and (f) to take whatever actions may be necessary to carry out the mission of the agency in situations of emergency."
12. 83 A.2d 482 (Conn.1951).
13. The seven states with statutes relating specifically to public school employment are: California, Connecticut, Minnesota, Nebraska, Oregon, Rhode Island, and Washington.

The four states with statutes relating to public employment in general are: Massachusetts, Michigan, New York, and Wisconsin.

A provision in the New Jersey Constitution and statutory provisions in Alaska, Florida, and New Hampshire either grant to public employees the right to present proposals to their public employers through representatives of their own choosing, or authorize public employers to enter into agreements with representatives of their public employees. Presumably, these provisions apply to public schools teachers and to school boards. However, there are no provisions expressly obligating public employers to bargain, negotiate or confer, nor are public employers who elect to do so required to follow any specific procedures.

14. California, Connecticut, Massachusetts, Michigan, Minnesota, New York, and Rhode Island.

15. There may be an implied obligation in the statutes of Oregon, Washington, and Wisconsin. The Nebraska statute provides specifically against any implied obligation.

16. See *Berkeley Teachers Association et al. v. Berkeley Federation of Teachers, American Federation of Teachers, AFL–CIO Local 1078 et al.* 56 L.C. 65, 938 (Calif.1967), for a judicial interpretation of this statute.

17. See, however, *Matter of Salem School Department* and *Salem Teachers Union, Local 1258, American Federation of Teachers,* and *Salem Teachers Association,* CCH *Labor Law Reporter,* State Laws 3, p. 60,911 (Mass. Sept., 1966), where the State Labor Relations Commission held that principals and other supervisory personnel should not be included in the teachers' bargaining unit inasmuch as the "duties, responsibilities and other conditions of employment (of supervisory staff) differ from those of a teacher . . . ."

18. This is not to say, however, that executives or supervisors are excluded from mere membership in the representative organization. See *Board of Education of School District, City of Hazel Park* and *Hazel Park Federation of Teachers,* 63 LRRM 1001 (Mich.1966); also *School Board of City of Grand Rapids* and *Grand Rapids Federation of Teachers,* 64 LRRM 1269 (Mich.1966).

19. See *Local 1067, West Milwaukee—West Allis Federation of Teachers and Wisconsin Federation of Teachers, AFL–CIO* and *Joint City School District No. 1 of the City of West Allis, et al.,* 54 LRRM 1337 (Wis.1963) where the State Labor Relations Board held that supervisory personnel may belong to an organization representing teachers if the presence of the supervisory personnel does not "establish domination or interference with the organization by the municipal employer employing such supervisory personnel."

20. See, for example, *Matter of Madison Teachers, Inc. v. Joint School District No. 8, City of Madison et al.,* 65 LRRM 2488 (Wis.1967) where Wisconsin's statute was interpreted to mean that adoption of a school year calendar "was a negotiable item since it had a direct and intimate relationship to teachers' salaries and conditions of employment."

21. The Minnesota statute requires the school board to meet and confer with

the recognized teacher organization or teachers' council with respect to
"conditions of professional service." It is expressly provided, however,
that " 'conditions of professional service' means economic aspects relating
to terms of employment, but does not mean educational policies of the
district." To further emphasize the distinction between economic issues
and educational policies, the statute expressly provides that "(w)ith respect
to conditions of professional service the parties shall meet and confer in
an effort to reach agreement. With respect to all other matters, the parties
shall meet and confer in order to afford a reasonable opportunity for the
expression of views and the exchange of information." In the statutes of
the other three states, both economic issues and educational policy issues
are within the scope of negotiations.

22. See, however, *Local 953* v. *School District,* 66 LRRM 2419 (Mich.1967)
where a state court held that a school district and a teachers' organization
may enter into a contract wherein it is voluntarily agreed that unresolved
grievances arising under the contract will be submitted to binding
arbitration.

23. See, for interpretation of New York's statute, *Board of Education of City
of New York* v. *Shanker, et al.,* 56 L.C. 65, 935 (N.Y.1967).

State Collective Negotiation Statutes

STATE	TYPE OF STATUTE		RIGHT OF TEACHERS TO BARGAIN THRU REPRESENTATIVES OF THEIR CHOICE		OBLIGATION ON SCHOOL BOARDS TO BARGAIN, ETC.		SCOPE OF NEGOTIATIONS		IMPASSE PROCEDURES				STRIKES BY TEACHERS	
	PUBLIC EDUCATION	PUBLIC EMPLOYMENT GENERALLY	FULL	PARTIAL	EXPRESSLY PROVIDED	NO PROVISION	ECONOMIC ISSUES	ECONOMIC AND EDUCATIONAL ISSUES	FACT FINDING	MEDIATION	ARBITRATION	OTHER	EXPRESSLY PROHIBITED	NO PROVISION
CALIFORNIA	X			X	X			X						X
CONNECTICUT	X			X	X		X			X	X		X	
MASSACHUSETTS		X	X		X		X		X		X		X	
MICHIGAN		X	X		X		X			X			X	
MINNESOTA	X			X	X		X					X		X
NEBRASKA	X			X		X		X	X	X		X		X
NEW YORK		X		X	X		X		X				X	
OREGON	X			X		X	X					X		X
RHODE ISLAND	X		X		X		X				X			X
WASHINGTON	X		X			X		X				X		X
WISCONSIN		X	X			X	X		X	X			X	

APPENDIX III

How and Where to Find Education Law

CONSTITUTIONS are adopted by "we, the people" and amended in the manner provided by the constitution. Statutes are enacted by legislative bodies elected by "we, the people," and court decisions are handed down by judges elected or appointed as provided for in constitutions or statutes.

The Federal Constitution and Federal Statutes are found in the United States Code. Federal Statutes are also found in the United States Statutes at Large. Periodically since 1913, the Congress of the United States, by Joint Resolution, has authorized the publication of an Annotated Constitution of the United States of America. The latest publication was authorized in 1960 by Public Law 86–754, which directed the Library of Congress "to have prepared a revised edition of the Constitution of the United States of America, Analysis and Interpretation, published as Senate Document Numbered 170, Eighty-second Congress, which shall contain annotations of decisions of the Supreme Court of the United States after June 30, 1952, construing the several provision of the Constitution . . . ." This latest revision was submitted in September, 1964 and includes annotations of U.S. Supreme Court decisions through June 22, 1964. There is also a United States Code Annotated which contains annotations and court decisions concerning congressional legislation. State Codes of General Laws normally include the state's constitution and statutes. Many states publish a Code of School Laws.

Court decisions are an important source of law, including education law, because courts are responsible for interpreting and construing constitutional and statutory provisions. Most states publish official reports of the decisions of their appellate courts, but the National Reporter System, published by the West Publishing Company, provides the quickest reporting of the decisions of all appellate courts in the country. While these reports are not official, they are widely used by members of the legal profession because of their special features. There are thirteen different reports and a weekly advance sheet is published for each of the thirteen reports. A table of statutes construed is included in each report and in each advance sheet. Of particular interest are the "head notes" for each decision reported, which refer the reader to Key Number Digests, including the American Digest System.

THE NATIONAL REPORTER SYSTEM

The Atlantic Reporter (Atl. or A.2d)—eight states: Maine, Vermont, New Hampshire, Connecticut, New Jersey, Pennsylvania, Delaware, and Maryland.

The Northeastern Reporter (N.E. or N.E.2d)—six states: Massachusetts, Rhode Island, New York, Ohio, Indiana, and Illinois.

The Southeastern Reporter (S.E. or S.E.2d)—five states: Virginia, West Virginia, North Carolina, South Carolina, and Georgia.

The Southern Reporter (So. or So.2d)—four states: Florida, Alabama, Mississippi, and Louisiana.

The Southwestern Reporter (S.W. or S.W.2d)—five states: Kentucky, Tennessee, Missouri, Arkansas, and Texas.

The Pacific Reporter (P. or P.2d)—fifteen states: Montana, Wyoming, Idaho, Kansas, Colorado, Oklahoma, New Mexico, Utah, Arizona, Nevada, Washington, Oregon, California, Alaska, and Hawaii.

The Northwestern Reporter (N.W. or N.W.2d)—seven states: Michigan, Wisconsin, Iowa, Minnesota, North Dakota, South Dakota, and Nebraska.

The New York Supplement (N.Y.S. or N.Y.S.2d)—Decisions of N.Y. Court of Appeals, Appellate Division of the N.Y. Supreme Court, and other lower New York courts of record.

The California Reporter (Cal.Rptr.)—Decisions of the California Supreme Court, District Courts of Appeal, and Appellate Department of Superior Court.

The Federal Supplement (F.Supp. or F.Supp.2d)—Decisions of the U.S. Court of Claims, U.S. District Courts, and U.S. Court of Customs.

The Federal Reporter (F. or F.2d)—U.S. Court of Appeals decisions.

The Federal Rules Decisions (F.R.D.)—Decisions of the U.S. District Courts involving federal rules of civil and criminal procedure.

The Supreme Court Reporter (S.Ct.)—U.S. Supreme Court decisions.

The American Digest System. The American Digest System, published by the West Publishing Company, is a series of digests of cases from 1658 to date, consisting of eight units:

1658 to 1896—The Century Digest
1896 to 1906—First Decennial Digest (25 volumes)
1906 to 1916—Second Decennial Digest (24 volumes)
1916 to 1926—Third Decennial Digest (29 volumes)
1926 to 1936—Fourth Decennial Digest (34 volumes)
1936 to 1946—Fifth Decennial Digest (49 volumes)
1946 to 1956—Sixth Decennial Digest (36 volumes)
1956 to date—General Digest, Third Series

Case digests in each of the eight units are arranged in the same order according to subject matter. For example, under the topic "Schools and School Districts," is the sub-topic "Private Schools and Academies":

Schools and School Districts

I. Private Schools and Academies
    Sec. 1. Establishment and Status in General
    Sec. 2. Incorporation and Organization
    Sec. 3. Public Aid
    Sec. 4. Regulation and Supervision
    Sec. 5. Property, Funds, and Liabilities in General
    Sec. 6. Governing Boards and Officers
    Sec. 7. Teachers and Other Instructors
    Sec. 8. Pupils, Tuition, and Discipline

The text material consists of short digests of all cases concerning the particular sub-topic which were decided during the period of time covered by a particular volume of the Digest.

The American Digest System includes a Table of Cases, which lists alphabetically the exact title of all cases referred to in the Digest. It also lists all the places where the text of each case may be found, and it lists the topic and key numbers of every point of law decided in each case, including information as to whether the case has been affirmed, reversed, or modified.

Corpus Juris Secundum. In contrast to the American Digest System, which is primarily concerned with court decisions, Corpus Juris Secundum (C.J.S.), also published by the West Publishing Company, is primarily concerned with case law principles; these principles are published in encyclopedic form. Case citations to support the principles stated in the text are found in the footnotes. As of 1966, C.J.S. consisted of one hundred and one volumes and five index volumes. Volume 14 deals with Colleges and Universities, and includes forty-four sub-titles. The case law principles relating to "Schools and School Districts" are found in Volumes 78 and 79 and include five hundred and twelve titles and sub-titles (Sub-titles 1 through 322 are found in Volume 78 and sub-titles 323 through 512 are found in Volume 79.) Sub-titles 3 through 11, for example, under "Schools and School Districts," relate to "Private Schools," i.e.:

    II. Private Schools
        Sec. 3. In General
        Sec. 4. Incorporation and Organization
        Sec. 5. Public Aid
        Sec. 6. Visitation, Supervision, and Control
        Sec. 7. Contracts
        Sec. 8. —— Contracts with Teachers and Instructors
        Sec. 9. ——Contracts for Instruction
        Sec. 10. Property and Conveyances; Liabilities
        Sec. 11. Discipline, Suspension, or Expulsion of Pupils

American Jurisprudence. American Jurisprudence (Am.Jur.), published by the Lawyers Cooperative Publishing Company and Bancroft–Whitney Company, follows the same encyclopedic style as Corpus Juris Secundum except that case citations are restricted to the more important or *leading* cases. As of March, 1968, it consisted of thirty-seven volumes of a second series which began in 1962, and fifty-eight volumes of the first series which began in 1936. Volume 55 of the first series deals with Universities and Colleges, and Volume 47 of the first series includes the material on Schools. As in Corpus Juris Secundum and the American Digest System, the material under these two topics is arranged according to sub-topics. For example, under "Schools" there is the sub-topic "Private Schools":

Labor Cases. Labor Cases (L.C.), published by the Commerce Clearing House, Inc., is a "Full text reporter of decisions rendered by Federal and State Courts throughout the United States on federal and state labor problems." The publication began in 1939, and has continued down to the present with yearly volumes. A Topical Index is included at the end of each volume and provides the reader with an accurate indication of the subjects with which the various cases reported in the particular volume are concerned. Labor Cases is kept current beyond the latest bound volume through insertions in a loose-leaf binder, the *Labor Law Reporter.*

The Labor Relations Reference Manual. The Labor Relations Reference Manual (LRRM), published by the Bureau of National Affairs, Inc., began publication in 1937. It contains "digest-summaries of all published decisions of the National Labor Relations Board and significant decisions of state labor relations boards . . . ." In addition, "all opinions relating to labor relations by the Supreme Court of the United States and the United States Courts of Appeals are reproduced in full text . . . (and) practically all other labor relations decisions of federal and state courts are included in text." Instructions for finding cases concerning a general subject (e.g., "Teachers," "Government Employees") are found in a loose-leaf binder, the *Labor Relations Reporter Master Index.* The Labor Relations Reference Manual is kept current through insertions in a loose-leaf binder, the *Labor Relations Reporter.*

Index to Legal Periodicals. This index consists of fourteen bound volumes, 1926 to 1967, with paperbacks thereafter. The major law schools in the country periodically publish articles, comments, and notes relating to various aspects of law. The Index to Legal

Periodicals refers to these articles, etc., under appropriate topics, such as Colleges and Universities, Education, Schools and School Districts, Teachers and Teaching.

Restatement of the Law. The Restatement is an attempt by the American Law Institute to reconcile the conflicts in court opinions (case law) as to principles and rules of common law, and to restate them in reasonably simple language. The first Restatements were published in 1945 and have been periodically revised in supplements. The publication of Restatement 2d began in 1964.

Glossary of Legal Terms

Abrogation—the act of abolishing or repealing, as by later enactment.

Action—a suit or a lawsuit.
    (a) Action at law—to obtain ordinary legal relief
    (b) Action in equity—to obtain equitable relief

Allegation—statement in pleadings, reciting what the pleader expects to prove.

Annotation—explanatory or supplementary note to, or commentary on, a principal text such as a constitution, statute, or court decision.

Amicus curiae—friend of the court, not a party to the action or directly involved, but who has an indirect interest and information bearing on a legal issue under consideration.

Appellant—a party taking an appeal from a decision of one court to another court for decision.

Appellate court—a court authorized to receive appeals from another court.

Appellee—a party against whom an appeal is taken.

Arbiter—a chosen or appointed umpire or judge.

Assault—the intentional invasion of a person's interest in freedom from apprehension of harmful or offensive bodily contact.

Battery—the intentional invasion of a person's interest in freedom from harmful or offensive bodily contact.

Caveat emptor—let the buyer beware.

Certiorari—a writ issued by a superior court directing an inferior court to send up for review the records and proceedings in a case.

Codification—process of collecting and scientifically arranging laws into chapters, subheadings, etc.

Common law—legal principles derived from usage and custom or from court decisions affirming such usages and customs, as distinguished from law created by constitutions and statutes and court interpretations thereof.

Consideration—an inducement, maybe an act, an amount of money or a promise.

Contract—an agreement for sufficient consideration to do or not to do a particular thing:

    (a) Unilateral contract—a promise for an act

    (b) Bilateral contract—a promise for a promise

Construe—determine the meaning.

Corporate body—sometimes referred to as a body corporate or a corporate entity—a legal creation or artificial person authorized to perform specific functions.

Criminal liability—liability to fine or imprisonment or both, as distinguished from civil liability to compensate by paying damages or doing or not doing a specific thing.

Damages—a money award as compensation or indemnity which may be recovered in court in a civil action.

Declaratory relief—a court decision which declares the rights of parties or expresses the opinion of the court on a question of law, without ordering anything to be done.

De facto—in fact, actually.

De jure—legally, as a matter of law.

Defendant—the party defending or denying; the party against whom relief or recovery is sought in a court decision.

Demurrer—allegation by one party in a court action which admits the matters of fact alleged by the other party to be true but, even so, are not of such legal consequence as to justify further proceedings in the case.

Dictum—statement of legal principle in a court decision which is not necessitated by the facts or the law of the case.

Ejusdem generis—of the same kind, class, and nature. When applied in statutory construction it means that where general words follow an enumeration of words with a specific meaning, the general words are construed as limited to matters of the same kind or class as those specifically mentioned.

Estoppel—a bar raised by the law which prevents a party from alleging or denying a certain fact because of his previous statements or conduct.

Ex delicto—from a fault, malfeasance or tort, as distinguished from **ex contracto** which means from a contract.

Ex parte—on one side only, a proceeding when granted for the benefit of one party only.

Ex rel.—legal proceedings instituted in the name and on behalf of the state but on the information and at the instigation of an individual who has a private interest in the matter.

Gerrymandering—altering abnormally or arbitrarily.

Indicia (of authority)—discriminating marks, or badges.

Injunction—a judicial order requiring a party to take or refrain from some specified action.

In loco parentis—in place of the parent; charged with some of the parents' rights and responsibilities.

In pari delicto—equally culpable or guilty.

In re—concerning. Designates a type of case.

Inter alia—among other things.

Jurisdiction—lawful right to exercise official authority.

Laches—failure to assert a right for an unreasonable length of time, to be differentiated from a statute of limitations.

Liquidated damages—a specific sum of money stipulated by the parties by contract as the amount of damages to be recovered by one party for breach of an agreement by the other.

Litigant—a party to a law suit.

Litigation—a judicial contest or the act of carrying on a suit in a law court.

Litigious—controvertible or disputable.

Mandamus—a command by a court that a certain act be performed.

Mandate—a judicial command.

Malfeasance—commission of an unlawful act.

Misfeasance—improper performance of a lawful act.

Nonfeasance—failure to perform a required duty.

Nonsuit—an official judgment dismissing a suit when the plaintiff either abandons it or fails to establish a cause of action.

Non obstante verdicto—notwithstanding the verdict.

Nuisance—a continuous condition or use of property in such a manner as to obstruct proper use of it by the public or by others lawfully having the right to use it.

Offeree—the party to a contract who accepts the offer, the promisee.

Offeror—the party to a contract who makes the offer, the promissor.

Plaintiff—a party who sues by filing a complaint.

Plenary—having full powers.

Petitioner—a party who presents a written application to the court.

Police power—power to enact laws for public health, safety, and general welfare.

Precedent—a judicial decision considered as furnishing authority on a similar question of law in a subsequent but similar case.

Privilege—a right or immunity enjoyed only under certain conditions.

Quantum meruit—as much as he deserves for his labor.

Quantum valebant—as much as the goods are worth.

Quasi—almost as if, quasi-judicial or quasi-legislative.

Quo warranto—by what authority. A method of trying the title to a public office.

Relator—substantially the same as a plaintiff.

Remand a case—to send a case back to the court where it was heard for further proceedings.

Respondeat superior—responsibility of one party for the acts of others under his supervision or control.

Respondent—a defendant in certain cases, usually the party against whom an appeal is taken.

Res ipso loquitur—the thing speaks for itself; rebuttable presumption of negligence.

Res adjudicata—a matter judicially decided.

Sanctions—provisions for securing conformity to law, such as penalties.

Scienter—knowingly; the party knew the circumstances.

Sine die—finally, as an adjournment without setting a day for reassembling.

Stare decisis—to stand by decided cases. Principle that when a court has declared a legal principle, it is the law until changed by competent authority.

Statute—a law resulting from the exercise of legislative power, as by the Federal Congress or state legislatures.

Supersedeas—a writ by an appellate court commanding a stay of legal proceedings.

Tort—a civil wrong not arising out of contract; an interference by one party, usually the defendant, with a legally protected interest of another party, usually a plaintiff.

Table of Cases